WITHDRAWN
UTSA LIBRARIES

*Palgrave Macmillan Studies in Banking and Financial Institutions*

Series Editor: **Professor Philip Molyneux**

The Palgrave Macmillan Studies in Banking and Financial Institutions are international in orientation and include studies of banking within particular countries or regions, and studies of particular themes such as Corporate Banking, Risk Management, Mergers and Acquisitions, etc. The books' focus is on research and practice, and they include up-to-date and innovative studies on contemporary topics in banking that will have global impact and influence.

Titles include:

Yener Altunbas, Blaise Gadanecz and Alper Kara
SYNDICATED LOANS
A Hybrid of Relationship Lending and Publicly Traded Debt

Yener Altunbas, Alper Kara and Öslem Olgu
TURKISH BANKING
Banking under Political Instability and Chronic High Inflation

Elena Beccalli
IT AND EUROPEAN BANK PERFORMANCE

Paola Bongini, Stefano Chiarlone and Giovanni Ferri (*editors*)
EMERGING BANKING SYSTEMS

Vittorio Boscia, Alessandro Carretta and Paola Schwizer
COOPERATIVE BANKING: INNOVATIONS AND DEVELOPMENTS

Allessandro Carretta, Franco Fiordelisi and Gianluca Mattarocci (*editors*)
NEW DRIVERS OF PERFORMANCE IN A CHANGING FINANCIAL WORLD

Dimitris N. Chorafas
CAPITALISM WITHOUT CAPITAL

Dimitris N. Chorafas
FINANCIAL BOOM AND GLOOM
The Credit and Banking Crisis of 2007–2009 and Beyond

Violaine Cousin
BANKING IN CHINA

Peter Falush and Robert L. Carter OBE
THE BRITISH INSURANCE INDUSTRY SINCE 1900
The Era of Transformation

Franco Fiordelisi and Philip Molyneux
SHAREHOLDER VALUE IN BANKING

Hans Genberg and Cho-Hoi Hui
THE BANKING CENTRE IN HONG KONG
Competition, Efficiency, Performance and Risk

Carlo Gola and Alessandro Roselli
THE UK BANKING SYSTEM AND ITS REGULATORY AND SUPERVISORY FRAMEWORK

Elisabetta Gualandri and Valeria Venturelli (*editors*)
BRIDGING THE EQUITY GAP FOR INNOVATIVE SMEs

Kim Hawtrey
AFFORDABLE HOUSING FINANCE

Munawar Iqbal and Philip Molyneux
THIRTY YEARS OF ISLAMIC BANKING
History, Performance and Prospects

Sven Janssen
BRITISH AND GERMAN BANKING STRATEGIES

Kimio Kase and Tanguy Jacopin
CEOs AS LEADERS AND STRATEGY DESIGNERS
Explaining the Success of Spanish Banks

M. Mansoor Khan and M. Ishaq Bhatti
DEVELOPMENTS IN ISLAMIC BANKING
The Case of Pakistan

Mario La Torre and Gianfranco A. Vento
MICROFINANCE

Philip Molyneux and Eleuterio Vallelado (*editors*)
FRONTIERS OF BANKS IN A GLOBAL WORLD

Anastasia Nesvetailova
FRAGILE FINANCE
Debt, Speculation and Crisis in the Age of Global Credit

Dominique Rambure and Alec Nacamuli
PAYMENT SYSTEMS
From the Salt Mines to the Board Room

Catherine Schenk (*editor*)
HONG KONG SAR's MONETARY AND EXCHANGE RATE CHALLENGES
Historical Perspectives

Noël K. Tshiani
BUILDING CREDIBLE CENTRAL BANKS
Policy Lessons for Emerging Economies

---

**Palgrave Macmillan Studies in Banking and Financial Institutions**
**Series Standing Order ISBN 978-1-4039-4872-4**

You can receive future titles in this series as they are published by placing a standing order. Please contact your bookseller or, in case of difficulty, write to us at the address below with your name and address, the title of the series and the ISBN quoted above.

Customer Services Department, Macmillan Distribution Ltd, Houndmills, Basingstoke, Hampshire RG21 6XS, England

---

# Affordable Housing Finance

Kim Hawtrey
*Professor of Economics, Hope College, USA*

© Kim Hawtrey 2009

All rights reserved. No reproduction, copy or transmission of this publication may be made without written permission.

No portion of this publication may be reproduced, copied or transmitted save with written permission or in accordance with the provisions of the Copyright, Designs and Patents Act 1988, or under the terms of any licence permitting limited copying issued by the Copyright Licensing Agency, Saffron House, 6-10 Kirby Street, London EC1N 8TS.

Any person who does any unauthorized act in relation to this publication may be liable to criminal prosecution and civil claims for damages.

The author has asserted his right to be identified as the author of this work in accordance with the Copyright, Designs and Patents Act 1988.

First published 2009 by
PALGRAVE MACMILLAN

Palgrave Macmillan in the UK is an imprint of Macmillan Publishers Limited, registered in England, company number 785998, of Houndmills, Basingstoke, Hampshire RG21 6XS.

Palgrave Macmillan in the US is a division of St Martin's Press LLC, 175 Fifth Avenue, New York, NY 10010.

Palgrave Macmillan is the global academic imprint of the above companies and has companies and representatives throughout the world.

Palgrave® and Macmillan® are registered trademarks in the United States, the United Kingdom, Europe and other countries.

ISBN-978-0-230-55518-1    hardback

This book is printed on paper suitable for recycling and made from fully managed and sustained forest sources. Logging, pulping and manufacturing processes are expected to conform to the environmental regulations of the country of origin.

A catalogue record for this book is available from the British Library.

A catalog record for this book is available from the Library of Congress.

10 9 8 7 6 5 4 3 2 1
18 17 16 15 14 13 12 11 10 09

Printed and bound in Great Britain by
CPI Antony Rowe, Chippenham and Eastbourne

Library
University of Texas
at San Antonio

*This book owes much to my wife, Jenny, who makes our house a home.*

# Contents

| | |
|---|---|
| List of Figures | x |
| Glossary of Abbreviations | xii |
| Preface | xvii |

**1  Introduction** — 1
  Aims and objectives — 3

**2  Housing Stress: Nature, Causes, and Consequences** — 6
  Introduction — 6
  What is "housing stress"? — 7
  The extent of housing stress — 12
  Economic costs of housing stress — 13
  Social costs of housing stress — 18
  Determinants of housing stress — 20
  Defining "affordable housing" — 23
  Conclusions and next steps — 24

**3  The Financial Dimension** — 26
  Introduction — 26
  The subprime credit crisis — 27
  Capital market failure — 37
  Toward a general equilibrium outcome — 41
  Economic benefits of greater flexibility in housing finance — 43
  Capital markets make housing "different" — 45
  Conclusions and next steps — 46

**4  Affordable Housing Finance in the US** — 49
  Introduction — 49
  US housing markets and policy — 50
  Housing finance in the US — 54
  American housing stress — 60
  The current debate in the US — 63

| | | |
|---|---|---|
| 5 | **Affordable Housing Finance in the UK** | **69** |
| | Introduction | 69 |
| | UK housing markets and policy | 70 |
| | Housing finance in the UK | 74 |
| | British housing stress | 77 |
| | The current debate in the UK | 81 |
| 6 | **Affordable Housing Finance in Australia** | **84** |
| | Introduction | 84 |
| | Australian housing markets and policy | 85 |
| | Housing finance in Australia | 90 |
| | Australian housing stress | 94 |
| | The current debate in Australia | 99 |
| 7 | **Capital Market Solutions** | **103** |
| | Introduction | 103 |
| | Investment hurdles | 105 |
| | Portfolio diversification | 108 |
| | From "beta" to "alpha" investing | 109 |
| | Developing a defined asset class | 111 |
| | How regulators can assist | 116 |
| | Conclusions and next steps | 125 |
| 8 | **Retail Finance Solutions** | **127** |
| | Introduction | 127 |
| | Affordability-based lending | 128 |
| | Shared equity | 132 |
| | Equity release | 138 |
| | Pooled investor vehicles | 140 |
| | Conclusions and next steps | 143 |
| 9 | **Public Sector Solutions** | **145** |
| | Introduction | 145 |
| | Incentives and disincentives | 146 |
| | Tax incentives | 149 |

| | |
|---|---:|
| Risk mitigation | 153 |
| Conclusions and next steps | 157 |
| **10 Future Directions** | **160** |
| *References* | 164 |
| *Index* | 177 |

# Figures

| | | |
|---|---|---|
| 1.1 | Housing affordability ratings (2008) by country (number of cities in each category) | 3 |
| 2.1 | Distribution of markets by housing affordability, 2008 (six countries) | 13 |
| 3.1 | US mortgage originations by product, 2001–2007 | 28 |
| 3.2 | Fall in stock prices during the year 2008 – US, UK, and Australian banks | 30 |
| 3.3 | Rating downgrades of global banks by Standard and Poor's | 31 |
| 3.4 | Arrears (30+ days) – by country | 31 |
| 3.5 | Trend in nonperforming loans – by country | 32 |
| 3.6 | Summary, by country, of 2008 official support measures (all currency in billions) | 33 |
| 3.7 | Projected final writedowns by loan category in the US | 35 |
| 3.8 | Bank credit growth and the financial crisis (annualized percentage change) | 35 |
| 4.1 | Evolution of the US housing finance system | 55 |
| 4.2 | Mortgage characteristics in the US | 56 |
| 4.3 | Growth in US mortgage debt as percent to GDP | 56 |
| 4.4 | US housing finance burden, 1996–2007 | 57 |
| 4.5 | US mortgage interest rate, 1973–2008 | 57 |
| 4.6 | US mortgage innovation index | 58 |
| 4.7 | US mortgage affordability index, 1973–2008 | 59 |
| 4.8 | US housing affordability, 1980–2008 | 61 |
| 4.9 | US city rankings by housing affordability, 2008 | 63 |
| 5.1 | All households by tenure – three countries | 73 |
| 5.2 | Mortgage characteristics in the UK | 75 |
| 5.3 | Growth in UK mortgage debt as percent to GDP | 76 |
| 5.4 | Evolution of the UK housing finance system | 78 |
| 5.5 | UK housing finance burden, 1996–2007 | 79 |

| | | |
|---|---|---|
| 5.6 | UK metros with lowest affordability | 80 |
| 6.1 | Mortgage characteristics in Australia | 91 |
| 6.2 | Growth in Australian mortgage debt as percent to GDP | 91 |
| 6.3 | Australian bank lending – by category | 92 |
| 6.4 | Share of banks and non-banks of Australian mortgage lending | 92 |
| 6.5 | Evolution of the Australian housing finance system | 95 |
| 6.6 | Cyclical nature of Australian housing finance | 96 |
| 6.7 | Proportion of Australians in housing stress – by category | 97 |
| 6.8 | Australian metros with lowest affordability | 98 |
| 6.9 | Price index of established houses (annual percent change)—Australia | 99 |
| 7.1 | Overview of links between housing financiers and investment fund managers | 106 |
| 7.2 | Credit markets' alpha opportunity set | 111 |
| 7.3 | Effect of greater capital market flexibility on the mixed asset-class efficient frontier | 112 |
| 7.4 | Usage of AVMs – by country | 114 |
| 9.1 | Housing taxes and subsidies – by country | 149 |
| 9.2 | Housing risk mitigation – by country | 154 |
| 9.3 | Overview of public sector solutions | 158 |

# Glossary of Abbreviations

| | |
|---|---|
| A2F | Access-to-finance |
| ABS | Asset-backed security |
| AFIC | Australian Financial Institutions Commission (Australia) |
| AHG | Affordable Housing Goal (US) |
| AHS | American Housing Survey (US) |
| AHNRC | Affordable Housing National Research Consortium (Australia) |
| AHURI | Australia Housing and Urban Research Institute (Australia) |
| AIP | Alternative investment product |
| ALMO | Arms-length Management Organisation |
| ARM | Adjustable-rate mortgage |
| ASX | Australian Stock Exchange (Australia) |
| AUS | Automated underwriting system (US) |
| AVM | Automated valuation model |
| BIS | Bank for International Settlements |
| CAR | Californian Association of Realtors (US) |
| CAHS | Comprehensive Affordable Housing Strategy (UK) |
| CCHPR | Cambridge Centre for Housing and Planning Research (UK) |
| CEHI | Cost-effectiveness in Housing Investment research program, University of Brighton (UK) |
| CDE | Community development entity (US) |
| CDFI | Community Development Financial Institution (US) |
| CDS | Credit default swap |
| CDO | Collateralized debt obligation |
| CIH | Chartered Institute of Housing (UK) |
| CHAS | Comprehensive Housing Affordability Strategy (US) |
| CHC | Community Housing Cymru (UK) |

| | |
|---|---|
| CML | Council of Mortgage Lenders (UK) |
| CMO | Collateralized mortgage obligation |
| CHFA | Community Housing Federation of Australia (Australia) |
| CHO | Community Housing Organization (Australia) |
| CLG | Communities and Local Government (UK) |
| CS | Communities Scotland (UK) |
| CSHA | Commonwealth State Housing Agreement (Australia) |
| DU | Desktop underwriter (US) |
| ECHP | European Community Household Panel (Europe) |
| ECSC | European Committee for Social Cohesion (Europe) |
| EFB | Essential function bonds (US) |
| EFI | Essential function instrument (UK) |
| ETI | Economically targeted investment |
| FDIC | Federal Deposit Insurance Corporation (US) |
| FHA | Federal Housing Administration (US) |
| FIRREA | Financial Institutions Reform Recovery and Enforcement Act of 1989 (US) |
| FMR | Fair market rent |
| FHFB | Federal Housing Finance Board (US) |
| FHFA | Federal Housing Finance Agency (US) |
| FHL | Federal Home Loan (US) |
| FDIS | Federal Deposit Insurance System (US) |
| FHA | Federal Housing Administration (US) |
| FRB | Federal Reserve Board of Governors (US) |
| FSA | Financial Services Authority (UK) |
| GFC | Global Financial Crisis |
| GEM | Growing-equity mortgage |
| GHB | Guaranteed housing bond |
| GPM | Graduated-payment mortgage |
| GSE | Government-sponsored enterprise (US) |
| HAI | Housing affordability index |
| HCA | Homes and Communities Agency (UK) |

| | |
|---|---|
| HECM | Home equity conversion mortgage (US) |
| HELOC | Home equity line of credit |
| HERA | Housing and Economic Recovery Act 2008 (US) |
| HFS | Housing finance system |
| HIA | Housing Industry Association (Australia) |
| HOLC | Home Owners' Loan Corporation (US) |
| HMDA | Home Mortgage Disclosure Act (US) |
| HRP | Housing Recovery Plan 2008 (Australia) |
| HUD | Department of Housing and Urban Development (US) |
| ISMIP | Income Support for Mortgage Interest Program (UK) |
| JCHS | Joint Center for Housing Studies (US) |
| JV | Joint venture |
| LCHO | Low-cost home ownership (UK) |
| LIHTC | Low-Income Housing Tax Credit Program (US) |
| LTFRM | Long-term fixed-rate mortgage |
| LTV | Loan-to-value |
| LVR | Loan-to-value ratio |
| MBA | Mortgage Bankers Association (US) |
| MBB | Mortgage-backed bond |
| MBS | Mortgage-backed security |
| MDO | Mortgage debt outstanding |
| MMMF | Money market mutual fund |
| NAHA | National Affordable Housing Agreement (Australia) |
| NAHP | National Affordable Housing Program (UK) |
| NAR | National Association of Realtors® (US) |
| NATSEM | National Centre for Social and Economic Modelling (Australia) |
| NCHF | National Community Housing Forum (Australia) |
| NHF | National Housing Federation (UK) |
| NHPAU | National Housing and Planning Advice Unit (UK) |
| NHS | National Housing Strategy (Australia) |
| NHAF | National Housing Affordability Fund (Australia) |

## Glossary of Abbreviations xv

| | |
|---|---|
| NICOHA | Northern Ireland Co-ownership Housing Association (UK) |
| NIFHA | Northern Ireland Federation of Housing Associations (UK) |
| NIHE | Northern Ireland Housing Executive (UK) |
| NLIHC | National Low-Income Housing Coalition (USA) |
| NMTC | New Markets Tax Credit Program (US) |
| NRAS | National Rental Affordability Scheme (Australia) |
| OECD | Organisation for Economic Cooperation and Development |
| OFHEO | Office of Federal Housing Enterprise Oversight (USA) |
| PCA | Property Council of Australia (Australia) |
| PHA | Public housing authority |
| PMI | Private mortgage insurance |
| PPP | Public–private partnership |
| PSID | Panel Study of Income Dynamics (USA) |
| RAM | Reverse-annuity mortgage (UK) |
| RBA | Reserve Bank of Australia |
| REIA | Real Estate Institute of Australia (Australia) |
| REMIC | Real estate mortgage investment conduit |
| RFC | Reconstruction Finance Corporation (US) |
| RMBS | Residential mortgage-backed security |
| RMS | Regulated Mortgage Survey (UK) |
| RSL | Registered Social Landlord (UK) |
| RTC | Resolution Trust Corporation (US) |
| S&L | Savings and loan (US) |
| SAA | Strategic asset allocation |
| SAAP | Supported Accommodation Assistance Program (Australia) |
| SAM | Shared-appreciation mortgage |
| SEH | Survey of English Housing (UK) |
| SEM | Shared-equity mortgage |
| SFHA | Scottish Federation of Housing Associations (UK) |
| SHA | State Housing Authority (Australia) |

| | |
|---|---|
| SHOTS | Securities Housing Trust Scheme |
| SML | Survey of Mortgage Lenders (UK) |
| SPL | Subprime loans |
| SPV | Special purpose vehicle |
| TIF | Tax Increment Financing (US) |
| TSA | Tenant Services Authority (UK) |
| USDA | Department of Agriculture (US) |
| UNCHS | United Nations Center for Human Settlements |
| WA | Welsh Assembly (UK) |

# Preface

At the time of writing, housing finance in the United States was in crisis and the world's economies were caught in the grip of the subprime mortgage meltdown. Against that backdrop, this book has been written with an eye to the future; a more sustainable future for housing finance and affordable housing in which capital markets play a smarter and less disruptive role in this essential sector of the economy.

Some background to the genesis of this book – the first, as far as I am aware, to be written specifically on the subject of affordable housing finance – may help the reader. This book emerges out of a decade of policy engagement by the author – a finance academic, industry consultant, and former banker – with the issue of finance for affordable housing. In 2000, whil I was based in Sydney, I was invited to chair a peak national housing committee dedicated to developing solutions in the Australian context: the Affordable Housing National Research Consortium (AHNRC). The consortium, comprising government officials and chief executives from leading national industry bodies, directed a large policy research grant, with the brief to engineer new ways to finance accessible housing.

The consortium's work is today regarded as a watershed: the resulting reports and papers (AHNRC, 2001; Hawtrey, 2001) have had far-reaching policy impacts in Australia, all the way to its Prime Minister's office. The proposals were formally endorsed by state governments around the country in a joint communiqué issued by Housing Ministers, and the financial model implemented by Adelaide City. National welfare groups ACOSS (Australian Council of Social Services) and Shelter embraced the proposals. On the national political stage, the research was adopted by the then Opposition as official party policy, and subsequently, in 2008, the newly elected Rudd Government introduced a new housing package that echoed the spirit of the consortium's work, with the promise of more to come.

Encouraged by the response to the consortium's white papers in policy circles, I began to plan a book-length treatment of affordable housing that would do justice to this emerging field of financial economics, one that would take experiences and ideas across continents. While incubating the plan of this book, I accepted invitations in Australia to join the national Panel of Experts on Housing at the Federal Department of Family and Community Services (FACS), and to present at the National Housing Conference, Cities Leadership Summit, Committee for Economic Development of Australia (CEDA) and National Housing Summit. These peak policy forums helped to further crystallize the concepts in this volume.

When 2007 arrived and I was about to begin work on this text, the housing crisis began to emerge in the US. Fortuitously (for this study), I had relocated to an academic post in the US where I could observe events in the world's largest economy at close quarters. The present volume was written through the height of the US liquidity crisis and the shakeout on Wall Street in 2008, and the economic fallout in 2009, a phenomenon that continues to reverberate around the world.

In the wake of the shakeout, it has become clear that affordable housing finance is a topic whose time has come. There is widespread agreement that this defining subprime episode, the largest macroeconomic upheaval of a generation, has its roots in the housing finance market, a fact that makes our subject matter pertinent for the entire economy, not just the housing sector. Unless we address the challenge of housing finance with sustainable long-term strategies, the seeds of a repeat mortgage crisis will remain to bear fruition sometime in the future.

Such is the setting and rationale for this tome. The book is written for a broad audience, both academic and professional, including housing lawmakers, industry associations, and bankers. I have sought to provide a readable yet systematic study that is integrated and international in nature, and accessible. Aware that the topic of housing appeals to a diverse readership including elected officials, urban planners, architects, environmentalists, engineers, social workers, and so on, I have tried to keep financial economics jargon to a minimum.

I believe that research think tanks and housing policy summits will find the volume useful, and it should also be accessible to non-profit community housing groups. In writing the manuscript, I have sought to make it suitable for undergraduate courses on Housing Economics and Policy, or similar. The text may also be of interest to those outside the field of housing who are nevertheless interested in funding for economic infrastructure in general.

Also, I hope the subject matter is interesting to average voters, and ordinary families facing the challenges of high house prices, rents, and mortgages.

This book could not have been completed without the help of several key individuals. My sincere thanks go to Renee Takken and Lisa von Fircks of Palgrave Macmillan for their extraordinary patience during the preparation of the manuscript. Also, thanks to series editor Philip Molyneux for encouraging and facilitating the books in this series.

I am grateful to Joy Ortiz for her generous assistance in keying in the large diagrams, and to John Stamolis for collating the data for several charts in Chapter 6.

A special word of gratitude to my colleagues at the Department of Economics, Management, and Accounting at Hope College, for their collegiality and friendship. Finally, thanks to my family for their enduring support (and many cups of coffee!) during the completion of this work.

Kim Hawtrey<br>
Professor of Economics<br>
Hope College<br>
Holland Michigan 49422-9000<br>
US

# 1
# Introduction

This book addresses the increasingly vexing and pressing global problem of housing stress, with particular emphasis on the financing dimension. It is about affordable housing, and housing finance, and how the two intersect.

The themes explored in this volume – the growing pressures on housing affordability and the imbalances in housing finance – have come into sharp relief since the onset of the global credit crisis of 2008. Housing finance has emerged as a major policy concern in most advanced economies in the wake of the recent banking turmoil. Significantly, the crisis, led by problems in the US subprime mortgage market, has its main roots in the very sector we are studying. Taking the history-making credit crisis as its point of departure, this volume looks at the dimensions of the problem, compares current policy approaches in several countries, and works towards a suite of solutions.

Many factors influence housing affordability, ranging from the spatial (planning, dwelling size, sustainable design, land supply, etc.) to the economic (efficiency, production, investment, incomes, rents) and from government policy (taxes, subsidies) to finance (interest rates, banking institutions, capital markets, financial innovation). Both owners and renters need to be examined, and the nature and dimensions of housing problems vary from one business cycle to the next. Having said that, the present text argues that the usual strategies for improving access to affordable housing such as zoning and building design, by themselves are insufficient, and that financial strategies for stimulating the supply of more affordable housing finance need to be at the forefront of a new wave of future housing solutions.

As demonstrated by the history-making subprime mortgage crisis, there is an urgent need for the two fields of affordable housing and capital markets to be satisfyingly integrated. Such is the aim of this book. The purpose here is to provide a fresh perspective on the challenge of affordable housing by placing particular emphasis on the role of financial market solutions.

Three advanced economies receive the most attention: the United States (where the mortgage crisis originated), the United Kingdom, and Australia. By the same token, the discussion in the book is broadly applicable to most OECD (Organisation for Economic Cooperation and Development) economies, subject to institutional details.

While the three economies treated in the text do not have a monopoly on the problem (or its solution), they are ideal as case studies because they share a common commitment to market-oriented housing, and all three have a ratio of mortgage debt to gross domestic product (GDP) well in excess of the OECD average.

Yet they also exhibit some key differences. The US is the source of the subprime crisis, which proved contagious to the UK, but not as damaging to Australian banking. The US has been at the frontier of financial market innovation, and its housing policy has emphasized financial measures more, relative to the UK and Australia. However, the UK has managed to outpace the other two in terms of rising mortgage debt ratios, and unlike Australian and US banks, British banks are known to lend more than 100 percent of the property value. Affordability in the US is easier: in 2008, no surveyed metropolitan market in the UK or Australia was classified as "affordable" for housing, unlike the US where over 70 cities were affordable (Figure 1.1).

The three countries exhibit alternative policy approaches. The United States has emphasized Government-Sponsored Enterprises (GSEs) and tax breaks for financing approved forms of housing. The UK, for historical reasons, has a larger public housing estate and provides a fascinating case of the move towards marketization. Australia has tended to rely on the government to directly provide public housing, supplemented by periodic stopgap measures such as first home buyer subsidy schemes. These curious differences make for a fascinating triangular case study.

Against that background, the book explores various potential generic ideas for improving future housing finance supply, particularly in Chapters 7 through 9. In those chapters, the text seeks to provide a forward-looking and hands-on menu of ideas that is globally applicable and grounded in financial economics. The aim is to present a range of creative and workable options, in order to stimulate debate and develop a practical way forward for decision-makers in the field such as bankers, elected officials, urban planners, financial economists,

|  | Affordable | Moderately unaffordable | Seriously unaffordable | Severely unaffordable | TOTAL |
| --- | --- | --- | --- | --- | --- |
| Australia | 0 | 0 | 3 | 24 | 27 |
| UK | 0 | 0 | 6 | 10 | 16 |
| US | 77 | 59 | 23 | 16 | 175 |
| TOTAL | 87 | 74 | 40 | 64 | 265 |

*Figure 1.1* Housing affordability ratings (2008) by country (number of cities in each category)

*Source*: 5th Annual Demographia International Housing Affordability Survey (Cox and Pavletich, 2009).

community housing groups, and housing policy summits. A subsidiary aim is to provide a text suitable for students and courses on housing economics.

## Aims and objectives

While research on affordable housing is plentiful, studies of affordable housing finance are less common, and are largely scattered and uncoordinated. Much of our knowledge is currently in the form of conference papers, commissioned reports, and government policy manuals that are not easy to access. The body of work in various housing journals has not been satisfyingly integrated. Moreover, there has been insufficient cross-fertilization of ideas between countries, despite the obvious global connectedness of housing finance markets as demonstrated by the 2008 subprime credit crisis. The time has come to integrate the debate and share insights across borders.

The present volume has three main objectives.

First, in Chapters 2 and 3, the text defines the nature of housing stress and makes the case for a capital markets solution. This section of the codex argues for the importance of financial solutions when tackling affordable housing. While the physical dimension of affordable housing – land, design, materials, building codes, zoning, etc. – cannot be ignored, such "bricks and mortar" issues have not been sufficient to explain the housing affordability crisis, nor have they prevented it from leading us into the deepest economic downturn in a generation. Instead the book will place "dollars and cents" (or "pounds and pence") squarely on the agenda, arguing that the banking and investment side of affordable housing offers the greatest scope for progress at the present time. The financial side of housing, more than the architectural dimension, has emerged in the twenty-first century as the generic economic problem requiring a tailored solution.

This proposition is evidenced by the prevailing subprime mortgage crisis, which is effectively reshaping the US economy. With 50 percent of the US$14.4 trillion (Federal Reserve Board, 2008; at the end of the third quarter 2008) in outstanding mortgages in the United States being intermediated through securitization, the disruption to market function from capital market sources has been significant. The thesis in this manuscript is that the resulting economy-wide shockwaves have their original roots in the housing market because they represent unresolved stress in aspirational housing finance. Finding new and better solutions for stimulating housing capital markets is an essential precondition for the resolution of our current economic troubles.

Second, in Chapters 4 through 6, the book presents a comparative intercontinental study of three housing markets. The dimensions of – and existing responses to – affordable housing stress are surveyed in the US, the UK, and Australia. In the process, these chapters unpack some of the classic issues surrounding housing markets, housing finance, and housing policy. It is remarkable how similar the experience is across countries, and how common the problems are across borders: "in recent decades, the median multiple [measure of housing affordability] has been remarkably similar among the nations surveyed" (Cox and Pavletich, 2009).

Third, in the trilogy of Chapters 7 through 9, the volume outlines what is meant by a "financial markets solution", and works through a list of what that might look like. Chapter 7 explores the new frontier in professional investment management known as "alpha" investing, and how this logically implies a seat at the capital market table for nontraditional asset classes, including multigrade mortgages. Chapter 8 canvasses options for retail banking solutions, including shared equity, pooled equity vehicles, and so on. Chapter 9 evaluates a number of different models for the government to stimulate private sector financial support for affordable housing. These include low-income housing investment tax credits, and low-income housing bonds.

The closing chapter assesses the policy judgments that will be required and suggests future directions for research into that elusive goal, sustainability in affordable housing finance.

Uniquely, this book analyzes the interaction between capital markets and housing outcomes. Rather than just calling for more public sector funding, this book highlights the potential role of private capital.

Although the role of the public sector is not lost sight of, this book aims to show the potential role of private funding mechanisms in improving the supply of affordable housing finance.

It is hoped this text on "home economics" will assist policymakers to formulate effective responses, and help inform decision-making by various private stakeholders in the future of affordable housing, notably bankers, investors, mutual fund managers, financial engineers, real estate bodies, social strategists, and policymakers.

# 2
# Housing Stress: Nature, Causes, and Consequences

## Introduction

This chapter provides an overview of housing stress and the closely related notion of housing finance stress. It defines housing stress and draws out implications of housing exclusion for the economy and society. The conventional determinants of housing affordability are canvassed, but then the text explains why we need to look beyond traditional affordability if we are to understand the global credit crisis and its financial roots.

We generally distinguish the question of affordable housing from that of outright homelessness which, although related, is a different issue. This is not to deny that a connection exists with street homelessness. On the contrary, evidence suggests there is indeed a strong "trickle-down" effect. Several studies have found evidence that tighter housing market conditions contribute to higher rates of homelessness, and that changes in the housing market had something to do with the dramatic rise in homelessness in the US after 1980 (see, for instance, O'Flaherty, 1995; Ying and Park, 2000; O'Flaherty and Wu, 2006). Although this book does not directly tackle the social policy challenge of people living on the street, nevertheless our topic has significant consequential ramifications for the shelter population, the outright homeless.

In this book, the term "affordable housing" relates to those who are housed, but are in housing stress. Our focus is on the economic policy challenge presented by mainstream cost-of-living concerns of typical wage earners, both low income and middle class. This is where our topic is focussed, on the intermediate group between those in poverty and the comfortable, working people who are employed and housed yet nevertheless frequently experience significant financial pressure or housing exclusion. This zone of "intermediate housing", also known as aspirational housing, contains huge populations suffering a type of economic stress that is often hidden. It is precisely this demographic subgroup whose aspirations drove the US housing boom and the subsequent subprime credit crunch.

## What is "housing stress"?

Housing affordability is a complex issue, yet it can perhaps best be defined using a common benchmark known as "housing stress". A reasonable setting of the benchmark, specifically chosen in order not to overstate the problem, is that households who pay more than 30 percent of their income on housing costs, whether renting or buying, are said to be in housing stress.

This widely used overall measure of housing-related hardship is internationally accepted and regarded as fairly conservative. In the US, the Fannie Mae Foundation has articulated the notion of affordability and housing stress. Affordability expresses the challenge each household faces in balancing the cost of its actual or potential housing, on the one hand, and its non-housing expenditures, on the other, within the constraints of its income (Stone, 2006b). In the US there is widespread acceptance that the ratio of housing cost to income is an appropriate indicator of affordability. The simple "rule of thumb" ratio was 25 percent of income until the early 1980s, but has been 30 percent since then.

Australia employs the same approach, ever since the official National Housing Strategy (NHS, 1991) defined housing affordability as a situation where "housing costs leave households with a sufficient income to meet other basic needs such as food, clothing, transport, medical care and education". Households paying more than 30 percent of their incomes in rents or mortgage payments are considered to be experiencing affordability problems. In particular, households falling in the lowest two income quintiles (lowest 40 percent) in the overall distribution of income, who pay above the threshold, are considered to be in housing stress. This more common measure of housing affordability is known as the "30/40 rule", and says that housing affordability is compromised when households in the bottom 40 percent of income distribution spend more than 30 percent of their household income on housing, adjusted for household size (Yates and Milligan, 2007).

The term "housing stress" is a technical economic term, not a psychological one (although it may easily involve mental trauma). It refers to housing-driven monetary hardship, and a more accurate term is "housing-induced financial stress". Shelter is here viewed predominantly from a budget point of view, like any other consumer item. The notion of housing-induced financial stress brings into view the residual effect of high housing costs. Households who pay more than one-third of their pretax income on housing costs will find it difficult to make ends meet with today's cost of living. In particular, this especially affects households in the lowest 40 percent income bracket – the "working poor" – but is not restricted to that group. Increasingly, middle-class two-income households can be prone to the experience of housing deprivation. There is also a group of people with defined characteristics that tend to suffer from housing finance stress: couples with a high number of dependents, those struck down by illness, victims of reversals of fortune after the boom in real estate markets, the uninsured, the elderly, students, the unemployed, and residents of certain geographic locations.

Accordingly, although personal experiences of housing stress are important and real, for public policy purposes and economic analysis, we employ objective and metric benchmarks to measure the phenomenon. These act as analytical indicators and normative standards of housing affordability that transcend unique individual experiences. In particular, they are used when assessing housing affordability problems, as well as for determining eligibility and payment levels for publicly subsidized rental housing and ownership programs.

Instead of the 30-percent rule, we can employ the "residual income" concept of housing affordability as an alternative. Housing is typically the largest and least flexible claim on after-tax income for most people, and other expenditures are limited by how much is left over. An affordability problem is said to exist if a household cannot meet its non-housing needs adequately, after paying for housing. The metric is the gap between housing costs and incomes. An advantage of this measure is that we can make comparisons. For example, suppose two households have comparable disposable incomes: one consists of a single person, while the other is a couple with three children. In this scenario, the larger household would have to spend substantially more for its non-shelter necessities than the smaller household, to achieve a comparable quality of life (Stone, 2006a). Conversely, if we compare two households of the same size but with different after-tax incomes, the lower-income household would have less left over than the higher-income household, in order for both to obtain a comparable standard shelter.

A drawback of this "financial residual" approach is that before we can calculate how much income is available for spending on housing, we must first assess how much income households need for non-housing expenses. This step requires a myriad of assumptions to be made about the representative household. Moreover, while the principal component of housing stress is high housing expenses relative to income, other stress conditions may also have an impact.

The US Department of Agriculture uses a multivariate definition to measure housing stress (USDA, 2004). Housing stress exists where 30 percent or more of households have one or more of the following conditions: lack complete plumbing (the home lacks essential bathroom facilities), or lack a complete kitchen, have more than one person per room, or pay 30 percent or more of income for owner costs or rent. This housing stress typology is employed by the USDA because it can help rural development planners identify counties with the greatest housing assistance needs.

Other ways of measuring housing stress include the value-to-income ratio and the payback period. The value-to-income ratio – also known as the median multiple – is the cost of a median house divided by the median family income. Depending on interest rates, a value-to-income ratio of less than two is generally "affordable" while a ratio greater than three is unaffordable. The payback period is the number of years that a median-income family would need to pay back a loan equal to 90 percent of a median home value at prevailing mortgage interest rates. Fewer than 10 years is very affordable, 10–20 is affordable, 20–30 marginal, 30–40 unaffordable, and more than 40 severely unaffordable (American Dream Coalition, 2009).

Housing-induced financial stress often reflects a type of hidden economic exclusion. This may occur simply when access to affordable housing is restricted due to insufficient supply, especially within a geographic distance from a person's place of employment. When more severe, housing stress may typically associate with rising rates of repossessions and foreclosures, and tenant evictions. Particularly vulnerable, in this view, are low-income households who have little left over to meet basic living costs after paying excessive housing costs. Through housing-related hardship, some households are forced into situations of overcrowding. Overcrowding, in turn, leads to other consequences. It may also transform into outright homelessness, a serious social problem and policy concern. In other words, there is a continuum of housing stress, not all of which is readily visible.

Looked at from this perspective, financial stress from housing will have indications that can be measured in terms of lack of access. In the UK, the Financial Services Authority (FSA) made use of the September

2003 National Statistics Omnibus Survey to assess how mortgage holders cope with a specified percentage increase in mortgage interest rates. The results were reported in the FSA's *Financial Risk Outlook* of 2004. Borrowers were asked what action they would take to cope with the increased cost of debt service if they were to struggle or fall behind on their loan repayments. Cutting back on other spending was nominated by 25 percent of respondents, a further 25 percent said they would talk to their lender to rearrange payments, and 23 percent said they would re-mortgage. Ten percent said they would dip into life savings or investments. Only 10 percent said that they would consider selling and moving to a different location. The Australian Household Expenditure Survey uses a list of indicators that comprises the following: could not pay utility bill on time, sought financial help from friends/family, could not pay auto renewal or insurance on time, pawned or sold something, went without meals, sought assistance from charity organizations, was unable to heat home (Yates, 2007). In the case of homebuyers, financial stress is felt when interest rates rise, pushing up repayments.

A conceptual problem with all the above measures, however, is they do not distinguish between a housing affordability problem and low income per se (Gans and King, 2003). The former, the specific housing dimension to the problem, can be thought of in terms of any gap that might exist between the underlying economic cost of housing supply on the one hand, and the price that must be paid by the renter or purchaser on the other. Glaeser and Gyourko (2002) argue that an affordability problem exists when housing is expensive relative to its physical cost of construction. This is helpful as it moves us closer to "housing affordability", purely conceived. Yet by including only physical production costs, Glaeser and Gyourko overlook a second important aspect: financing costs.

Housing, by its very nature, involves the use of financial instruments such as mortgages. Often, the eventual cost of the financial side of housing can turn out to rival the cost of physical production. It is not unusual for the total payments made by the borrower over the lifetime of an annuity mortgage to amount to 200 or 300 percent of the original loan. This is surely a significant consideration, and must be included as part of the "supply" cost of housing in the economy.

Difficulty meeting housing payments is one of the key indicators of financial stress in a rubric developed by the Australian government. On that definition, a respondent is considered to have faced financial stress if they had experienced one or more of the indicators over the past year, including "unable to pay the mortgage or rent on time" (Australian Bureau of Statistics, 2006).

Not surprisingly, lack of housing affordability, more often than not, is a matter of lack of housing finance affordability. Access to, and cost of, finance is therefore an important but often overlooked measure of housing stress. When a household is making a decision to buy a house, the biggest barrier is often its ability to qualify for a sufficient mortgage. Home lenders will take into account the size of the borrower's deposit, which determines the loan-to-value ratio (LVR), and mortgage burden, or ability to service the loan, measured by the ratio of loan repayments relative to the customer's monthly income. If the prospective borrower cannot bridge the "deposit gap", this is one form of housing finance stress. In some countries, lenders are prepared to advance the whole value of the property, and the deposit requirement evaporates. In this situation, the size of the deposit required diminishes as a binding constraint on obtaining finance. Yet that is only half the equation. The repayments fraction – the proportion of household income consumed by mortgage payments – may still be a limiting factor. If this proportion is higher than 30 percent of income, then it violates the 30-percent rule from the outset. Or if subsequently house prices fall, or the mortgage interest rate resets higher after an agreed "honeymoon" period, or if the householder suffers an unexpected loss of livelihood, then financial stress can result down the track.

The combined constraint – deposit hurdle coupled with repayments burden – forms a benchmark for housing finance stress. We can label this the "access-to-finance" indicator of housing finance stress. The Access-to-Finance (A2F) indicator is a bivariate benchmark for housing finance stress where, either because of the deposit hurdle or the repayments burden, or both, a household is unable to afford a mortgage. Generally, A2F will closely reflect the ratio of mortgage servicing costs to income. We will refer to this A2F indicator throughout the text, and report relevant trends in the data, especially in Chapters 4 through 6.

One study classifies mortgage stress into two categories. "Mild" mortgage stress is said to be present when households have re-prioritized and curtailed spending to pay the mortgage, but there is no significant risk of default. "Severe" stress is when households are having difficulty making regular mortgage repayments, are at significant risk of default, or have defaulted or commenced a forced sale (Johnson, Manning and Disney-Willis, 2007).

In summary, the preferred measure in this book will be the A2F dual indicator, the constraint that combines deposit gap plus income multiple. By extension, this can also encompass the 30-rule and 30/40 rule, which are essentially income multiples, but can apply to renters as well as buyers. We will thus pay attention, during the discussion that ensues, to the efficient delivery of financial services for housing, for that will affect the fundamental global cost of housing in the economy.

## The extent of housing stress

Estimates of the extent of housing stress vary by country and also by the measure employed. In the US, one in three American households spends more than 30 percent of income on housing, according to the Joint Center for Housing Studies (2008). Another reliable source similarly estimates that 95 million people, or 30 percent of the population, have housing problems including a high-cost burden, overcrowding, poor quality shelter, and homelessness. One in seven spends more than 50 percent, around 40 million Americans (National Low Income Housing Coalition, 2004).

In the euro area, taking the European Community Household Panel (ECHP) as reference, analysis of the nature and extent of the persistence of housing deprivation using a cross-sectional view shows that around 20 percent of the population appears to be experiencing housing stress at a given point in time. However, longitudinal analysis of the flows into and out of housing deprivation shows a staggering 50 percent have gone through some kind of housing deprivation, at one time or another (Ayala and Navarro, 2007). The results suggest not only that there are groups running a greater housing deprivation risk but also that some face a greater probability of being in this state on a persistent basis.

In Australia, research by the National Centre for Social and Economic Modelling (NATSEM) released in 2008 shows that 23 percent of low- and middle-income households are spending one-third or more of their gross income on rent or the mortgage. This represents a rise of 25 percent since 2004. Around six percent of lower-income households are paying more than 50 percent of their income on housing, according to recent research by the Australian Housing and Urban Research Institute (AHURI). A consumer survey by J.P. Morgan and Fujitsu Consulting in 2008 found that four percent of all households are suffering from "severe" levels of mortgage stress, based on the more stringent criterion of facing a significant chance of defaulting on their home loan.

Admittedly, the figures mentioned above were mostly of those before the credit crisis. Since the crisis, the housing price "bubble" has burst and it might be assumed that housing stress has eased somewhat. While that is partly true, by no means has the problem of housing stress gone away.

Figure 2.1 provides an international, postcrisis overview of housing affordability problems. The 2009 *Demographia International Housing*

| Rating | Number of markets | Percentage |
|---|---|---|
| Severely unaffordable | 64 | 24.2 |
| Seriously unaffordable | 40 | 15.1 |
| Moderately unaffordable | 74 | 27.9 |
| Affordable | 87 | 32.8 |
| TOTAL | 265 | 100.0 |

*Figure 2.1* Distribution of markets by housing affordability, 2008 (six countries)

Source: 5th Annual Demographia International Housing Affordability Survey (Cox and Pavletich, 2009).

*Affordability Survey* provides the latest comparative ratings for 265 metropolitan markets in Australia, Canada, Ireland, New Zealand, the UK, and the US. The survey is unique in providing standardized comparisons of housing affordability between international housing markets. Data apply to the third quarter of 2008.

To rate housing affordability, the survey employs the ratio of median house price to median household income multiple ("median multiple"). The median multiple metric is recommended by the World Bank and the United Nations. A rating of "affordable" applies if the multiple is 3.0 or less. A city is said to be "unaffordable" if it has a multiple of more than 3.0. This lack of affordability is "serious" if the score is more than 4.0, and "severe" if it is more than 5.0.

The survey covers 265 major cities in six countries, including the US, the UK, and Australia. As the table shows, despite the global slowdown and drop in house prices in the crisis-ridden year of 2008, some 68 percent of housing markets internationally remained "unaffordable", postcrisis. Of these, one-fourth are ranked "severely" unaffordable, with median multiples above 5.0.

The credit crisis did not make it easier to access finance. Lenders tightened eligibility criteria to access loans and, house prices slumped; many people's mortgages became "underwater". Further analysis is provided in Chapters 4 through 6, where we show that housing stress remains a reality, even after the credit crisis.

## Economic costs of housing stress

In the UK, the Cost-effectiveness in Housing Investment (CEHI) research program proposed the notion of the "exported" costs of inadequate housing. The CEHI argued that poor living conditions can be expected to generate additional costs to key non-housing service providers, including the following:

- The education service: poor, overcrowded and noisy home conditions impede learning.
- The police and judicial services: poor housing and environmental design and construction is associated with a higher incidence of some crimes.
- The emergency services: poor housing conditions and heating/cooling increase the risks of accident and fire.
- The energy supply services: poorly designed housing uses excess energy and produces ecological damage.

The CEHI team termed these costs "exported costs" because they are generated by underinvestment in one sector (housing in this case) and then effectively outsourced to others.

On account of these exported costs of housing deficiency, housing access and affordability have important implications for the economy as well as for the fabric of the community (Hamnett, 1996b; Heady, 1997).

For instance, if lack of affordable housing for essential workers (nurses, firefighters, teachers, janitors, bank tellers, and so on) close to the inner city restricts labor supply, an adverse side effect will be a rise in costs of production. The economic performance of cities and the growth of employment in metro areas, especially in the high phase of a business cycle, has been shown to be related to the prevailing human capital mix (Owyang et al., 2008). Housing exclusion raises issues for the economic competitiveness of a borough, county, city, state, or nation; consequences of housing stress include the erosion of economic capital (Erbas and Nothaft, 2002). Job creation is related to housing-induced constraints on employment growth in metropolitan areas (Saks, 2008). A 2006 industry report in Australia found evidence that a generation of low-skilled low-paid hospitality workers, transport operators, sales clerks, hospital staff and the like did not have adequate affordable housing options close to work (Property Council of Australia, 2006).

Employment outcomes are distorted as a consequence of supply falling short of demand in a range of essential occupations. In order to function properly, cities need plenty of lower paid service workers. If routine office processors, waiters, shop assistants, bus drivers and the like are unable to afford to live anywhere near the centers of economic activity, job mismatches persist, and transactions costs rise. The regional economy suffers because of the inefficiency of workers or due to labor shortages. These problems are clearly evident in intensive world cities and regions like London, New York, and Sydney. This in turn forms a significant barrier to attaining full industrial efficiency as firms seek to minimize their costs and make location decisions, and unwanted restrictions may therefore be imposed on the growth of metro areas if housing problems choke the supply of vital human capital. An affordable, safe, and cohesive urban environment is critically important to attract and retain these workers.

Reduced effective access to the labor market is often a corollary of housing exclusion, for those who are job-seeking. Lower cost housing is generally geographically concentrated in areas of low employment, which in turn can markedly reduce the job prospects of households in those localities: the "spatial concentration of unemployed people may hamper contacts with those who have a job; in this way, no information is exchanged on job openings" (Van Kempen and Priemus, 1999). In a vicious circle, poor job prospects reduce lifetime earnings and the capacity to meet long-term housing costs.

Housing tenure also promotes educational outcomes (Mueller and Tighe, 2007). Children who live in poor housing have lower educational attainment and a greater likelihood of being impoverished and unemployed as adults (Harker, 2006). Children living in temporary, overcrowded, or otherwise inadequate housing may suffer educational disadvantage. Poor housing leading to poor health can adversely affect school attendance and performance, and insecurity of tenure and frequent forced moves will disrupt a child's schooling and may lead to truancy. Using the US Panel Study of Income Dynamics to explore the impact of housing on children's productivity through educational attainment, researchers have found that the children of homeowners are significantly more likely to achieve a higher level of education and, thereby, higher level of earnings (Boehm and Schlottmann, 1999). Evidence from Australia also supports the link between housing and education (AHURI, 2005).

Children of homeowners are more likely to stay in school (by 7–9%), and daughters of homeowners are less likely to have children by the age of 18 (by 2–4%) (Green and White, 1997). Owning a home leads to improved test scores in children (9% in math and 7% in reading) and reduced behavioral problems, by three percent (Haurin, Parcel, and Haurin, 2002).

There is a large body of evidence that links poor housing conditions to a range of serious health problems and costs (for example, Bonnefoy,

2007; Marsh, 2000). Research has established a link between living conditions and health promotion strategies (Ambrose, 2001; Thomson et al., 2001). Research published by the British Medical Association shows a correlation between ill health and poor housing, especially damp and inadequately heated houses (Thomson et al., 2002; Marsh et al., 2004). The large variations in seasonal mortality in the UK have been associated with dismal housing conditions (Clinch and Healy, 2000). Healy (2004) reports that fuel-poverty and poor health are linked. After studying the UK data, Ambrose concludes that "it follows that investment in sufficient housing of a quality to safeguard health should be seen as a preventative healthcare measure" (Ambrose, 2003).

In the Australian context, research for the National Health Strategy and other works (AHURI, 2002) established a strong correlation between low economic status and poor health.

In the US, it has been shown that the number of low-income families that lack safe and affordable housing is related to the number of children that suffer from asthma, viral infections, anemia, stunted growth, and other physical problems (Sandel and Zotter, 2000). Children in problem-housing are at an increased risk of viral or bacterial infections, and have a greater chance of suffering mental health and behavioral problems (Harker, 2006). Housing deprivation leads, on average, to a 25 percent greater risk of disability or severe ill health across a person's lifespan, and those who suffer housing deprivation as children are more likely to suffer ill health in adulthood, even if they live in non-deprived conditions later in life (Marsh et al. 2000).

Homeownership is an important vehicle for lifetime wealth creation. In the UK, between 1998 and 2005, while average incomes of first-time buyers rose by 60 percent, the average houseprice for first-time buyers rose further still by 136 percent (HM Treasury, 2006). Empirical evidence using the US Panel Survey of Income Dynamics (PSID) shows that owning a house is positively and significantly associated with wealth accumulation over time (Di et al., 2007). In other research, housing tenure choices were found to affect household net wealth levels even after controlling for other factors such as initial wealth, location, income, education, and other personal characteristics (such as propensity to save) that might influence the rate of wealth accumulation, and even during periods when alternative investments produced higher than normal returns and rents grew slowly. For low-income minority families, median average annual housing-related wealth appreciation in the US context is estimated at $1712 per person; this wealth is achieved both through equity and forced savings resulting from mortgage repayment (Boehm and Schlottmann, 2004).

Home ownership has been found to increase intergenerational wealth accumulation through improved educational achievement in children, which leads to greater earnings when these children enter the workforce (Boehm and Schlottmann, 2002). Housing stability aids the educational prospects of children to the extent that it assists the accumulation of human capital and the future quality of the economy's labor force.

Housing finance and tenure are significant in explaining financial exclusion. Increasing debt burdens put financial pressures on mortgagees, which can lead to foreclosure and make debt a pathway to financial exclusion and social "residualization" (Carbo, Gardner and Molyneux, 2005).

Home ownership imparts stability. According to the US data, those who become owners of a house typically own it for seven years before moving to another house. Homeowners live in larger, higher quality units; they enjoy better housing services with costs that fall over time; and they stand to make considerable returns if they remain owners for a longer time (McCarthy, Van Zandt and Rohe, 2001).

In connection with enhancing household equilibrium, research has found that improved housing tenure reduces the frequency of individual job instability, both in terms of switching between different local jobs and new jobs outside the local labor market (Munch, Rosholm and Svarer, 2008). In addition, home ownership reduces the risk of unemployment and has a positive empirical impact on wages. These results are robust to statistical diagnostic tests, notably to different strategies for correcting for the possible endogeneity of the home-owner variable. Boehm and Schlottmann (2006) find that families in owned homes exhibit an increased probability of staying put over time, while those in rental units are more likely to move. These differences are important because of their potential implications for long-term neighborhood stability and the associated effect on economic stability.

Home ownership contributes to enhanced economic security of households to the degree that it makes for a more stable workforce and for a greater resilience of consumers to bad times. In particular, across a life cycle, security is achieved through secure tenure (in case of renters) or by equity formation (in case of home owners). The latter opens up possibilities to withdraw equity in order to, say, retire early or increase consumption. This can be achieved through re-mortgaging or by moving and scaling down. In this way, asset accumulation in housing, perhaps with periodic equity release, helps to mitigate cyclical economic problems among the population, such as periods of unanticipated unemployment, or the economic deprivation characteristic of some elderly households. Research demonstrates that an important corollary of housing investment is low housing expenditures in older age, as a result of debt repayments at an earlier age (Turner and Yang, 2006).

Improved housing access and stability also have significant positive distributional effects. Unlike the sharp division between the landed gentry and those without property in the preindustrial era, modern society gives many the chance to own real estate. In turn, this allows the vast majority to accumulate lifetime wealth, which acts to counteract the tendency toward a grossly unequal distribution of economic benefits. However, net differences still exist on account of differences in household composition and variations across countries in the size of the owner-occupied sector.

## Social costs of housing stress

Housing stress impacts negatively on the formation of "social capital". Social capital refers to the mutual trust and civic behaviors that facilitate communal engagement. Cities and suburbs function as a complexity of multi-nodal metro structures, and the associated interactional linkages, flows, and networks, within and beyond metropolitan boundaries, have great significance for the maintenance of social cohesion and community energy or atrophy (European Committee for Social Cohesion, 2000).

Housing plays a key role in the formation of social capital through a complex process involving both form and function. Architecture, for instance, can act as an important determinant of social cohesion. If the social cohesion role of housing is weakened by housing exclusion and housing instability, then civic equity and urban connections are likely to suffer, in turn hampering the promotion of a sustainably compact socio-urban form. Where social capital disintegrates, so does social cohesion. Where this occurs, segments of the community will experience social exclusion; in effect, they will be prevented from full participation in the life of the community.

In support of this, research by urban economists suggests a relationship between housing structure and social fabric (Temkin and Rohe, 1998). In communities where residents are more likely to be socially connected with their neighbors, they will be more involved in local politics and better linked with the public infrastructure and space around them. Street crime (robbery, auto theft) will be less common where there is more affinity between people and the streets that surround them. Social capital literature documents a flow-on effect from such civic connection to economic outcomes such as income growth, with implications for economic performance (Glaeser and Sacerdote, 2000). One of the key factors enhancing this sense of social unity is housing stability.

Further evidence in this direction, that housing strengthens communities, is provided by DiPasquale and Glaeser (1998) who demonstrated that homeowners are more likely to know their Congressional representative (by ten percent) and school board head by name (by nine percent), and are more likely to vote in local elections (by 15 percent) and work to solve local problems (by six percent). Another US study found that homeowners are more likely to be satisfied with their homes and neighborhoods, and more likely to volunteer in civic and political activities (Rohe, Van Zandt, and McCarthy, 2000).

The links between crime and inadequate housing are complex. A range of factors, including poor housing, affects crime levels. In the US context, resident ownership is strongly related to better building security and quality, and to lower levels of crime (Saegert and Winkel, 1998). In a British study, Barrow and Bachan (1997) compared crime levels and costs across London's public housing estates. They found, for example, that the annual cost of dealing with crime in the deteriorated and stigmatized London estate of Stepney was more than four times that of the level for the newer and better-resourced Paddington estate. Evidence such as this suggests that providing housing that is both appropriate and affordable is one of a number of strategies necessary for dealing with problems of crime.

Inadequate housing can contribute to family dysfunction and breakdown. McCaughey (1992), in a study of 33 families, has documented how, in cases of housing deprivation, normal family and parenting relationships are threatened and how they are difficult to re-establish if broken. Without secure tenure over housing of a reasonable basic standard, large enough to meet the minimum requirements for the shelter of a household, given its size and composition, normal "family life" is more difficult to sustain. A survey in Australia found serious social problems associated with financial stress and anxiety. More than half of the total sample surveyed (58%) said that financial stress had had an impact on themselves, on their family, or on the broader community in the past six years. In particular, 5.8 percent of households said financial stress had contributed to relationship breakdown, 3.5 percent said it had led to substance abuse, 3.3 percent said it contributed to increased gambling, and 1.3 percent said worry about money contributed to violence in the relationship (Wesley Mission, 2006).

Humanly speaking, housing plays an important role in society's vision of the quality of life of its citizens, or the lack thereof. In particular, it forms part of the jigsaw puzzle that is poverty. In recent years, there has been a school of thought arguing the multi-aspectual nature of poverty, that poverty consists not simply of monetary deprivation but also of a network of social exclusions. According to this view, poverty refers not only to a lack of income but also to an inadequate participation in different domains of life, such as employment, education, housing, and health. One study estimated the relative importance of housing problems as a dimension of poverty in four European countries, including the UK, and concluded that housing problems occupy a large part of everyday life for the poor in those countries (Dewilde and De Keulenaer, 2003).

In summary, the evidence is compelling, that adequate and affordable housing is a necessary ingredient in the achievement and maintenance of an inclusive and cohesive society (Phibbs, 2000). The housing stock, in other words, functions at two levels: it makes up an integral part of hard infrastructure of the economy and, at the same time, forms a part of "soft infrastructure" of the society in which the economy is nested, the so-called social capital (Putnam, 1998).

This survey of the range of largely interdependent, housing-related social and economic costs is significant by any measure for the households that experience them, and for the governments that must deal with their consequences.

## Determinants of housing stress

Housing affordability and the level of housing exclusion are complex phenomena that reflect a myriad of factors. The usual drivers of the housing market include home affordability. Affordability reflects slow or booming home starts and sales, trends in home prices, changes in the inventory of new and existing homes for sale, and rises or falls in percentage points in mortgage rates.

Influences on housing affordability fall into four broad categories.

- Spatial: zoning, dwelling size, estate design, land supply.
- Economic: production, income, rents, demography.
- Government policy: taxes, subsidies, regulations.
- Financial: interest rates, banks, capital markets, investment.

Spatial factors such as urban density, dwelling design, and geography play a role in housing affordability and the dynamics of housing deprivation. So too do physical plant considerations, including new construction rates, deterioration rates, and initial stocks. The debate over urban renewal ("brownfield" development) versus urban sprawl ("greenfield" development) is relevant, with research showing that land supply and demand matter.

For instance, Miceli and Sirmans (2007) examine the link between the holdout problem and urban sprawl, and find that developers attempting land assembly often face a potential holdout problem that raises the cost of development. To minimize this extra cost, developers prefer land whose ownership is less dispersed. This creates a bias toward development at the urban fringe where average lot sizes are larger, resulting in urban sprawl, which may finally help keep housing costs down. Either way, this example illustrates the potential role of land use patterns and metropolitan space pressures.

Arguably, house prices are about the proverbial "location, location, location". Competing demands for limited space in cities generate an urban equation that yields its own inevitable price outcome: if the prices and rents of dwelling units increase faster than incomes in the inner locations of major cities, as is often the case, then housing problems increase. With few exceptions, rents and prices of fully detached houses have grown faster than the household incomes of the lower 40 percent income group in major metropolitan regions in advanced countries. House prices and rents have risen strongly across most cities in the current decade, which has simply priced most low-income earners, as well as many middle-income earners, out of the housing market.

Yet the spatial factor can be exaggerated, and may in fact operate in reverse over time. A global sample of 120 cities by the World Bank in 2005 found that the built-up area densities of cities decreased significantly between 1990 and 2000, at an average rate of 1.7 percent per annum. Other historical data on 30 cities suggest that the decline in average urban densities is almost a century old in many cases, not simply a passing phenomenon but a secular trend, a consequence of improved living standards and a host of technological innovations that have made urban transport cheap and efficient (Angel, 2009).

Zoning rules, nevertheless, can clearly cause local bottlenecks in key localities. Aura and Davidoff (2008) analyze the effects of supply constraints on housing prices in the US, and conclude that a coordinated loosening of official restrictions across jurisdictions could have large price effects. Other evidence on housing supply regulations and their effect on metropolitan areas reveals that locations with relatively few barriers to construction, experience more residential construction and smaller increases in house prices in response to an increase in housing demand (Saks, 2008). For cities to expand, the supply of land must not be artificially constrained. Land supply bottlenecks lead to increases in land prices and, since land is a major housing input, to increases in house prices. The more stringent the restrictions, the less the housing market is able to respond to increased demand and the more likely the house prices are to increase. And when residential land is very difficult to come by, housing becomes unaffordable. There is a body of empirical evidence to prove that placing restrictions on urban land supplies has led to serious house price escalation (Cox and Pavletich, 2009).

For our purpose, it is important to note that at the low-income end of the market, space and location can clearly make for a significant mismatch problem. Shortages of low cost rental dwellings are more intense in some regions and subregions than others. For example, vacant low-rent houses available in the outer suburbs do not significantly ease affordability problems in the inner cities.

Macroeconomic variables also influence housing affordability. These include labor market participation, inflation rates, household incomes, and migration. Often, to the casual observer, it appears that these are easing the situation, yet that conclusion is not always valid. Consider the effect of GDP growth. Over time, average real household income in industrial nations has risen, and other things remaining equal, housing affordability should improve. However, other things have not been equal. While full-time employment has remained relatively strong in industrialized countries (at least prior to the global credit crisis) and average earnings have risen, generally in line with the consumer price index, the growth in national income has not been equally shared. The result is that real household incomes in many cases have actually fallen for key household groups, notably the bottom two income quintiles (lowest 40%).

A further important observation, as numerous researchers have pointed out, is the broad shift away from permanent, full-time employment toward part-time and casual employment. This makes it harder to qualify for, and service, a bank loan. So, in particular regions and demographic segments, housing affordability problems may actually be increasing, despite people being in "steady" employment, the so-called working poor.

Government housing assistance policy is the third important factor in housing affordability. Traditionally, government policy has focussed on social welfare measures, in the form of subsidies paid directly to households, such as rent assistance. Governments, especially in the UK and Australia, in the role of the landlord, are also engaged in providing public housing estates. These policy initiatives have been the subject of extensive debate, with some critics pointing to the problem of "ghettoization" and others calling for the government to step back from the role of owner of estates, to instead play the role of facilitator or broker of housing solutions.

In the US, emphasis has been placed on rent ceilings and mortgage support. Tax settings and accounting rules, including allowable depreciation rates on property, also enter the equation. We will return to these policy issues in later chapters.

Last, but by no means the least, financial considerations play a key role in affordability. Indeed, the major theme of this dissertation is that their role is often underestimated. Discussion about financial effects on housing needs to be based on retail banking mortgage terms and market hurdles. Chapter 3 will deal in detail with the financial dimension to housing stress.

## Defining "affordable housing"

Ultimately, housing affordability is all about the oldest theory in economics: supply and demand. But is simple affordability the real issue? The use of the phrase "affordable housing", by commentators and also in the title of this text, is deliberate. It means more than just house affordability, in two important respects.

First, when housing adequacy is expressed using the term "affordable housing", it implies that affordability is not a characteristic of housing per se, rather it is a "relationship between housing and people" (Stone, 2006a). Affordable housing is a three-dimensional notion, a triangulation that asks: affordable to whom, on what standard of affordability, and for how long? Further, argues Stone, while housing affordability is an indicator, affordable housing carries the connotation of a standard. An indicator is an empirical metric, usually of the relationship between housing costs and incomes. A standard, on the other hand, is a normative specification of the appropriate value that an indicator should or should not take (Baer, 1976).

Second, buying a house requires the wherewithal to cover the purchase price, and the capacity to take on a large, long-term debt obligation. Lack of cash and credit therefore act as constraints, and in the new post-crisis financial environment, any buying boost resulting from the sharp drop in mortgage rates for prime borrowers will be largely offset by the rising proportion of would-be homebuyers who can no longer get credit at any rate, as banks scale back loans to match their shrinking assets. This factor, the financial dimension, is a function of conditions in the capital market, not the housing market. As one commentator puts it, "this aspect of the credit situation is not captured in the home affordability index" (Haughey, 2008).

Third, affordable housing is not the same as "social housing". Publicly owned public housing, and the closely related "community housing" sector, make up social housing and can be thought of as an extension of the government's social security services. By contrast, affordable housing addresses the gap experienced by many working and middle-income households in the private sector whose incomes are not sufficient to allow them to access adequate housing in the market. In the US, where the term originated, "affordable housing" means housing that is privately owned or rented and meets certain affordability benchmarks (Davis, 1994).

In summary, our topic of "affordable housing finance" implies more than just house affordability.

## Conclusions and next steps

We can think of a housing spectrum, ranging from "over-housed" to "under-housed". At one end of the spectrum, some consumers have no affordability problem whatsoever and enjoy a wide range of housing choices, and the ratio between the number of persons in the household and the number of rooms in the dwelling is more than comfortable for present and future needs. At the opposite end, there are households for whom the cost of obtaining satisfactory dwellings with sufficient functional characteristics to meet essential needs exceeds what they can afford, and who have limited options. In between is a mainstream group which has access to housing and housing finance but feels the pressure of paying the rent or the mortgage, and is vulnerable to negative trends such as rising prices or interest rates.

In accordance with the above-mentioned spectrum, think of the housing population in three cohorts: the comfortable, the aspiring, and the excluded. The second and third groups are of the most interest to our subject. As a general rule of thumb, these households make up around 50 percent of the population, 30 percent being middle-class homeowners (or aspiring homeowners) and 20 percent being the chronically under-housed who are unable to afford a decent place to live that meets their reasonable needs.

Lack of housing access, adequacy, affordability, and finance in turn produces negative externalities – unpriced, unintended costs – that are borne by the economy and community. The direct costs of poor housing include bottlenecks in attracting workers to growing industries, and adverse impacts on the health and educational opportunities of household members. Impacts on the community include declining social cohesion and erosion of social capital. A common scenario would be the social exclusion of a significant section of the population from the normal avenues of participation in society.

In this chapter, we viewed housing mainly as a consumer item. In the next, we consider housing in its asset role, as an investment. Residential real estate accounts for around half of all the tangible capital assets in the developed countries of the world (Caplin et al., 2003). The housing industry is well in excess of US$40 trillion; housing is the most valuable asset category on earth. Yet the retail financial markets for housing, and our capability to trade housing as a capital market asset, remain surprisingly underdeveloped.

This is evident from the financial market failure of 2008. As we will discover, bankers tried in vain to bridge the gap in housing finance in recent years by multiplying subprime loans. Housing demand is not going to go away anytime soon, it is a basic human necessity. Instead, housing finance markets will need to evolve once again and become better equipped at handling mortgage finance of multiple varieties. Chapter 2 elaborates this line of thought.

# 3
# The Financial Dimension

## Introduction

The demand for housing finance comes from purchasers of dwellings. Because of the long-term and expensive nature of housing, buyers usually are not in a position to pay cash and therefore require an annuity mortgage. Long-term finance is therefore a critical component of the price of housing, which makes it different from most other commodities in the economy. House buyers fall into two categories: owner-occupiers who purchase to live in the dwelling and landlords who purchase in order to rent the dwelling. The latter includes governments, which purchase dwellings – existing or new – in order to rent them, usually at a below-market rental.

The supply of housing finance comes from savers looking for a place to invest their money long term, with a steady cash flow. These savers may include individual savers, but these days the bulk of the funds are likely to come from mutual funds and pension funds, operated by professional investment managers. Indeed, one of the major developments in recent times has been the re-intermediation of savings, away from traditional bank deposits into managed funds and hedge funds and the like. This has restricted banks' ability to raise their own retail funding for mortgage lending, and forced them to increasingly source that funding from the wholesale capital markets. This is not necessarily a bad thing, but is significant and forms part of the background to the subprime credit crisis.

The housing finance system refers to the entire mechanism for gathering savings and funnelling them to purchasers. Through this mechanism, the housing finance architecture facilitates the effective demand for housing. It needs to do this efficiently. By improving the flexibility of the housing finance market, we enhance the efficiency of the housing market itself and lower the real cost of housing. By continually evolving and improving its performance, through innovating and refining its technological capability, the housing finance infrastructure can enhance flexibility in the market and make a material contribution to economic welfare.

Not only does the housing finance system need to be efficient, it also needs to be sustainable. If the financing system turns dysfunctional, the funds of savers will no longer be channelled to investors efficiently, and housing finance would consequently become more expensive, or less accessible due to rationing, or both. For the ordinary investor, such as a home-buyer, the deposit hurdle would rise, the monthly mortgage repayment burden would increase, and the A2F (Access-to-Finance) housing stress indicator would undergo a step change. Since finance is a critical component of the price of housing, affordability would deteriorate. Thereby, efficiency and flexibility of the sector would regress.

In 2008, the global financial system experienced an exceptional episode of instability, led by the crisis in the United States subprime mortgage market. With the onset of the global credit turmoil, the housing finance infrastructure became dysfunctional, and affordable housing finance became a topic whose time had come.

## The subprime credit crisis

There is widespread agreement that the economic upheaval, the defining macroeconomic episode of our time, originated in the housing finance market, and that this was driven by the subprime mortgage sector, which is also known as the "Alt-A" or "non-conforming" sector. The crisis had been building for some time. The seeds of the problem lay in the accumulation of assets, especially securitized loans in the market for residential mortgage-backed securities (RMBS), whose liquidity and credit quality were less reliable than usual: the household sector equivalent of corporate "junk" bonds. The process of securitization entails the bundling together of underlying mortgages and their removal from the originating institution's balance sheet, with ownership transferred by sale to the wider investment community. Securitized instruments trade on the secondary market, where they are bought and sold by third parties, not by the originator of the underlying assets nor necessarily by the initial investor. The idea of securitized mortgage markets goes back at least to the early 1960s (Jones and Grebler, 1961).

At the retail level, a typical experience ran something like this. In 2005, a couple had already purchased a home, financed with a 30-year fixed-rate prime mortgage based on a sound credit history. A mortgage broker in town called one evening offering to refinance their loan, with a new product that promised to allow them the flexibility to choose from different payment options varying from one month to the next. What was not made clear was that this was a "negative amortization" loan, with a ballooning principal that buried the couple deeper into debt even as they thought that they were paying down their mortgage balance. Other products around at that time included the so-called Ninja loans ("no income, no job, no assets") and "liar" loans (no paperwork check of borrowers' income). This story, which did not have a happy ending, was played out many times, as hundreds of billions of dollars worth of these loans "reset" to higher monthly payments once the honeymoon period expired. Hence the term "predatory lending". This is the subprime credit crisis in microcosm.

Securitizers then took the new loans and turned them into RMBS, and sold them on the capital market. Credit rating agencies like Moody's and Standard & Poor's acquiesced, assigning solid ratings and making these bonds look competitive with prime paper. Figure 3.1 shows how the pattern of US lending shifted sharply after 2003, from traditional prime loans toward subprime loans.

The business model of lenders in the US had shifted; lenders were collecting lucrative fees just for writing new loans. Those involved in

|      | Prime | | | Non-Prime | | | | |
|------|------------|-------|-------|---------|-------|------|----------------|-------|
|      | Conforming | Jumbo | Total | Sub-prime | Alt-A | FHA | Home equity | Total |
| 2001 | 57.1 | 20.1 | 77.2 | 7.2  | 2.5  | 7.9 | 5.2  | 22.8 |
| 2002 | 59.1 | 19.8 | 78.9 | 6.9  | 2.3  | 6.1 | 5.7  | 21.1 |
| 2003 | 62.4 | 16.5 | 78.8 | 7.9  | 2.2  | 5.6 | 5.6  | 21.2 |
| 2004 | 41.4 | 17.6 | 59.1 | 18.5 | 6.5  | 4.6 | 11.3 | 40.9 |
| 2005 | 34.9 | 18.3 | 53.2 | 20.0 | 12.2 | 2.9 | 11.7 | 46.8 |
| 2006 | 33.2 | 16.1 | 49.3 | 20.1 | 13.5 | 2.7 | 14.4 | 50.7 |
| 2007 | 49.1 | 13.9 | 63.0 | 7.3  | 10.8 | 4.4 | 14.6 | 37.1 |

*Figure 3.1* US mortgage originations by product, 2001–2007

*Source:* Adapted from Inside Mortgage Finance, *2008 Mortgage Market Statistical Annual.* Figures show percent share of all mortgage originations.

the deals made their cut, then passed the risk onto a third or fourth party. Instead of keeping the risky loans in their own portfolios, the lenders, that originated the mortgages, resold them to Wall Street investment houses. Those firms then packaged them up with other mortgages and sold them to investors as high-yield mortgage-backed securities (MBSs).

The whole process was predicated on the idea that real estate prices would keep rising. But by 2006, the market began to soften, and then to tumble. All of a sudden, those households who had taken the "new loans" found themselves underwater, owing more on their new houses than the houses were worth. It all turned out to be just a "house of cards", as the report on US television current affairs program 60 Minutes put it.

The problem was that secondary credit markets had not priced and graded many mortgages accurately. Credit market conditions in the US and Europe seriously deteriorated in 2007, reflecting heightened counterparty risk concerns among major financial institutions. As the level of uncertainty escalated, lenders in the US and Europe became increasingly reluctant to supply financing; this was a problem for institutions that depend heavily on wholesale funding. This led to acute balance sheet pressures on banks and severe strains in the global interbank funding network. In response, central banks supplied emergency liquidity and national economic authorities arranged injections of taxpayer-funded capital for specific institutions that were under stress.

In the years prior to the crisis, the wholesale mortgage market appeared to evolve and deepen. Securitization was supposed to be aiding the pricing and trading of risk. New types of mortgage products were created, and for a period, mortgages became more liquid instruments. Computerization and metrics such as credit scores reduced the costs of making loans and led to a "commoditization" of mortgages. Yet in one important respect, capital markets did not mature. As the US Federal Reserve Chairman Bernanke notes, "a key function of efficient capital markets is to overcome problems of information and incentives in the extension of credit" (Bernanke, 2007). In the traditional model of mortgage markets, based on portfolio lending, banks lent on their own account and had strong incentives to invest in gathering information about borrowers. In contrast, when loans are securitized and originators have little financial or reputational capital at risk, the danger exists that the originators of loans will be less diligent, and "the failure of investors to provide adequate oversight of originators and to ensure that originators' incentives were properly aligned was a major cause of the problems that we see today in the subprime mortgage market" (Bernanke, 2007b).

As 2008 unfolded, it became increasingly clear that the dislocation in the global financial system was of historic proportions, starting with the failure of the two largest US mortgage corporations: Fannie Mae and Freddie Mac, and of Wall Street stalwart Lehman Brothers. The four big investment banks in the US were either shut down (Lehman) or sold off (Merrill Lynch) or turned into bank holding companies (Morgan Stanley, Goldman Sachs). The period of greatest intensity in the crisis, September and October of 2008, finally revealed just how deep and widespread the distress of banks is in the US, the UK, and Europe.

Figure 3.2 shows the drop in stock prices of US, UK, and Australian banks in the crisis-ridden year 2008. Most US banks and mortgage lenders recorded huge declines, in the range of 60–90 percent. The slump in the UK FTSE financial index (right hand side of chart) was in roughly the same ballpark as US banks. In Australia, the ASX Banks index fell by a more modest 43 percent.

Reflecting the debacle, on 17 December 2008 Standard and Poor's downgraded 11 major intercontinental banks (Figure 3.3).

Focussing on housing loan arrears, shown country-wise in Figure 3.4, we see that they began to run higher in the US as the crisis mounted, with the 30+ days arrears rate on all mortgages up from 4.3 percent

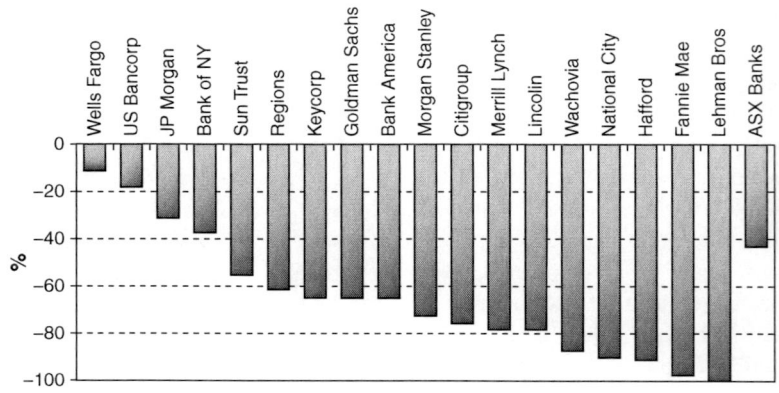

*Figure 3.2* Fall in stock prices during the year 2008 – US, UK, and Australian banks

*Source:* Chart data from *Federal Reserve Bank of St. Louis Review*, 91(1), January 2009; London Stock Exchange FTSE Banks index; Australian Stock Exchange (ASX) Financial sector index. Figures for US are for year ending November.

|  | Previous S&Ps rating | New S&Ps rating |
|---|---|---|
| Bank of America | AA− | A+ |
| Barclays PLC | AA | AA− |
| Citigroup | AA− | A |
| Credit Suisse | AA− | A+ |
| Deutsche Bank | AA− | A+ |
| GoldmanSachs | AA− | A |
| HSBC* | AA− | AA− |
| JP Morgan | AA− | A+ |
| MorganStanley | A+ | A |
| Royal Scotland | AA− | A+ |
| UBS | AA− | A+ |
| Wells Fargo | AA+ | AA |

*Figure 3.3* Rating downgrades of global banks by Standard & Poor's

Source: Standard and Poor's. S&P's scale is AAA, AA+, AA, AA−, A+, A, A− (L toR: high to lower ratings).
*HSBC was not downgraded.

|  | Arrears (%) |
|---|---|
| Australian mortgages | 1.13 |
| UK Prime RMBS | 2.90 |
| US mortgages | 6.40 |

*Figure 3.4* Arrears (30+ days) – by country

Source: Adapted from Reserve Bank of Australia. Data are for September 2008.

in 2005 to 6.4 percent in 2008. In the UK, the share of rated (prime) securitized mortgages that were 30+ days in arrears edged from 2.3 percent in 2005 to 2.9 percent in 2008. Australia's arrears rate, by contrast, remained low, near historical levels.

Figure 3.5 displays the trends in loan quality during the crisis. Impaired loans (most of which are mortgage-related) rose sharply in the US as the credit turmoil took hold. There was also an increase in impaired loans in Australia, although more modest. Anecdotal evidence suggests a rise also occurred in impaired loans in the UK in the crisis-ridden year 2008.

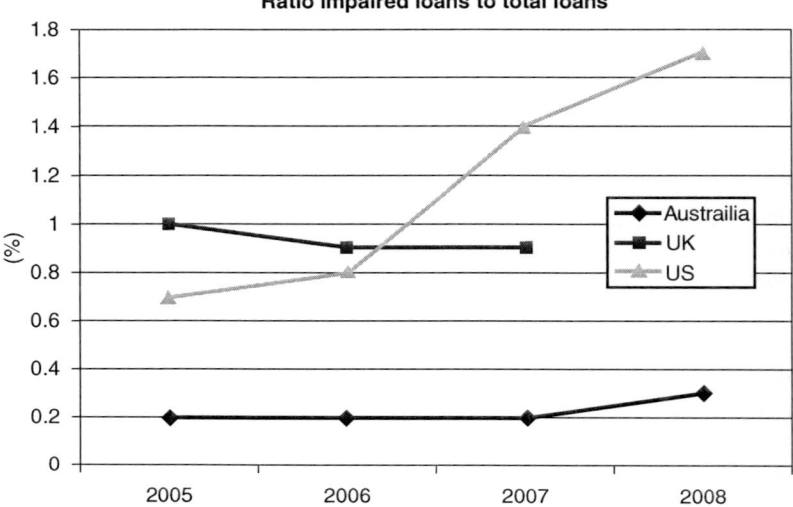

*Figure 3.5* Trend in nonperforming loans – by country

*Source:* Chart data from *Global Financial Stability Report*, International Monetary Fund, Washington DC, October 2008. Data show loans in 60+ days arrears, as percentage of total loans outstanding.

The cost of the collapse was high for taxpayers. A comparison of the major "bailout" packages across various countries is presented in Figure 3.6, including that for the US, the UK, and Australia. The November 2008 US bank bailout package cost taxpayers around US$700 billion, and in the February 2009 economic "stimulus" package, Washington spent a further US$800 billion. Firms and households are paying a further heavy price because of layoffs, business closures, lost investment opportunities, and wealth erosion due to stock market losses.

In Figure 3.6, bank "bail-outs" proper are summarized in the first column. Almost all the countries listed doled out a package each to rescue individual banks, defined as the injecting of capital directly into those firms. The bailouts in some countries were more extensive (Germany, Netherlands, US, UK) and in one case, the banks have been nationalized (Iceland).

In the case of the US, beginning September 8, 2008, the government announced the US$700 billion Troubled Asset Relief Program (TARP), of which around US$250 billion was earmarked for direct bank bailouts. At the time of writing, 52 banks had been funded by the program including the likes of Citibank ($45 billion), Bank of America ($45 billion), J.P.Morgan Chase ($25 billion), Wells Fargo ($25 billion), Goldman Sachs

| Country | Capital injection | Purchase of assets | TOTAL |
|---|---|---|---|
| Australia | — | $A8 | $A8 |
| Austria | €15 | — | €15 |
| Belgium | €4.4 | 2.5 | €6.9 |
| Canada | — | CAD$25 | CAD$25 |
| France | €41 | — | €41 |
| Germany | €130 | — | €130 |
| Greece | €5 | — | €5 |
| Iceland | Nationalized | Nationalized | 100% |
| Italy | As needed | — | As needed |
| Netherlands | €46.8 | — | €46.8 |
| Spain | — | €50 | €50 |
| South Korea | — | KRW1,000 | KRW1,000 |
| Switzerland | CHF6 | US$60 | US$60+ |
| USA | US$250 | US$450 | US$700 |
| UK | £50 | — | £50 |

*Figure 3.6* Summary, by country, of 2008 official support measures (all currency in billions)

*Source:* Adapted from Bank of England, *Financial Stability Report*, Number 24, October 27, 2008.

($10 billion), Morgan Stanley ($10 billion) and Merrill Lynch ($10 billion), Bank of New York Mellon ($3 billion), and State Street ($2 billion), as well as US Bancorp, Suntrust, Washington Mutual, National City, Countrywide, First Horizon, Indy Mac, Wachovia, PNC, Regions Financial, Fifth Third, and Keycorp. Regarding the US response, it is significant to observe that this was the second major US taxpayer-bailout in 20 years; the other had resulted from the US Savings and Loans crisis in the 1980s.

On October 8, 2008, UK authorities announced a comprehensive and system-wide support package that addressed directly the weaknesses in UK banks' balance sheets and involved a government-supported recapitalization scheme for UK banks, involving big name institutions like Abbey, Barclays, HBOS, HSBC Bank plc, Lloyds TSB, Nationwide Building Society, Royal Bank of Scotland, and Standard Chartered. For example, a capital of £37 billion was injected into RBS, HBOS, and Lloyds. Assessing the UK bailout package, the Bank of England said the measure represented "the largest UK government intervention in financial markets since the outbreak of the First World War" (*Financial Stability Report*, Number 24, October 27, 2008, p. 32).

In Australia, no bank bailout package was necessary. The Federal Government did, however, in November 2008, introduce for the first time in that country, a guarantee scheme for large deposits and wholesale funding, a plan it had previously announced in October. The Australian Prudential Regulation Authority supported the move. The government arrived at its decision on depositor guarantees not to head off potential bank losses, but rather, in the Reserve Bank of Australia's words, to "promote financial system stability in Australia, by supporting confidence" during a time of acute uncertainty (*Financial Stability Review*, October 2008). Australian bank deposits were already safe, legislatively speaking, with or without the government's new guarantee: there was already a depositor priority scheme in place under the Banking Act which gives depositors first claim on the assets of a bank. Notwithstanding this, practical advantages of the new guarantee scheme include the removal of potential uncertainty on the timeliness of payment in the event of a claim, and removal of the competitive distortion created by foreign guarantees previously enacted by governments overseas.

In early 2009, both the US and the UK, recognizing that the banking crisis was larger than originally imagined, announced further phases in their bank rescue operations. The UK government said on January 19, 2009 that it would commit tens of billions of pounds of additional funds to extend its rescue plan, centered around an effort to insure banks against further losses, similar to the US plans unveiled then to cap losses at Citibank and Bank of America. In the US, the new Obama administration announced in mid-February that it would introduce a second bank rescue package, involving the purchase of impaired assets for quarantining into a "bad bank". The White House also introduced a US$75 billion plan to support the housing sector, in February 2009.

The final extent of the bailout bill may not be known for some time, years perhaps, because of the complexity and time-consuming nature of the cleanup. Yet it is likely to total around $500 billion in the US. This estimate is based on the projections for total final writedowns from the subprime crisis and is shown in Figure 3.7.

By October 2008, US financial institutions had incurred losses on their portfolio estimated at more than three percent. IMF projections suggest that by the time the dust settles from the current crisis, US writedowns will amount to as much as five to six percent of the portfolio.

European banks also incurred huge loan writedowns. As of October 2008, Europe, as a whole, had already incurred a total of US$220 billion in loan losses, according to the IMF. This is equal to around two-third of the US losses of US$325 billion to date. Based on a pro rata basis, we

|  | Amount outstanding US$b | Losses as of Oct 2008 US$b | (Percentage of loans) | Total projected writedowns US$ | (Percentage of loans) |
| --- | --- | --- | --- | --- | --- |
| Housing | 4,700 | 170 | (3.6) | 265 | (5.6) |
| Personal | 1,400 | 45 | (3.2) | 80 | (5.7) |
| Business | 3,700 | 110 | (3.0) | 195 | (5.2) |
| TOTAL | 9,800 | 325 | (3.3) | 540 | (5.51) |

*Figure 3.7* Projected final writedowns by loan category in the US

*Source:* Adapted from *Global Financial Stability Report*, International Monetary Fund, Washington DC, October 2008; figures are in US$billion unless otherwise stated.

|  | Housing | | | Business | | |
| --- | --- | --- | --- | --- | --- | --- |
|  | Pre-crisis | → | 2008 | Pre-crisis | → | 2008 |
| Australia | 12.7 | → | 9.2% | 18.3 | → | 8.9% |
| UK | 10.6 | → | 4.4% | 19.2 | → | 7.2% |
| US | 11.7 | → | 2.7% | 14.3 | → | 3.4% |

*Figure 3.8* Bank credit growth and the financial crisis (annualized percentage change)

*Source:* Adapted from Bank of England; ECB; Federal Reserve; RBA Pre-crisis figures are annual average credit growth for 2005–2007. Figures for 2008 are up to September.

can project that banks in the Euro area will ultimately see writedowns of around US$350 billion resulting from the crisis.

The economic effect of the crisis was that credit lines dried up and macroeconomic conditions deteriorated into recession by 2009. The slowdown in credit included housing. Figure 3.8 shows how mortgage lending slowed in all three countries under study.

Undoubtedly, many of the "usual suspects" played some part in the crisis, such as unchecked balance sheet growth, conflicts of interest, and a complex web of business deals. Yet all of these are responsible at par for the course in the world of banking most of the time, and do not by themselves fully account for what happened. The 2008 credit crisis points beyond these factors, to market failure in the provision of affordable housing finance.

As many as five years earlier, some observers had expressed fears that Fannie and Freddie were adding to the risks that might be posed to the US Treasury by displaying inadequate accounting and financial controls

(Poole, 2003). Baker Botts law firm (2003) performed an investigation into Freddie Mac's accounting practices and concluded that "disclosure processes and practices fall below the standards required of a registered public company". Green and Wachter (2005) concluded that both companies clearly "failed to perform one of the most basic functions of a publicly traded company"; that is, to report earnings correctly and according to generally accepted accounting practices.

Similarly, an analysis by the OECD (Organisation for Economic Cooperation and Development) pinpoints transparency and information, as critical to the strength and safety of financial markets (Lumpkin, 2008):

> In many instances of systemic instability, multiple factors have been involved ... poor governance and internal management, inadequate control of operational risks, and inadequate disclosure and lack of transparency.

This has become even more important as the banking industry has grown in complexity, a fact highlighted by the credit crisis. According to another official commentary (Schich, 2008):

> [t]raditional distinctions between different financial activities, including banking, securities dealing, and asset management, have become more blurred. As well, closer and more complex inter-linkages in the financial system have facilitated spillover effects and implied that the systemic risk factors that (commercial) banks are exposed to are more universal.

That is to say, the subprime crisis of 2008 stemmed, to a significant degree, from a breakdown in credit risk information and lack of transparency.

One response might be to retreat from secondary mortgage markets and restrict activity only to prime lending. Yet this draconian prescription has never applied to corporate debt, even in the wake of the junk bond crisis of the 1980s, and as outlined in the previous chapter, housing stress is an economic pressure in the real economy that is not going to go away any time soon. Sticking our heads in the sand and thereby trying to pretend that affordable housing finance needs will magically take care of themselves is not a realistic response. Instead, we need an intentional strategy to ensure that the financial infrastructure is in place to handle affordable housing finance better, next time around.

The banking system attempted to respond to the question of affordable housing finance in a somewhat haphazard fashion, during the pre-crisis years. This well-intentioned response unfortunately explains the eventual onset of the crisis of 2008. The response was not properly grounded in well-developed financial procedures and capital market infrastructure. The failure of the experiment demonstrates that the housing finance system needed, as a partner, a more competent and flexible wholesale capital market for prime and subprime housing finance that correctly facilitated the orderly issuance, purchase, pricing, and trading of housing-backed securities of various investment grades.

The view in these pages is that the arbitrage point in affordable housing in the twenty-first century increasingly lies within the financial domain. It can be argued that a form of capital market failure, revolving around the question of credit information transparency and symmetry, is the essential cause of the global credit crisis. This highlights the central importance of the finance dimension in addressing the housing sector of the economy.

## Capital market failure

At one level, the 2008 crisis came about because of cyclical macroeconomic factors: an upswing in housing prices, accommodating government policies during the Bush administration years, and competitive pressures prior to the crisis that saw banking firms falling over each other to expand lending. We might add some poor business practices by banks that encouraged higher-risk lending practices by staff, and a proliferation in products offering loan incentives, such as easy initial terms, to customers.

At another level, however, it can be argued that the situation developed in the way it did because of structural deficiencies in capital markets. One symptom of this is that credit-rating agencies, the very capital market professionals who are supposed to detect problems in credit instruments, did not see the crisis coming. These agencies are now under scrutiny for having given investment-grade ratings to securitized vehicles that were essentially subprime, such as MBSs and collateralized debt obligations (CDOs). Generous ratings by these credit rating agencies encouraged investors to buy securities backed by subprime mortgages, and the reliance on these ratings led many investors to treat securitized products based on sub-standard mortgages as equivalent to higher quality securities, in the opinion of many observers.

Another pointer is the fact that the market is taking so long to regroup. This suggests a classic information problem. After the initial shock received from unexpected news, when the market temporarily becomes illiquid due to uncertainty, financial markets normally recover quickly with trading resuming around new consensus price levels (Sy, 2008). However, following this crisis, the market did not recover quickly. By 2009, a full year into the crisis, many parts of the credit market remained closed to new lending and the situation was still a long away from resolution. This suggests that the information set is insufficient to unlock the market, since we need to translate individual loan data to prices for securities with credit risk. This critical step appears to be beyond the capabilities of the credit risk models in use at the time. In March 2008, in testimony before the US House of Representatives, Charles Prince, CEO of Citigroup, one of the largest banks in the world, admitted that the credit risk models used at Citigroup and in the industry were wrong. In early May 2008, Standard & Poor's announced that it would stop rating certain types of mortgage-backed bonds citing the reason that "the market segment does not allow meaningful analysis".

The credit crisis has as its roots the many US mortgages issued in recent years to subprime borrowers, defined as those with lesser ability to repay a standard loan based on normal criteria. Once housing prices started to drop in 2007 in many parts of the US, refinancing became more difficult. Defaults and foreclosures increased dramatically as initial "honeymoon" terms expired; home prices failed to go up as anticipated, and adjustable-rate mortgages (ARMs) interest rates reset higher. High default rates emerged on many subprime loans as well as on ARMs.

The underlying problem, however, is asymmetric and incomplete information, not risk. Credit markets always carry risk, yet most of the time operate normally. However, on this occasion, in this market segment, at this time in history, information about risk was wildly inaccurate. Capital markets did not evaluate the credit risks systematically.

The subprime crisis reflects information problems that are well known in economic theory. The problem of motivating one party to act on behalf of another is known as "the principal–agent problem". The problem arises when a principal compensates an agent for performing certain acts that are useful to the principal and costly to the agent, and where there are elements of the performance that are costly to observe. For instance, whenever a bank lends to a mortgage customer, the bank cannot be 100 percent certain of the customer's capacity to repay the loan. Similarly, when an investor buys an RMBS from a bank, the investor cannot fully know the credit quality of the underlying mortgages. In other words, the principal–agent problem is present for all contracts that are written in a world of information asymmetry, uncertainty, and risk. Here, principals do not know enough about whether (or to what extent) a contract has been satisfied. The solution to this information problem is to ensure the provision of appropriate incentives so that agents act in the way principals wish.

The emergence of capital markets as a source of housing finance has a somewhat checkered history. It was motivated by limitations inherent in the traditional "maturity transformation" role that banks perform, where they rely on short-term deposits to fund long-term mortgage lending. Over time, this motivated major innovations in financial instruments, which had the effect of linking mortgage lending more closely to capital markets at large. Fed Chairman Ben Bernanke has called this shift, from reliance on specialized portfolio lenders financed by deposits to a greater use of capital markets, the "second great sea change in mortgage finance, equalled in importance only by the events of the New Deal" (Bernanke, 2007a).

In general, however, capital markets have simply not developed sufficient functionality with respect to originating and pricing housing finance other than prime home loans. This reflects historical attitudes. Large wholesale investors – mutual funds, pension funds, hedge funds, unit trusts, and the like – have traditionally shunned investment in "low-cost housing". Conventional wisdom has always held that the reason these investors have tended to shy away from this type of investment is on account of the fact that it typically provides lower returns and higher property risks.

Against this, however, is the observation that for years, investors have been willingly investing in corporate bonds, that is, non-mortgage bonds that are B and C graded. This is evidence that sophisticated investors will buy lower-grade paper, provided the minimal informational requirements are met. Indeed, we know from portfolio theory that holding a mix of paper, of varying risk and return characteristics, improves the optimality of a portfolio by reducing the portfolio's risk, for a given rate of return.

This suggests that an alternative plausible explanation exists as to why professional investors have tended to shy away from low-income housing investment in the past. This explanation has to do with the lack of transparency and information, two factors essential to the proper functioning of capital markets. The multigrade market has not developed a suite of instruments for affordable housing bonds to parallel that in the corporate bond market. There has been (and still is) a lack of information about the risk and return performance of different possible grades of non-prime mortgage vehicles. Because no market sector has existed for such instruments, housing bonds with a B or C grade are perceived by fund managers as suffering from low liquidity. Poor detailed market information and the dearth of trades of such investments only add to the drawbacks and have acted to further retard the evolution of a bona fide non-prime sector. This general proposition is supported by research findings. For instance, Diaz-Serrano (2005) concludes, "there exist credit market imperfections".

By mid-2007, when it was recognized that significant asset and loan serviceability deterioration had occurred in the US housing market, uncertainty spread to the secondary market for CDOs, where the demand for credit-linked products declined significantly. This resulted in significant uncertainty regarding the pricing of these instruments. In this environment, the accounting standards applicable for valuing and reporting asset values became particularly significant, and "the sharp re-pricing of credit was amplified by the great opacity of new instruments, such as structured credits, and of the distribution of exposures across the system" (Hronsky and Robinson, 2008). This led to a crisis of confidence in valuations, as market participants wondered about the size and character of their own exposures and those of others. The financial crisis, in other words, was not a repudiation of multigrade mortgage debt per se, but rather an exposure of blind spots in the credit intelligence infrastructure. Fed Chairman Ben Bernanke confirms: "The adjustable-rate subprime mortgages originated in late 2005 and in 2006 have performed the worst, in part because of slippage in underwriting standards, reflected for example in high loan-to-value ratios and incomplete documentation" and "investor uncertainty has increased significantly, as the difficulty of evaluating the risks of structured products that can be opaque or have complex payoffs has become more evident" (Bernanke, 2007b).

The good news is that information problems can be addressed and either rectified or at least alleviated. Notwithstanding the suspicion that will persist until the dust settles from the current crisis, there is no logical reason why – down the trail – a wholesale housing paper market could not evolve, akin to the corporate paper market, with fifteen grades ranging from AAA down to C−, along the lines of Standard & Poor's or Moody's rating scale. In such markets, however, monitoring the originators and ensuring that they have incentives to make good loans will be critical. The glimmer of hope from the 2008 crisis is that we are seeing a reassessment of the importance of informational quality in mortgage capital markets. Clearly, the originate-to-distribute model is already being modified to provide stronger protection for investors and better incentives for originators to underwrite prudently. This is a wholesale capital markets task, a mission best implemented by large investment professionals, and is discussed in Chapter 7.

The tragedy is that this essential functionality of the wholesale capital market was not already well established prior to the 2008 crisis. Given the information infrastructure vacuum, and faced with the growing demand for affordable housing credit, retail bankers took upon themselves the task of originating and pricing housing debt of varying grades. This was a disastrous approach. After more than one hundred years of restricting themselves to standard prime home lending, retail bankers inexplicably departed from the script and began taking on the role of wholesale capital markets.

One explanation from economic theory is that when financial markets start to exhibit "convex payoffs", where the relationship between risk and return becomes non-concave or abnormal, the markets move closer toward a casino environment. Perverse rewards induce an incentive to gamble. Complexity, asymmetric information, and leverage – all combined to increase the reward for gambling in the period before the crisis.

Risk and return are supposed to have an inverse relationship, and this is meant to reflect in securities' prices. Accordingly, the credit crisis reflected the mispricing of MBSs. In turn, this stemmed from a lack of foresight and sophistication on the part of wholesale capital markets about the growing significance of sub-grade housing finance in the economies of the twenty-first century, which explains the lack of preparedness by those markets to put in place the credit data necessary to properly price and trade housing-backed paper of varying grades. In turn, the absence of fully developed pricing of risk and return compromised the secondary mortgage market on which the modern housing finance system depends. As US Treasury Secretary Henry Paulson put it, "[o]riginators had weak incentives to maintain strong underwriting standards, particularly at a time when securitizers, credit rating agencies, and mortgage investors did not conduct due diligence sufficient to align originator incentives with the underlying risks" (*President's Working Group on Financial Markets Policy Statement*, US Treasury, March 13, 2008).

## Toward a general equilibrium outcome

It is useful at this point to look at some "home economics": the housing market from the perspective of modern economics. In economic theory, agents maximize their target variable subject to a set of natural constraints. If the theory is one of general equilibrium, the solution will represent the global optimum allowable by the state of nature, the best possible outcome. But if artificial limits exist, such as barriers to market entry or incomplete markets, the model will restrict economic agents to a "corner solution", a compromise outcome that is second to best.

A corner solution for the demand and supply of housing finance will be suboptimal, for households and the economy, because it will involve a loss of welfare, compared with the ideal (first-best) solution. Such a corner solution almost certainly obtains in real world housing markets of advanced countries. The principle reason is that mortgage markets are incomplete. At the retail level, an "all-or-nothing" constraint applies: a non-shared lender-issued debt-only annuity mortgage, or nothing. And at the wholesale level, transparent and liquid markets do not exist for all feasible grades of mortgage credit. This is essentially what caused the credit crisis, and points to the potential welfare gains if such markets were to become fully developed. The degree to which credit restrictions are binding on households is partly a function of the range of mortgage products on offer, but is also a reflection of the range of credit instruments the market is capable of pricing and trading.

Historically, advanced industrial countries have essentially operated with a financial market for housing that is limited to a corner solution. Only one grade of home loan has been available – prime – rather than a spectrum of housing loans varying from AAA to C− in quality. And only one funding channel for increasing the supply of housing has effectively existed, namely standard retail bank mortgages, rather than a variety of retail and wholesale debt and equity channels. This is in contrast to the corporate finance sector, where papers of many different grades are on offer and several financing paths are available, direct or indirect, intermediated or non-intermediated. Moreover, research shows that the bank-mediated channel is homogenized by the effect of Basel risk-based capital requirements on financial institutions (Calem and LaCour-Little, 2004). This results in significant divergence between regulatory and economic capitals, and highlights the incentive problems inherent in simplified methods of capital regulation.

From the point of view of economic theory, mortgages have been a narrowly confined market in terms of the range of options, characterized by rigidities. This is not unrelated to the swings and imbalances that characterize most housing markets. The market for owner-occupied housing is often inefficient and adjusts slowly to changes in market conditions. Disequilibrium in the housing market can originate from supply-side disturbances and can also arise from demand disturbances. Although price changes guide the market toward a new equilibrium eventually, inefficiencies have been shown to impede market clearing, and housing is characterized by sustained periods of disequilibrium (Riddel, 2004).

Some commentators argue that the expansion of structured credit products including CDSs and CDOs during the past decade both contributed to, and was supported by, a strengthening of the originate-and-distribute (O+D) business model of financial intermediation. Increasingly, rather than holding the credits they originated, credit institutions would sell them off, possibly after having repackaged them, into the capital markets. Yet it is significant that once money was lost from the MBSs, withdrawal from the market by investors gave rise to a modern version of a "run on the banks" in the financial system. The failure of the MBS market might not have been so evident or debilitating for the economy, if the dependence on credit originated from retail banks had not been so great.

Although the so-called intermediation efficiency is generally high in developed countries – reflecting a set of institutional factors, risks (such as interest rate, credit, and liquidity risks), and legislative conditions that affect the cost of intermediating housing loans – the fact remains that this is prime retail conduit with prime retail credit market horizons. The common boom–bust cycle in housing markets can in large part be attributed to this lack of flexibility. And the subprime crisis, viewed from this perspective, can be interpreted as an attempt by the economic actors involved to expand the possibilities, and create more room to move along the spectrum of risk and return.

The clock will not be wound back to the days when banks and capital markets were largely separated. The activities of financial institutions have become much more closely intertwined with capital markets, and banks have moved beyond their traditional role to effectively act as agents for the capital market, and offer a much broader range of financial engineering. Likewise, banks have become much more reliant on capital markets for their own risk management and funding, to the point where disruptions in capital markets in the future will have a serious impact on their ability to operate.

## Economic benefits of greater flexibility in housing finance

Improving the flexibility – reducing the rigidity – of housing finance markets matters for the housing sector, and for the economy as a whole.

There is general recognition about the importance of the interactive nexus between housing and the macroeconomy (Leung, 2004; Berry, 2006). Many researchers, however, tend to operate with a Real Business Cycle model of the housing sector. Yet the evidence – and events during the credit crisis of 2008 and subsequently – points to the financial sector as a potentially powerful explanation of housing cycles, and that house prices and supply are very much related to liquidity effects. Housing is a major purchase requiring long-term financing, and well-functioning housing finance systems are those that enable the provision of long-term finance, in particular. The extent to which markets enable the provision of housing finance across a wide range of credit grades is therefore a major economic question for the twenty-first century.

In particular, credit frictions make a major difference. Research has found that frictions in credit markets used by households amplify and propagate the effect of shocks on housing investment, house prices, and consumption. Using data from the British Household Panel Survey to investigate the incidence of housing finance problems, evictions, and repossessions, researchers aver that negative financial surprises are an important route into financial difficulties, controlling for other changes such as divorce or loss of employment (Böheim and Taylor, 2000). By the same token, favorable financial developments can have a positive effect: the effect of structural changes in credit markets that lower the transaction costs of additional borrowing decrease the effect on house prices and housing investment (Aoki et al., 2004).

In a similar vein, Jin and Zeng (2004) develop a dynamic stochastic general equilibrium model of the business cycle properties surrounding residential investment and house prices, incorporating monetary frictions and credit market activities. The model generates the high volatility of residential investment in the house investment goods producing sector, as well as the pro-cyclicality of house prices, and shows how monetary policy and nominal interest rates play a special role in the determination of house prices. Credit shocks generate remarkably volatile residential investment and house prices.

In the US situation, one study measured the relative importance of credit, income, and wealth constraints on home purchase. The results show that financing constraints continue to have an important impact on potential home buyers. The wealth constraint still has the largest impact, but credit constraints have grown in importance as well as a barrier to homeownership, mostly reflecting an increase in the number of households with impaired credit quality (Barakova et al., 2003). This reinforces the need for capital markets to rate and price different levels of mortgage debt accurately.

In the context of the UK, analysis of the effects of financial liberalization, proxied using the rising average loan–value ratio for first-time buyers, shows that greater flexibility in housing finance raises the consumption of housing relative to that of non-housing goods and services (Pain and Westaway, 1997).

A more flexible financial infrastructure can be expected to raise the elasticity of real housing supply. In turn, this should help mitigate the boom–bust cycle in housing. Recent research suggests that locations with more elastic housing supply have fewer and shorter bubbles, with smaller price increases. In particular, US data show that price run-ups are almost exclusively experienced in cities where housing supply is more inelastic (Glaeser et al., 2008).

Differences in the supply of housing generate substantial variation in house prices across the US, and because house prices influence migration, the elasticity of housing supply also has an important impact on local labor markets. Furthermore, housing supply constraints alter local employment and wage dynamics in locations where the degree of regulation is most severe (Saks, 2008).

In summary, a more flexible housing finance system will moderate the boom–bust cycle, impart better economies of scale, remove rigidities, and better act to stimulate private investment in affordable housing, and help correct the shortage of low-cost dwellings.

## Capital markets make housing "different"

Housing finance, more often than not, is a sine qua non of housing affordability and accessibility. While it is undoubtedly true that physical supply, demand, allocation, and equilibrium – not to mention government policy – play an important role in the market for housing, just like they do for any other commodity, housing is not like any other commodity.

Housing has a set of characteristics which together make it different, notably spatial fixity and complexity (Arnott, 2001). The long-lastingdurability and heterogeneous nature of housing, with its wide variation in the quality distribution of housing units, makes housing different from the vast majority of goods and services (Sweeney, 1974). A house is the single most important purchase most people make in their lifetime, and has the dual characteristics of consumption and investment. Research indicates that housing's asset nature, with its uncertain potential to generate capital gains, affects housing demand in surprising ways. An analysis of the formulation of expectations about housing prices using data from Florida, a state known for periodically booming real estate markets, shows an increase in housing prices actually increases the demand for owner-occupied housing. This suggests that, in a price boom, housing's role as an investment asset dominates its role as a consumption good, resulting in an upward-sloping demand curve (Dusansky and Koç, 2007).

Most importantly, housing requires a mortgage, or some form of financing. This inextricably links housing with the financial system in a manner that is not like other commodities, and makes our A2F measure of housing stress highly relevant.

Affordable housing economic models and solutions need to be careful not to simply treat housing like any other good or service. The capital market failure in dealing with subprime-grade housing credit provides an important clue about the significance of the financial dimension of the housing market.

## Conclusions and next steps

This chapter has pointed at capital market failure to explain the 2008 financial crisis, specifically the lack of informational infrastructure needed to support a fully articulated market in multigrade mortgage debt. It has argued that our financial system needs to develop the capability to cater to the variety of scenarios and borrowers in a modern industrial economy, as has already been developed in the corporate debt market.

The most basic proposition in financial economics concerns the role of risk and return in motivating investors. This applies when it comes to the interaction between affordable housing and the capital market. Various classes of rational investors, both retail and wholesale, are willing to entertain the potential role of affordable housing in diversifying portfolio risk, yet investor appetite mostly goes unsatisfied due to a lack of historical benchmark data on risk and returns to determine pricing. The solution is a new set of debt and equity instruments capable of being priced and traded by mutual fund managers within standard trustee guidelines.

The lack of sophistication of capital markets in relation to subprime housing credit that effectively produced the 2008 credit crisis will, until resolved, continue to limit the flexibility of the economy, and constrain housing finance markets to a corner solution. Greater informational efficiency is required: cross-country research has demonstrated that, controlling for country size, economies with stronger credit information systems have deeper housing finance systems (Warnock and Warnock, 2008).

We have seen that housing affordability problems are an increasingly common experience internationally, and that many housing finance flashpoints are common across countries. The speed with which the subprime crisis got transmitted across intercontinental borders surprised most observers, and demonstrated the fact that more and more we are becoming part of a "one-world" economy. There would seem to be a link between the housing debate and the growth of globalization. Indeed, Clapham (2006) goes so far as to argue that the discourse of globalization has dominated housing policy in the UK over the past decade, and that this is reshaping Britain's housing policy response.

The credit frictions in housing are amplified across the economy by housing's financial accelerator. Lack of flexibility and transparency in housing capital exacerbates the real economic cycle, and tends to exclude large-scale involvement by institutional investors. In this environment, chronic and excess demand (supply shortages) persist at the low-cost end of the housing market in most countries. Contrary to conventional economic theory, excess demand in this segment does not automatically bring forth a corrective supply response. The essential reason is that the housing market is at a corner solution, and will remain so until the market develops a more effective infrastructure.

Post-crisis, we need to work toward a more flexible and sustainable capital market solution for housing mortgage, including both mortgage and non-mortgage types. The efficiency of the housing finance system is of interest to households, financial intermediaries, and policymakers. Public housing authorities, used to seeing themselves essentially as landlords, need to embrace financial market solutions as a key ingredient in the overall policy package and become more skilled in analyzing professional securities markets. Currently, however, this is inhibited by a lack of capital market expertise in official circles and housing policy departments.

The interaction of finance with housing means our real estate economics needs to account for the unique capital market characteristics of housing as a consumer-investor commodity.

This raises three important questions.

For investors, housing finance creates the potential for long-dated "capital market" style instruments, but unlike the corporate debt market, the depth and breadth of secondary market trading remains immature. The challenge of enhancing the capital market for housing finance, of varying grades, and overcoming the problems evident in the subprime crisis, is discussed in Chapter 7.

For consumers, housing involves the single most important financial decision most people would make in their lifetime. Unlike a house, a

30-year credit instrument does not attach to everyday purchases such as a book or an iPod. Curiously, despite the importance and size of retail housing finance, consumer banking is restricted to a surprisingly narrow suite of products, revolving around the traditional annuity mortgage. Potential solutions to this will be covered in Chapter 8.

For governments, affordable housing and finance poses a set of policy and regulatory questions. To what extent should the public sector be involved in housing finance, directly or indirectly? What are the effects of incentives and disincentives on private patterns of behavior? We will consider that topic in Chapter 9.

Before that, however, we survey the situation in three countries that have quite different housing finance systems.

# 4
# Affordable Housing Finance in the US

## Introduction

This chapter surveys housing markets, housing stress, and housing finance in relation to the US experience, before and after the credit crunch. The chapter also reflects on the current debate in the US about housing.

With the 2008 credit crunch and housing correction, the US market has gone through the biggest cyclical downturn in decades. This is not the first time house prices have fallen. Between 1992 and 1996, there had been a drop in US housing prices. That episode also saw high default rates on subprime mortgages, but the difference in that case was these instruments were still a small fraction of the market. From 1996 to 2006, prices rose sharply and the US experienced a housing boom. During this period, despite the increasing share of subprime mortgages, default rates were low because house values kept rising. As the market innovated and grew more confident, subprime mortgages were increasingly securitized, and sold widely around the world.

That brings us to the subprime credit crisis of 2008. The correction in the market saw total home sales fall sharply. Existing dwelling sales fell 13 percent, and sales of new homes fell 26 percent, in the space of a single year in the midst of the downturn, as reported by Harvard University's 2008 *State of the Nation's Housing* report. Housing construction also nosedived: new housing starts and permits both fell from around from 1.5 million per month in mid-2007 to just 0.5 million by end-2008, according to Commerce Department figures.

In the crisis year of 2008, for the first time since record keeping began in 1968, the national median single-family home price as reported by the US National Association of Realtors (NAR) fell, by 6.1 percent, to US$2,17,900. Similarly, the S&P/Case Shiller US National Home Price Index registered a decline of 8.9 percent. Out of a total of 144 metro markets, sales prices during the downturn year fell back to 2006 levels in 12 cities, to 2005 levels in 35 cities, to 2004 levels in 19 cities, and to 2003 or earlier levels in 16 cities. And this was not the bottom; prices declined further after these figures were collated.

While these cyclical movements are significant, we need to look behind them to the root structural causes in US housing, and beyond them to the lessons we can learn for the future, especially in relation to affordable housing finance.

## US housing markets and policy

The United States (US) has a long tradition of government-supported financial assistance for affordable rental and home purchase utilizing sophisticated market techniques. Figure 4.1 provides an overview.

The role of the U.S. Department of Housing and Urban Development (HUD) is expanding home ownership, increasing access to affordable housing, fighting housing discrimination, eliminating chronic homelessness, and improving communities. HUD also works to increase public awareness of fair housing laws.

The Federal Housing Administration (FHA) provides mortgage insurance on loans made by FHA-approved lenders for single family and multifamily homes, and is the largest insurer of mortgages in the world. Over 34 million properties have been insured since its inception in 1934, when Congress created the FHA under the National Housing Act. The goals of the organization are to improve housing conditions, to provide an adequate home financing system through mortgage insurance, and to stabilize the mortgage market. The FHA became a part of the Department of Housing and Urban Development's Office of Housing in 1965. The FHA is the only government agency that operates entirely from its self-generated income and costs the taxpayers nothing. The proceeds from the mortgage insurance paid by the homeowners are captured in an account that is used to operate the program entirely (HUD, 2009).

FHA mortgage insurance provides lenders with protection against losses as the result of homeowners defaulting on their mortgage loans. The lenders bear less risk because FHA pays a claim to the lender in the event of a homeowner's default. Loans must meet certain requirements established by FHA to qualify for insurance. Unlike conventional loans that adhere to strict underwriting guidelines, FHA-insured loans require very little cash investment to close a loan, and this gives more flexibility in calculating household income and payment ratios. The cost of the mortgage insurance is passed along to the homeowner and typically is included in the monthly payment. FHA loans are insured through a combination of a small upfront mortgage insurance premium (UFMIP), as well as a small monthly mortgage insurance premium. A borrower with an FHA loan always pays the same mortgage insurance rate regardless of credit score. Conventional mortgage insurance premium rates factor in credit scores, whereas FHA mortgage insurance premiums do not.

Several other agencies have a role in US housing. Indeed, the plethora of agencies could be part of the explanation for the confusion that has emerged in the US market. The Federal Deposit Insurance Corporation (FDIC) is an independent agency of the federal government and insures deposits at banks and savings and loan institutions. Fannie Mae is the largest secondary mortgage market company in the US and was chartered in 1938 by the Congress. Freddie Mac is a secondary mortgage market company that was chartered in 1970 by the Congress.

Ginnie Mae is an entity that was established by the Congress in 1968 to provide insurance for mortgage-backed securities (MBSs) backed by federally insured or guaranteed loans, mainly those insured by the FHA or guaranteed by the U.S. Department of Veterans Affairs. The Federal Home Loan (FHL) Banks, are 12 independent but cooperative banks that provide liquidity to thrifts, and are regulated by the Federal Housing Finance Board (FHFB). The Federal Housing Finance Agency (FHFA) regulates Fannie Mae, Freddie Mac, and the 12 FHL banks. As of 2009, these government-sponsored enterprises provide more than $6.2 trillion in funding for the US mortgage markets and financial institutions.

Fannie Mae and Freddie Mac are examples of "government-sponsored enterprises" (GSEs). A GSE is a privately held company created by the Congress to reduce the cost of capital for certain borrowing sectors of the economy. In 1968, two agencies were formed: the Government National Mortgage Association (Ginnie Mae) and the Federal National Mortgage Association (Fannie Mae), which became a privately owned GSE, authorized to operate in the secondary market for conventional as well as guaranteed mortgage loans. In 1970, to compete with Fannie Mae in the secondary market, another GSE was created, the Federal Home Loan Mortgage Corporation, or Freddie Mac.

These agencies played a central role in the build up to the subprime credit crisis. In the early 1980s, Freddie Mac introduced collateralized mortgage obligations (CMOs), which separated the payments from a pooled set of mortgages into "strips" carrying different effective maturities and credit risks. From 1980 onward, the outstanding volume of GSE MBSs has risen from less than $200 billion to more than $4 trillion today (Bernanke, 2007b). An example is Fannie's "Alt-A" mortgages, a category between prime and subprime, involving loans where borrowers do not fully document their incomes. Alongside these developments came the establishment of private mortgage insurers, which competed with the FHA, and private mortgage pools, which bundled loans not handled by the GSEs, including loans that did not meet GSE eligibility criteria, the so-called non-conforming loans. Today, these private pools account for around $2 trillion in residential mortgage debt.

The U.S. Department of Housing and Urban Development operates voucher programs to assist needy tenants. Voucher eligibility is income-tested, and federal regulations govern how rent is determined for housing choice voucher programs. Section 8 Rental Voucher Program increases affordable housing choices for very low-income households by allowing families to choose privately owned rental housing. A state public housing authority (PHA) generally pays the landlord the difference between 30 percent of household income and the PHA-determined payment standard – about 80–100 percent of the fair market rent (FMR). The household may choose a unit with a higher rent than the FMR and pay the landlord the difference or choose a lower cost unit and keep the difference. To qualify, households typically have incomes up to 80 percent of area median income levels. The voucher programs help more than 1.4 million households in the US.

However, opponents of Section 8 contend that funds have not been targeted to the neediest families, and that horizontal inequity results from offering assistance to some, but not all, households with like characteristics. Funds have typically not been sufficient to serve all eligible families, and a simple proposal for better targeting is to decrease the subsidy at each income level by the same amount. Crews Cutts and Olsen (2002) argue for converting the Section 8 program into an entitlement program for the poorest eligible families.

The low-income housing tax credit (LIHTC) program was introduced in the Tax Reform Act of 1986, based on Section 42 of the Internal Revenue Code, to provide the private market with an incentive to invest in affordable rental housing. Federal housing tax credits are awarded to developers of qualified projects. Developers then sell these credits to investors to raise capital (or equity) for their projects, which reduces the debt that the developer would otherwise have to borrow.

Because the debt is lower, a tax credit property can in turn offer lower, more affordable rents. Provided the property maintains compliance with the program requirements, investors receive a dollar-for-dollar credit against their federal tax liability each year over a period of ten years. The amount of the annual credit is based on the amount invested in the affordable housing. On average, around 70,000 dwellings per year have been constructed or redeveloped under this program.

The Community Reinvestment Act (CRA), enacted in 1977, is also a significant factor in the supply of affordable housing in the US. The CRA requires federally regulated banking institutions to meet the "full range" of community credit needs. In practice, this entails provision to sections of the population underserviced by mainstream financial institutions. Access to affordable housing by low-income households and other minority groups is included within the scope of the CRA, and banks have seen this as one means to meet their CRA requirements. CRA-inspired mortgage loans for affordable owner occupation, in comparison to conventional loans, exhibit one or more "affordable loan" characteristics, such as reduced down payment (deposit), higher loan-to-value (LTV) rates, flexible employment (income) history hurdle, and reduced interest rates.

Essentially, funding for affordable housing finance in the US includes tax credits for housing bonds, and below-market interest rate loans. In contrast to the UK and Australia, conventional public housing represents only about one percent of the total housing stock in the US, and does not figure prominently in housing strategy. Only three percent of the population lives in "social housing" in the US, as against 20 percent in the UK (Scanlon and Whitehead, 2004).

At the same time, in the US there are many community-based, nonprofit organizations operating at the local and regional levels committed to assisting people with low to moderate incomes into owner occupation. In general, these organizations seek to bring together representatives from local government, state government, the private sector and/or nonprofit sector to leverage expertise, contacts, and access to funding sources. The effectiveness of these activities is given underlying support by pieces of legislation such as the CRA of 1977 and the LIHTC program outlined above.

As in the UK and Australia, there is no capital gains tax on the principal residence in the US. Private landlords do pay capital gains tax. Mortgage interest payments are tax deductible for homeowners, which does not apply in the UK or Australia. Tax settings are explored in more depth in Chapter 8.

## Housing finance in the US

At the start of the 1950s, American mortgage debt was equal to 20 percent of total household income; by the mid-2000s it had risen to 76 percent of income. Similarly, mortgage debt was 15 percent of household assets back then, but rose to over 40 percent of household assets in the current decade (Green and Wachter, 2005).

Recall from Chapter 2 that we are interested in applying the A2F (Access-to-Finance) dual indicator, supplemented by the 30/40 rule, to measure the extent of housing stress. Indicators of access to finance-related affordability constraints include the loan-to-value ratio (LVR), changes in ratio of mortgage debt to national income, ratio of median family income to mortgage qualifying income, the mortgage repayments burden as proportion of annual income, and similar.

As shown in Figure 4.2, the typical LTV ratio of US mortgages is 75 percent, which is higher than in the UK and Australia. The LTV is the amount of mortgage loan borrowed divided by the market value of the house used as collateral, and is the arithmetic complement of the percentage of down payment paid in purchasing a house. Lenders in the US will lend almost up to the full value of the property, up to 97 percent.

The flexibility of the US market is demonstrated by the availability of fixed-rate loans beyond 20 years in maturity, a product not offered in the UK or Australia (compare also Figures 5.1 and 6.1).

Figure 4.3 shows how the mortgage-to-GDP ratio has increased over time. The US ratio of mortgage debt to GDP has grown to over 75 percent, higher than the OECD average of 56 percent.

In keeping with the above, the US housing finance burden has been on a worsening trend. As Figure 4.4 shows, the ratio of mortgages outstanding continues to climb, relative to household disposable income. The ratio is now over 100 percent.

The rate of home ownership in the US is 69 percent (HUD, 2006). This is roughly equivalent to the UK at 71 percent, and Australia at 69 percent (Scanlon and Whitehead, 2004). Fueling home buying, the mortgage rate has fallen and remained low by historical standards (Figure 4.5). The proportion of US owner-occupiers with mortgages is 62 percent, about equal to the UK (60 percent) but higher than Australia (45 percent).

Unlike in many other countries, home mortgage interest is a tax-deductible expense in the US. Mortgage interest is reported on Form 1040, Schedule A along with other itemized deductions such as real estate property taxes, and charitable contributions. Taxpayers paying mortgage interest therefore receive a government subsidy to invest in housing.

*Affordable Housing Finance in the US* 55

|  | Institutions | Products | Legislation |
|---|---|---|---|
| Up to 1960s | • Creation of FHL Banks (1934)<br>• Creation of Fannie Mae (1938)<br>• Creation of FHA, FDIC, FSLIC, and private mortgage insurance companies (1934)<br>• Privatization of Fannie Mae and creation of Ginnie Mae (1968) | • Fully amortizing loans with monthly payments<br>• Fixed interest rate and longer than 20-year loan term<br>• Maximum LTV up to 80%<br>• Underwriting guidelines set by Fannie Mae (1954) | • National Housing Act (1934)<br>• Housing Act (1949)<br>• Regulation Q (1966) |
| 1970s to 1980s | • Creation of Freddie Mac (1970)<br>• New investors into the market: mutual funds, pensions (1980s)<br>• S&L Debacle (1980s) and creation of RTC (1989) | • Introduction of ARMs (1982)<br>• First MBS issuance by GSE, Freddie Mac (1971); first private MBS by Bank of America (1977)<br>• First CMO issuance (1984) | • Removal of bank interest rate ceilings (1980s)<br>• FIRREA (1989) and Basle I (1980s)<br>• Basle I bank capital adequacy framework (1980s) |
| 1990s to 2000s | • Creation of OFHEO (1992)<br>• HUD affordable housing goals for GSEs (1992) | • AUS, mortgage score, AVM models (1990s–2000s)<br>• HELOC, second mortgages, etc (1990s–2000s)<br>• Expansion of credit derivatives (1990s–2000s) | • Minimum and Risk-Based Capital Rules for GSEs<br>• Basle II bank capital adequacy framework (2000s)<br>• Fannie Mae and Freddie Mac put into conservatorship (2008) |

*Figure 4.1* Evolution of the US housing finance system

*Source:* Adapted from HUD, 2006

Affordable loan products in the US today are mostly low down payment mortgages, and interest-only and payment-option loans. When the collateral values are too high, however, the monthly mortgage

| Metric | Indicator |
|---|---|
| Typical LTV | 75% |
| Maximum LTV | 97% |
| Usual length to maturity | 30 years |
| Fixed-rate (>20 years) available? | Yes |

*Figure 4.2* Mortgage characteristics in the US

*Source:* Adapted from Green and Wachter (2005) and Scanlon and Whitehead (2004).
*Note:* LTV = Loan-to-Value ratio.

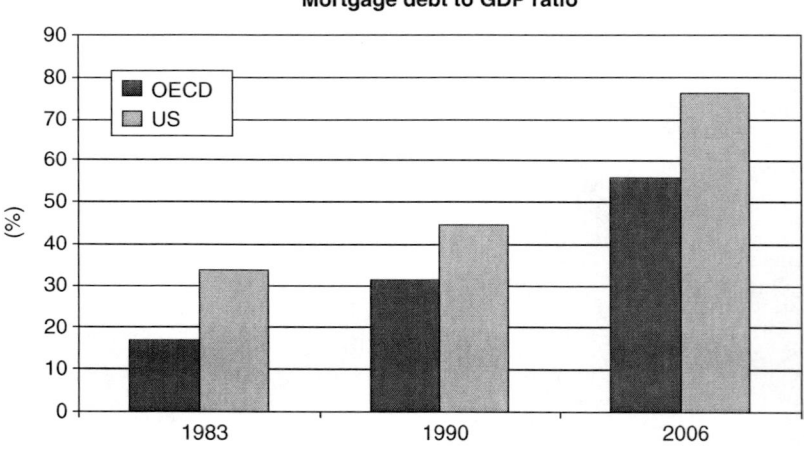

*Figure 4.3* Growth in US mortgage debt as percent to GDP

*Source:* Chart data from International Monetary Fund, *World Economic Outloook*, Data forum, September (2008). Figures for OECD are the average ratio across 16 industrialized countries, including the US.

payment becomes more burdensome to typical households, given other constant lending terms. At this point, government-subsidized finance kicks in. The US government's "housing guidelines" stipulate the volume of affordable mortgages GSEs are supposed to purchase each year. Since 2001, the goal was for low-to-middle income mortgages to account for 50 percent of homes financed by Fannie and Freddie. This was raised from 40 percent in the 1990s. This is an ambitious target and consequently had a huge effect on the mortgage market.

The shift to mortgages being funded by capital markets rather than by deposit-takers arguably began in the late 1960s, with the creation of

Affordable Housing Finance in the US 57

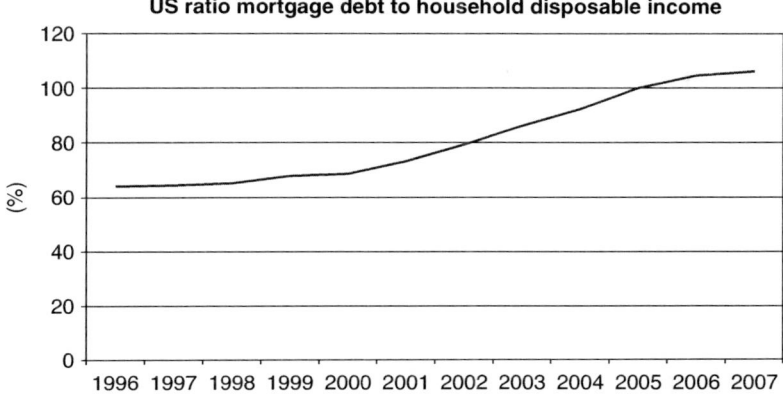

*Figure 4.4* US housing finance burden, 1996–2007

*Source:* Chart data from Organisation for Economic Cooperation and Development (OECD), *Economic Outlook*, No. 84, October 2008, Annex table 58.

*Figure 4.5* US mortgage interest rate, 1973–2008

*Source:* Chart data from US Department of Housing and Urban Development. Figures show annual average "composite" rate, a weighted mix of fixed and adjustable mortgage rates, excluding fees and charges.

Fannie Mae and Freddie Mac. As Green and Wachter (2005) point out, the federal charters that were granted to Fannie and Freddie required them to promote liquidity in the secondary market for mortgages as well as to originate mortgages.

Also around the same period, macroeconomic conditions shifted. Higher inflation in the 1970s made it harder for depositories to fund long-term, fixed-rate mortgages as nominal interest rates rose and banks found their hands were tied due to Regulation Q, a federal rule that placed a ceiling on the rate they could pay depositors. The resulting outflow of deposits led to a major structural change in US mortgage markets and, ultimately "a transformation of the housing finance system" (Green and Wachter, 2005, p. 7).

The industrial structure of affordable mortgage lending in the US, defined as home lending to low- and middle-income families and those living in underserved areas, consequently underwent significant change during the past few decades. The mix of institutions evolved, with affordable mortgage lending increasingly done by mortgage company subsidiaries of depositories, rather than savings institutions themselves (Nothaft and Surette, 2001). The reason probably has to do with cost savings, increased channels of product distribution, and attempts by banks to improve their reported performance in terms of the CRA.

The rise of mortgage companies in turn has raised concerns about the provision of prime housing credit to those in underserved areas, yet data indicate that affordable lending increased most among mortgage companies, and declined for depositories. Also, it is notable that the subprime market has been dominated by mortgage companies, not banks, which was possibly a factor in the lax credit assessment kills in recent years.

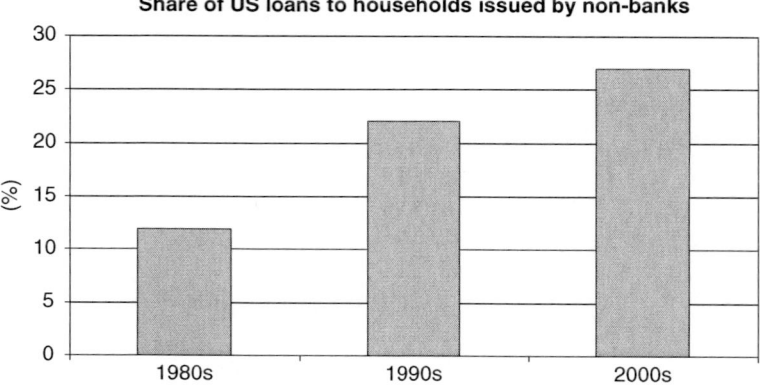

*Figure 4.6* US mortgage innovation index

*Source:* Chart data from International Monetary Fund, *World Economic Outloook*, Data forum, September (2008).

The progress toward financial innovation in the US is shown in Figure 4.6, using decade averages. The degree of change in the US has been much higher than in the OECD, where the average share of household loans issued by non-bank lenders is just five percent in the 2000s. Around 82 percent of Americans have a fixed-rate mortgage, much higher than in the UK (25 percent) and Australia (15 percent).

The easing in affordability since the crisis is confirmed in Figure 4.7 which shows the overall affordability index for US housing, 1973–2008. A rise in the line indicates affordability has improved.

The US mortgage market structure was reasonably successful for a long time. Access to mortgage credit widened over time. Notably, loans to sub-prime borrowers accounted for about 13 percent of outstanding mortgages in 2006 (Bernanke, 2007b). Initiatives by GSEs with affordable products have made a difference. For instance, products such as Freddie Mac's "Alt 97", introduced in the early 2000s, which permits the three percent down payment to come from non-borrower sources, have been shown to have a large impact on the home ownership propensities of all underserved groups: one study found a 27 percent increase in the relative probability of home ownership for young households, a 21 percent increase for Blacks, and a 15 percent increase for central city residents (Quercia et al., 2003).

Indeed, the general approach to housing finance, the "US model", has made a major impression on other countries. In the 1990s, one

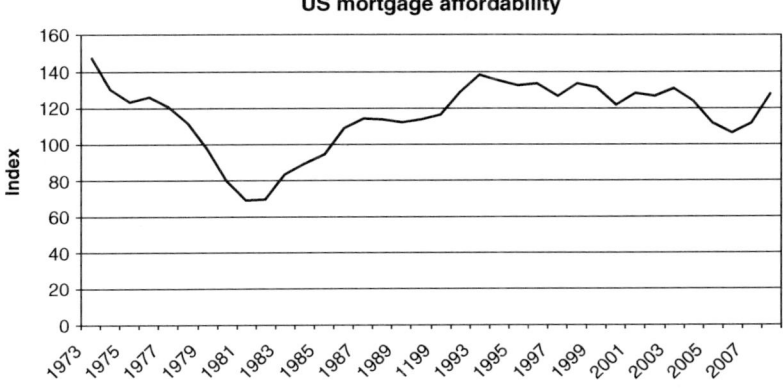

*Figure 4.7* US mortgage affordability index, 1973–2008

*Source:* Chart data from US Department of Housing and Urban Development. Figures show "composite" affordability, the ratio of median family income to mortgage qualifying income. Values over 100 indicate the typical family has more than sufficient income to purchase an average home.

particular aspect, mortgage securitization, came into fashion worldwide. At least 24 countries in six continents have issued MBSs in some form (Diamond, 2000).

However, for all its virtues, the US approach obviously contains imperfections. Writing in 2005, before the crisis emerged, Green and Wachter surveyed the complex web of securitized derivatives that entangled the mortgage market and expressed apprehension: "These financial instruments are crucial to the ability of the US to finance its unusual mortgage structure, because they allow investors to manage the complicated interest rate risk embedded in the U.S. mortgage. No other country, so far as we can tell, has anything like the panoply of financial products in the United States" (p. 17). The central role played by Fannie Mae and Freddie Mac in the US mortgage market in the run up to 2008, by raising funds to issue securitized mortgages and by playing an active role in the secondary market for MBSs, in hindsight was problematic. What has now become clear, in the wake of the credit crisis, is that this institutional framework failed to adequately answer the question of how Fannie and Freddie distributed the risk from mortgages across the economy. This represented a huge gamble by the US housing finance system.

The bubble eventually burst, and a period of mortgage turmoil followed. In its 2008 *State of the Nation's Housing* report, the Joint Centre for Housing Studies noted that the number of homes in foreclosure proceedings nearly doubled to almost one million in the space of a year. In the hardest-hit states, such as Ohio, the foreclosure rate jumped up to 1 in 25 loans. The foreclosure rate on all subprime loans doubled in the same year from 4.5 to 8.7 percent, and the rate on adjustable-rate sub primes more than doubled from 5.6 to 13.4 percent.

## American housing stress

Prior to the credit crisis of 2008, that is, at a median stage in the economic cycle, around 30 percent of American households spent more than 30 percent of income on housing and qualified as being in housing stress, according to the Joint Centre for Housing Studies (2008). In the five years upto 2006, the number of severely burdened renters in the bottom-income quartile grew by 1.2 million, while the number of severely burdened homeowners in the two middle-income quartiles rose by 1.4 million (Joint Centre for Housing Studies, 2008). Almost half of all households in the bottom-income quartile were severely burdened.

Around that time, there was not a single county in the US where, for instance, a full-time minimum wage worker could afford even a one-bedroom apartment at what the Department of Housing and Urban Development determines to be the FMR (National Low Income Housing Coalition, 2006).

Of the nation's 2000-plus nonmetropolitan counties, 302 were defined as housing stressed according to the US Department of Agriculture's most recent county typology, using data collected *before* the worst of the housing price bubble. In these counties, at least 30 percent of households failed to meet widely used household-level standards for minimum basic amenities, including housing expenses not exceeding one-third of income, household members not outnumbering rooms, or the dwelling not having incomplete plumbing or kitchen. In nonzero housing stress counties, 28 percent of households exceeded the expense/income threshold, while seven percent of homes were crowded and two percent lacked either complete plumbing or kitchens (USDA, 2004).

Housing stress counties were found to have higher proportions of minorities and higher unemployment rates. These counties contain 16 percent of all nonzero households, but nearly twice that share of all African-American households (30 percent). An even higher concentration of Native American (48 percent) and Hispanic (37 percent) households were found in housing stress counties. The unemployment rate in housing stress counties (8.4 percent) was above that in other

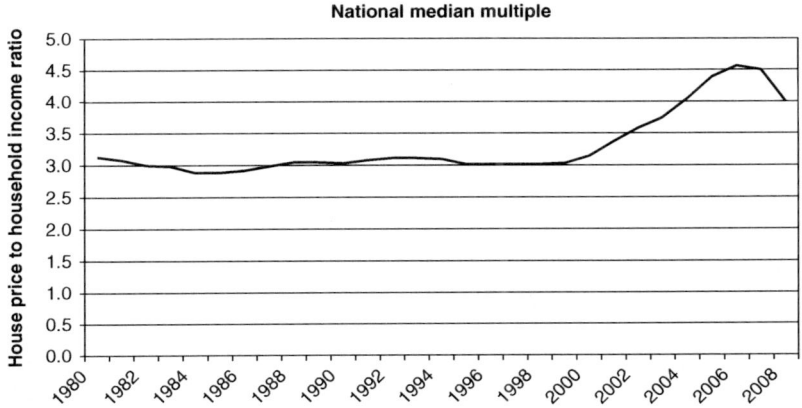

*Figure 4.8* US housing affordability, 1980–2008

*Source:* Chart data from Joint Center for Housing Studies, 2007 for 1980 through 2006, and 2007 and 2008 figures based on Cox and Pavletich (2009). Data show median house price to median household income ratio.

counties (5.7 percent). Geographically, housing stress counties are clustered mainly in the southeast and the west of the country (USDA, 2004).

Figure 4.8 summarizes the overall housing affordability picture. A rise in the index indicates increasing housing stress. In the years leading up to the crisis, housing stress was rising sharply. Since the crisis-induced economic slowdown, average affordability in the US market has eased.

The 2009 Demographic *International Housing Affordability Survey* (Cox and Pavletich, 2009) provides the latest comparative ratings for metropolitan markets in the US and five other countries. To rate housing affordability, the survey employs the ratio of median house price to median household income multiple ("median multiple").These are then classified into a four-stage scale of affordability as follows: Affordable (3.0 or less), Moderately unaffordable (3.1–4.0), Seriously unaffordable (4.1–5.0), and Severely unaffordable (5.1 and over).

In the 2009 survey, the median multiple is generally 3.0 or less in many housing markets of the US and Canada, which corresponds to "affordable". Internationally speaking, the US stands out in the survey: out of a total of 265 markets worldwide included in the 2009 survey, all markets rated "affordable" are in North America. This includes three markets with population above one million (Atlanta, Dallas-Fort Worth, and Houston), and a number of markets with more than 0.5 million. As we will learn in Chapters 5 and 6, housing affordability in other countries has not eased in the wake of the credit crisis to anywhere near the same degree. In the same survey, Australia, Ireland, New Zealand, and the UK are found to have no cities classified as "affordable" (see Figure 5.6).

Another set of rankings on a domestic comparison basis is produced by Sustain Lane (2009). These are shown in Figure 4.9, and use US Census Bureau data on average housing prices and average income levels to determine city housing affordability. They provide a differentiation within the US, from most affordable to least affordable.

The US has a more unequal housing market than other countries. The gap of 7.3 is wide, between the most affordable (1.8) and least affordable (9.1) markets. This compares with a gap of just 2.3 for the UK (4.6, 6.9) and 4.8 (9.6, 4.8) for Australia. US housing is less egalitarian.

Regarding housing finance specifically, the housing affordability problem has two sides, buying and renting, and each exhibits unique characteristics. Using the widely accepted ratio of housing costs to income as the measure of housing cost burden, Kutty (2007) examines annual trends in rents, owner costs of housing, home prices, and incomes over the period 1975–2001. The changes in the affordability situation over time are analyzed separately for renters and for owners. Research shows that the housing affordability problem for renters has

| More affordable | Affordable | Mixed | Unaffordable | More unaffordable |
|---|---|---|---|---|
| San Antonio | Houston | Albuquerque | Portland | San Jose |
| Fort Worth | Omaha | Cleveland | Minneapolis | Honolulu |
| Arlington | Philadelphia | Milwaukee | Denver | Miami |
| El Paso | Detroit | Mesa | Atlanta | Boston |
| Memphis | Baltimore | Austin | Las Vegas | San Diego |
| Oklahoma City | Columbus | Virginia Beach | Chicago | New York |
| Indianapolis | Jacksonville | ColoradoSprings | Fresno | Oakland |
| Louisville | Dallas | Tuscon | Sacramento | Long Beach |
| Tulsa | Charlotte | Phoenix | Seattle | Los Angeles |
| Kansas City | Nashville | New Orleans | Washington | San Francisco |

*Figure 4.9* US city rankings by housing affordability, 2008

*Source:* Adapted from Sustain Lane (2009).

been largely income-driven; on the other hand, for owners, changes in affordability have been related to changes in mortgage costs.

An emerging problem is that the subprime housing downturn has considerably restricted the new supply of affordable housing. This is significant because about 14 percent of the low-cost rental stock, with rents under $400, built before 1940 was permanently removed in the decade prior to the crisis. Nationwide, the number of housing permits issued fell 35 percent in a two-year period, including a 42 percent reduction in single-family permits. Completions of for-rent units in multi-family structures fell to just 169,000, down 38 percent from 2000. The rental share of all multifamily completions dipped below 60 percent for the first time in 43 years of record keeping (Joint Center for Housing Studies, 2008). This comes on top of long-term trend declines in the dwelling inventory in many cities, such as Buffalo, St. Louis, Cleveland, Detroit, and Pittsburgh which lost large fractions of their dwelling units. One study of population changes from 1970 through 2000 for 351 US cities found substantial stock declines, as high as 50 percent, in many cities (Goodman, 2005).

## The current debate in the US

Until recent events overtook the debate, most commentators would have agreed with HUD when it asserted that "the U.S. experience demonstrates that increased funding through MBSs and other means leads to more affordable lending" (HUD, 2006). The evidence was the steady increase in the home ownership rate and various lending products targeting low-income and other consumer cohorts. In regard to affordable housing in particular, it could also be said that various policies instituted in the US induce lending and funding institutions to better serve under-served population groups. For example, the housing goals GSEs, plus measures such as the CRA requirements, and the loan limits for FHA insurance and GSE mortgage purchases, fall under this heading. Affordability in the US is significantly better than in the UK or Australia, which do not share these features.

In view of the crisis, it is no longer so easy to make these claims for the US housing finance system. We now know that the techniques pioneered in the US system must be combined with sound risk-sharing arrangements among various intermediaries, and more prudent risk measurement by investors. By the time the crisis arrived, an estimated 2.2 million subprime home loans made in recent years have already failed or will end in foreclosure (King et al., 2006). In 2008, the crisis year, Fannie and Freddie were recording losses at the rate of around $20 billion per annum, and rising, as defaults piled up and investors dumped RMBS. The two companies guarantee so many mortgages (around US$2.5 trillion of single-family mortgages, around one-quarter of US loans outstanding), that even a small rise in defaults translates into billions of dollars of losses. About five percent of the borrowers guaranteed by Fannie and Freddie have credit scores below 620 (Wall Street Journal, March 11, 2008). Fannie estimates its overall exposure to subprime loans at about US$50 billion, and to Alt-A loans at a much larger sum of US$350 billion.

On September 7, 2008, at the height of the crisis, the US director of the FHFA announced the decision to place two GSEs into conservatorship: Fannie Mae and Freddie Mac. The move was fully supported by Treasury Secretary Henry Paulson, who went on record to say: "I attribute the need for today's action primarily to the inherent conflict and flawed business model in the GSE structure, and the ongoing housing correction". Fed Chairman Ben Bernanke also endorsed the decision, because it would "ensure the financial soundness of those two companies".

At the time of writing, it is unclear how long the recovery in the US housing market will take. Judging by history, it might be a long process. Of the 139 metros that saw their nominal OFHEO house price index values fall in the recession of late eighties and early nineties, 18 took ten years or more to return to peak prices, and another 56 took five to nine years (Joint Center for Housing Studies, 2008).

A more optimistic view was provided in February 2009 by Moodys Investor Services which published its post-crisis outlook for US housing. Moodys expected that by the end of the unprecedented downturn, the national Case-Shiller house price index would record a total peak-to-trough decline of 36 percent. House prices would decline by double digits (peak to trough) in nearly two-thirds of the nations' 381 metro areas, and in about ten percent of metro areas to exceed 30 percent(Zandi et al., 2009). The bright spot on the horizon was that house prices were expected to stabilize by the end of 2009.

The crisis clearly represents a watershed point, an opportunity to rethink federal housing policy. Various contributors are getting involved in the debate about the future form of the housing finance system (for example, see Rosenthal and Strange, 2008). The weaknesses of the US system should be corrected, but without losing the gains. Equally, the housing policies of the past arguably involved sometimes contradictory objectives, such as more affordable housing units simultaneously with housing finance policies that artificially inflated prices, like Freddie Mac and Fannie Mae, policy vehicles that put too much faith in borrowing without the usual rigors of market discipline.

So far, it is unclear that the lessons of the crisis are being taken on board. In 2008, at the height of the problems, Fannie and Freddie announced the Home Savers Advance program, offering borrowers in arrears as much as US$15,000 to catch up on their repayments. The money is in the form of a 15-year unsecured loan, and can be based simply on "verbal confirmation of financial capacity". Payments on the new loan kick in after six months, on top of the borrower's original monthly mortgage payments (which they were behind on to start with). Is this the right way to begin a new chapter in US affordable housing finance, post-crisis?

The economic rescue packages announced by Washington in the wake of the crisis have met with mixed success. In February 2009, a US housing official urged Congress to overhaul a $300-billion federal mortgage guarantee fund that was meant to help struggling homeowners avoid foreclosure, but has failed to catch on. The Hope for Homeowners program was one of the first federal responses to the housing market crisis. Approved by Congress in July 2008, it was launched in October with estimates that it would assist as many as 400,000 mortgage borrowers. But by February 2009, only 451 applications to participate have been received, 25 loans have been closed, and the FHA has insured no loans

(Reuters, February 3, 2009). The program was meant to help distressed homeowners switch out of burdensome, adjustable-rate mortgages into more affordable government-backed ones. But it has had little impact, and HUD official Meg Burns told a House committee hearing, "changes are needed as quickly as possible". She said the FHA has received more than 66,000 phone inquiries about Hope for Homeowners, but "overly restrictive eligibility standards and extremely high costs to consumers" had discouraged participation.

The US$800 billion economic stimulus package introduced by President Obama in February 2009 included a First-time Homebuyer Credit for $8000. Qualified first-time home buyers receive a $7500 discount (couples) or $3750 discount (singles) on their tax bill to the IRS (Internal Revenue Service), as an extra payment added on top of their current refund. Taxpayers, in other words, get everything they are already entitled to, plus the credit. The benefit is "refundable", which means the dollar-for-dollar reduction in their tax liability even continues beyond zero. So, for instance, if a home buyer's regular tax bill is $3000 before the credit, the total bill drops below zero and the federal government owes the home buyer $5000. Or to provide another example, if the individual owed $6000 and had $6700 withheld during the year, he or she would ordinarily receive a $700 refund but instead, the qualifying homeowner will receive a net refund check for $8700.

On February 18, 2009, the Obama administration announced an emergency housing rescue package worth US$75 billion, aimed at helping as many as nine million homeowners refinance their mortgages or avert foreclosure. There were two main parts to the plan. First, to help "responsible homebuyers", those who are current on their mortgage repayments but who cannot refinance to lower interest rates because the equity value of their property has fallen below qualifying levels. The second part of the plan aims at keep four million borrowers in their homes who are at risk of foreclosure, the "at risk homebuyers", by giving incentives for lenders to revise the terms of credit to a more affordable level. To qualify, a homeowner's LVR must exceed 105 percent. An additional US$200 billion was also expected to be used in backing failed government mortgage giants Fannie Mae and Freddie Mac.

Some criticized the Obama package for its selectivity. There are an estimated 80 million homeowners in the US, with around 50 million being current mortgage borrowers, but the plan helped less than one in five of these. Some proposed instead an across-the-board rescue approach, for example, by providing subsidized loans to all home buyers at below-market interest, or refinancing aid for all borrowers. The historical relationship between interest rates and housing prices suggests that this proposal will increase housing prices by at most five percent, say Glaeser and Gyourko (2008). A five-percent price rise will do little to stem foreclosures in markets where prices have already fallen by 30 percent, they argue. Subsidized lending encourages overbuilding and over-borrowing, and when governments lend, taxpayers have an exposure to potential defaults. Those same authors argue that federal housing policy should ensure that our poorest citizens are able to live in decent housing, and should address the high housing costs facing many middle-income Americans.

Kutty (2007) recommends that housing policy aimed at rental housing adopt a counter-cyclical focus, which it currently seems to lack.

Have the American GSE affordable housing goals increased the supply of mortgage credit? In the 1980s, housing market policymakers were concerned that Freddie and Fannie were not adequately facilitating the financing of affordable housing for low- and moderate-income families. To address these concerns, HUD established quantitative Affordable Housing Goals (AHGs) requiring GSEs to increase their purchases of mortgages for homes located in low-income neighborhoods.

Research indicates that the AHGs increased the supply of mortgage credit available to target households, after controlling for other mortgage market factors (Ambrose and Thibodeau, 2004). Another study however, based on GSE loan purchase activity in California, suggests little efficacy on the part of GSE home loan purchase goals in elevating the home ownership and housing conditions of targeted and underserved neighborhoods (Bostic and Gabriel, 2006). Önder (2002) also examines the impact of FHA mortgage insurance activity on home ownership, at two levels: census tract and metropolitan area. Making use of the Home Mortgage Disclosure Act dataset combined with the US Census, the findings indicate that FHA programs are of limited effect in the achievement of home ownership. Where a significant positive effect is detected, it tends to be of greater assistance to Whites relative to Blacks.

A further study to assess the impact of affordable lending efforts on home ownership rates focussed more narrowly on the impact of using flexible underwriting guidelines, primarily changes in the down payment and housing burden requirements. The impacts of changing these underwriting guidelines are compared with those resulting from lower borrowing costs, using the 1995 American Housing Survey (AHS). The findings indicate that affordable lending efforts are likely to increase home ownership opportunities for underserved populations, but that impacts may not be felt equally by all groups.

In particular, recent movers and central city households receive smaller gains than for other households. Consistently, changes in underwriting guidelines are found to have greater impacts than changes in the costs of borrowing for all groups (Quercia et al., 2003).

Clearly, affordable housing in the US remains a persistent challenge. The number of "severely-burdened households" in the US, defined as those paying more than half their income for housing, is put at 17.7 million households. More than one out of six children (12.7 million) live in households paying more than half their income for housing. Nearly one in five low-income families, and nearly one in four low-income minority families, reported living in structurally inadequate housing (Joint Center for Housing Studies, 2008).

As the subprime crisis revealed, the benefits of the US system to mortgage borrowers came with their own set of risks. Fannie Mae and Freddie Mac malfunctioned in a way that has cost the American taxpayer a lot of money, and led to a systematic crisis in financial markets. But we should not be too quick to toss the baby out with the bathwater. As one commentator has put it, "the benefits from the current U.S. system of mortgage finance for borrowers and macroeconomic stability are also real and should not be lightly discarded" (Green and Wachter, 2005).

Of particular interest in moving forward is the future of subprime capital markets. Subprime loans fell from 20 percent of originations in 2006 to just three percent after the crisis hit (Joint Center for Housing Studies, 2008). This raises the important question of the future of the "US model": can it be revitalized, in a new and more sustainable form? Once the dust has settled, can private capital markets pick up where they left off, only this time do it better? If Fannie and Freddie were indeed useful in developing the US market for mortgage capital, could their functions now be replaced by fully private agents? We return to these questions in Chapter 7.

# 5
# Affordable Housing Finance in the UK

## Introduction

This chapter surveys housing markets, housing stress, and housing finance in Britain, and reflects on the current debate in the United Kingdom (UK) about housing.

To set the discussion in context, it is relevant to rehearse the depth of the impact on Great Britain of the global mortgage crisis and the associated banking debacle. House prices in the UK fell 16 percent in 2008, the year of the crisis. The macroeconomy went into recession: real GDP growth was negative in two successive quarters, the September and December quarters of 2008, which is the accepted economic definition of recession. This was the worst performance by the economy since 1980. The British pound fell by around 30 percent during the year of the crisis, to a 23-year low of US$1.3600 by early 2009. In turn, this led to talk of nationalization of banks. The Bank of England cut its key interest rate to 1.5 percent, the lowest level in three centuries, the entire 315 years of the Bank's history. The country's main prudential regulator, the Financial Services Authority (FSA) stepped up its surveillance, requiring banks to submit disclosures on risk and performance on a weekly basis, rather than on monthly or quarterly bases. For its part, the UK government announced two rescue packages for the financial sector, amounting to a total of around 350 pounds sterling, and introduced other extraordinary measures, such as the Home Repossession (Protection) Bill 2008–09, which was adopted in February 2009.

At the same time, with the way UK house prices have risen in recent years, even since the market, affordability remains difficult for many. There are 1.7 million British households on council waiting lists for rented accommodation, and the national average house price is increasingly getting out of reach for many.

## UK housing markets and policy

Relative to the US and Australia, urban space is at a premium in the UK. Urban development in the UK has an ancient history and is as much the product of the constraints of the past as of the present. London, for example, had a population of 845,000 in the year 1800 and occupied 40 square kilometers, at a gross density of 211 persons per hectare. Today, it has a population of ten million people and occupies 1855 square kilometers, at a lower gross density of 54 persons per hectare (Cox and Pavletich, 2009). This shows the interplay of old and new: London is a crowded city, a legacy of earlier times, yet the average density of London has declined over the past 200 years, reflecting modern factors such as improved urban planning, as well as better transport links and communications. Houses in the UK are typically significantly smaller than in the "new world" countries. Average dwelling size in the UK is around 800 square feet (75 square meters), compared to 2150 square feet (200 square meters) in the US and 2200 square feet (210 square meters) in Australia (*Demographia Survey*, 2005).

An important factor in shaping British housing was the Second World War, when nearly four million English homes were destroyed or damaged. After the war there was a major boom in council house construction, which continued well into the 1950s. This helps account for house size: atypical postwar three-bedroom semi-detached council house was built on a square grid measuring $7 \times 7$ yards ($6.4 \times 6.4$ sq. m) with a maximum density of 12 houses per acre (around 337 square meters per house). The postwar effect also means that a high proportion of homes in the UK are previously council-owned, and explains why community-based housing plays such a strong role in the UK approach, even today. The council house is effectively the dominant form of public housing in Britain. Therefore, in the UK, public housing is often referred to as "council housing", based on the historical role of boroughs.

An important shift occurred in the 1980s, due to initiatives of the Thatcher government that restricted council housing construction and provided financial support to other forms of affordable housing. The Housing Act of 1980 introduced the opportunity to purchase for public tenants, and the Thatcher government's Right-to-Buy scheme offered council tenants the opportunity to purchase their housing at a discount of up to 60 percent. The 1988 Housing Act introduced mechanisms for "demunicipalising" social housing by allowing the stock to be transferred to housing association (HA) management. Under the Decent Homes Program, council-owned stock began to be transferred to HAs, arms-length organizations that manage local housing estates. Often the tenants continued to occupy the dwellings, and the housing stock remained the property of the council. Consequently, while the long tradition of promoting affordable housing through frugally built and locally managed estates continued, the locus of control shifted from councils to HAs. By the mid-1990s, 1.5 million public housing dwellings had been sold to tenants at subsidized values, and 185,000 former council dwellings had been transferred to HAs (Kleinman, 1996).

HAs today are local, semi-independent, not-for-profit organizations known as "Registered Social Landlords" (RSLs). They may also be referred to as Large Scale Voluntary Transfer organizations or Local Housing Companies. Some are trusts, co-operatives, and companies. Examples include the Hornsey Housing Trust, London and Quadrant Housing Group, Metropolitan Housing Partnership, Nottinghill Housing Association, and Leeds Federated Housing Association. RSL rents are commonly higher than for council housing; however, the Government has introduced a rent re-structuring policy, which aims to bring council and RSL rents into line by 2012. Some UK councils have transferred their entire housing stock to RSLs. Besides taking over the management of existing estates, RSLs are now also the conduits of most publicly funded new housing. Funding for new dwelling construction comes from subsidies (termed "social housing grants") which amount to sizeable public investments allocated to HAs by the government for use in development projects. From 2003 onward, in an effort to seek greater value for money, much of the funding has been channelled to a more select group of around 80 RSLs that have achieved partner status through Partner Program Agreements.

Owing to the growing importance of HAs, the industry organizations that represent them are increasingly becoming significant players in UK housing. There are four industry bodies representing HAs, corresponding to the four regions listed above. They are the National Housing Federation (NHF), Scottish Federation of Housing Associations (SFHA), Community Housing Cymru (CHC) in Wales, and Northern Ireland Federation of Housing Associations (NIFHA). The largest, the NHF (formerly the National Federation of Housing Associations), represents 1300 housing organizations as members, owning or managing approximately two million homes that house five million people across England. The mission of the NHF is to support and promote the work that HAs do, and provide leadership of the housing policy agenda nationally and locally. SFHA has 210 member associations and was established in 1975. CHC provides around 95,000 homes and housing services throughout Wales.

HAs are funded and regulated by a central housing agency. For four decades, the Housing Corporation (1964–2008) was the umbrella body that oversaw new affordable homes and regulated HAs in England. It ceased to operate on November 30, 2008. The Housing and Regeneration Act 2008 created a new framework for funding and regulating affordable housing, one that is likely to last for many years to come. It swept away the old regulatory structure, abolished the Housing Corporation, and established two new agencies: the Homes and Communities Agency (HCA) and Tenant Services Authority (TSA).

The HCA is responsible for the land as well as the money to deliver new housing, community facilities, and infrastructure. Its mandate is to ensure that homes are built in an economically sustainable way, as well as to promote good design. The HCA has a brief to base its approach on the government's regeneration framework, *Transforming Places Changing Lives*; to encourage decisions to be made as locally as possible; and to ensure that access to jobs is a key decider in the location of new social housing. The TSA acts as a new watchdog for social tenants by regulating housing landlords, setting high standards of management across HAs, and listening to tenant concerns. The TSA relates its brief to the government's white paper *Communities in Control*, and has powers to cut red tape for high performing RSLs and the ability to take action where tenants do not get a fair deal. From 2010, the TSA will regulate all providers of social housing and they will all be known as "Registered Providers" irrespective of their private, public, for-profit, or not-for-profit status.

There are also three other umbrella agencies, by geographic region. In Scotland, the oversight role is performed by Communities Scotland (CS), in Wales by the Welsh Assembly (WA), and in Northern Ireland by the Northern Ireland Housing Executive (NIHE).

One important way in which these agencies support affordability is that low-income households in rental accommodation are eligible for rent rebates or rent allowances, known as the "Housing Benefit".

In 2008, the UK government introduced the over-arching National Affordable Housing Program (NAHP), aimed at increasing the supply of affordable homes in England. From 2008 to 2011, the HCS will invest £8.4bn in affordable housing through the NAHP, and the program's development partners will deliver 180,000 new affordable homes. Each year, a proportion of the homes built will be made available for low cost home ownership and affordable rent. A 2:1 split is anticipated, with two-thirds for affordable rent through RSLs, and one-third for affordable sale through the HomeBuy Scheme. Before applying for funding, housing providers must first be awarded Investment Partner status through the prequalification process. Accredited Investment Partners that meet Specialist Provision requirements can then bid for funding.

Overall, the UK places a much stronger emphasis on social housing than Australia or the US. Figure 5.1 compares household tenures across the three countries. Some 20 percent of all British households are social renters. This reflects the historical development described above.

As in the US and Australia, there is no capital gains tax on the principal residence in the UK. Historically, mortgage interest payments were tax deductible under the Mortgage Interest Relief at Source (MIRAS) scheme, as still applies in the US, but this was progressively reduced and finally abolished in April 2000. As in Australia, but unlike the US, a transfer tax applies on home sales in Britain, on a sliding scale ranging between one and four percent depending on the property value. This tax is relatively low by the standards of the European Union (EU). In terms of the private rental sector, landlords can claim standard depreciation allowances, but unlike Australia's "negative gearing" arrangements, the UK does not allow losses from private renting to be offset against income from other sources for tax purposes.

Work estimating the price elasticity of supply of new housing for the UK over the entire twentieth century is consistent with the above historical survey. Flow estimates of the supply elasticity give strong evidence of a regime shift before and after World War II. Before the war, the implied UK price elasticity was found to be between 1 and 4, but postwar it was between 0 and 1, when the council housing program was introduced. These UK elasticities are lower than those for the United States: between 4 and 10 before the war, and between 6 and 13 afterwards (Malpezzi and Maclennan, 2001). Supply of new dwellings in the US market appears to be far more responsive to prices than in the UK.

|  | Owner occupied | Private renting | Social renting |
|---|---|---|---|
| Australia | 70 | 20 | 5 |
| UK | 71 | 10 | 20 |
| US | 69 | 30 | 3 |

*Figure 5.1* All households by tenure – three countries

*Source:* Adapted from Scanlon and Whitehead (2004).

## Housing finance in the UK

The UK has overtaken Germany as the largest residential mortgage market in the EU (European Mortgage Federation, 2007). The advancing maturity of the British housing market has much to do with improvements in the housing finance industry. Studies show that the housing finance system has been an important driver for transactions of residential properties in the UK. Using data for England and Wales, Ortalo-Magné and Rady (2004) find that the credit market liberalization of the 1980s raised the level of housing transactions and contributed to making for a period of exceptionally high transaction levels, particularly through changes in housing demand from first-time buyers.

In the UK mortgage market, most borrowing is funded by either mutual organizations such as building societies and credit unions or by proprietary lenders, that is, banks. Since 1982, when the market was substantially deregulated, there has been substantial innovation and diversification of strategies employed by lenders to attract borrowers. This has led to a wide range of mortgage types. For instance, the industry offers interest-only, endowment, pension-linked, buy-to-let, right-to-buy, flexible repayment, self-certifying, and foreign currency mortgages, and so on. A variety of mortgage interest rate options exist too, including variable, fixed, discount, tracker, and capped rate loans. Recent innovations in the UK market include base rate trackers and flexible mortgages that allow the borrower to vary the repayments. Offset mortgages have also appeared, involving linked savings and mortgage accounts, with savings offset against mortgage balance and interest netted to give tax advantages.

However, the market is still wary of fixed-rate mortgages, by US standards. Five years ago, variable rate mortgages accounted for 35 percent and fixed rate for 25 percent (Miles, 2004). Other shares were 18 percent for discount, 17 percent for tracker, and two percent for capped mortgages. Today, there are signs that this is changing. According to the more recent YouGov survey, around half of existing borrowers (49 percent) have fixed-rate mortgages of some description, with younger households much more likely to have them (68 percent of those under 35 years of age). At the same time, consumer attitudes toward long-term fixed rate mortgages (LTFRMs) remain hesitant, with people opting for lower rates in the short term and preferring to take their chances in the long term: less than ten percent of the Britons surveyed said that they would be comfortable choosing an LTFRM (Pannell, 2007). The consensus among observers is that, in the absence of a major policy intervention from the government, the take-up of LTFRMs looks set to remain below the US in the foreseeable future. This means the British population will continue to bear the interest rate risk entailed in variable mortgages.

Reflecting Right to Buy and other factors, including financial liberalization, home ownership has risen steadily in the UK from 57 percent in 1980 to 71 percent today (Williams, 2007; Downie and Robson, 2007). However, recent survey evidence suggests that the total number of English households in home ownership has actually fallen since 2005 (SEH, 2007), calling into question the Labour government's major 2005 refocus of housing policy toward home ownership, when the then Chancellor Gordon Brown declared "we will extend home ownership towards 75 per cent" HM Treasury and OPDM (2005b). Pannell (2007), however, provides evidence from the 2007 British Market Research Bureau (BMRB) survey in relation to housing aspirations that 78 percent of households indicate ownership is their preferred tenure in two-years time.

The proportion of British owner-occupiers with current mortgages is 60 percent, which is about equal to the US (62 percent) but higher than Australia (45 percent).The loan-to-value (LTV) ratio is a proxy for borrower gearing (the home buyer's debt-to-equity ratio) and measures the size of the mortgage relative to the house price. The average LTV of British mortgages is 69 percent, below that of the US (75 percent) but above that of Australia (63 percent). There is evidence that the UK ratio has been rising further (European Mortgage Federation, 2007). More striking, however, is the maximum LTV: financiers in the UK will lend more than the value of the underlying property (Figure 5.2). This is not usually the case in Australia or the US, where bankers view the practice with greater skepticism.

Growth in UK mortgage debt as a ratio to GDP has outpaced that of the Organisation for Economic Cooperation and Development (OECD), and is over 80 percent (Figure 5.3). The ratio is also higher than that in the US, though broadly comparable with that in Australia.

| Metric | Indicator |
| --- | --- |
| Typical LTV | 69% |
| Maximum LTV | 110% |
| Usual length of contract | 25 years |
| Fixed-rate (>20 years) available? | No |

*Figure 5.2* Mortgage characteristics in the UK

*Source:* Adapted from Green and Wachter (2005), and Scanlon and Whitehead (2004).
*Note:* LTV = Loan-to-Value ratio.

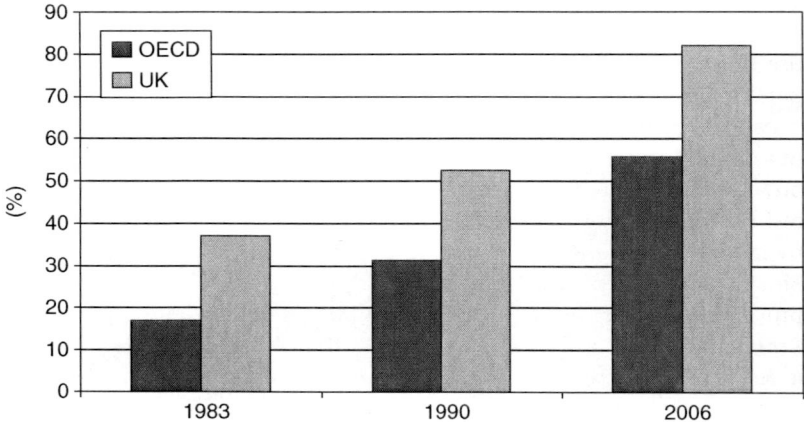

*Figure 5.3* Growth in UK mortgage debt as percent to GDP

*Source:* Chart data from International Monetary Fund, *World Economic Outloook*, Data forum, September (2008).

The degree of mortgage market concentration is not high in the UK by European or Australian standards, but is above than that of the US. Market concentration provides an indication of the level of competition within a market as it measures the extent to which leading lenders are able to dominate the market. The market share of mortgage loans outstanding held by the top five mortgage lenders in Britain is around 60 percent. Denmark (80%), Portugal (75%), Netherlands (70%), Italy (70%), and France (70%) have more concentrated mortgage markets. But the figure compares with just 37 percent in the US (Mercer Oliver Wyman, 2003). Although the UK market is less concentrated, the rate of return on mortgage lending is the highest in Europe, at 0.46 percent of mortgages outstanding. By comparison, the return to banks in Italy is 0.33 percent, and even lower in Germany (0.18%) and France (0.16%).

British lenders are in the process of significantly changing their methods of credit risk assessment, with a rapid rise in the use of innovative underwriting tools in the industry. A 2006 survey shows nearly half of all lenders using a credit score model compared with only ten percent before 2000 (Van Dijk and Garga, 2006). The proportion of lenders using Automated Valuation models (AVMs) rose virtually from zero in 2003 to around one-third at the end of 2005, and usage is expected to increase further over the next few years. AVMs are typically used for secondary lending decisions, such as valuing properties for re-mortgage and additional advances. In some countries, financial regulation aimed at maintaining prudent lending standards is delaying growth in AVM use (Downie and Robson, 2007). However, this does not seem to be a particular barrier in the UK.

Research indicates that the introduction of automated credit scoring helped give impetus to the subprime market in the UK from 2000 onward (Stephens and Quilgars, 2008). The UK is the largest market for residential mortgage-backed securities (RMBS) in Europe and has grown by more than 500 percent in the 2000s. Nevertheless of all mortgages outstanding in Britain, around 90 percent are still funded with retail funding, and only ten percent with capital market instruments such as RMBS or covered bonds (Earley, 2005). The flexibility of the UK market is less than that of the US. Britain has a comparatively lower level of securitization and, unlike the US, relies heavily on depository institutions, rather than on capital markets, to fund mortgages.

A major HM Treasury report, the *Miles Review*, identified this lack of a deeper market in longer-term fixed-rate mortgages as resulting in a number of "detailed funding issues" for the system, including difficulties in hedging pre-payment risk, lack of liquidity in fixed-market derivatives, illiquidity at the long end of the swaps market, limits on the use of wholesale funds by building societies, and issues related to capital requirements on lenders (Miles, 2004).

Besides mainstream home buyers and investors, the financial system also impacts HAs and households seeking to purchase low-cost housing from HAs. Both groups have been adversely affected since the global credit crisis. The cost of borrowing has increased, so HAs face higher costs. Those with higher debt ratios, and those who need to refinance frequently, are more vulnerable. Recent survey evidence suggests that some HAs could experience cash flow problems in the wake of the crisis (Whitehead et al., 2008). HAs reported a fall in enquiries about and sales of affordable units, probably reflecting uncertainty in the housing market combined with falling prices. Figure 5.4 shows the evolution of UK housing.

## British housing stress

Since low-income renters are largely taken care of through the sizable social housing system in Britain, measures of housing stress in the UK context typically focus on home buying rather than on renting. The margin of arbitrage tends to be around Low Cost Home Ownership (LCHO).

|  | Institutions | Products | Legislation |
|---|---|---|---|
| Up to 1960s | • Council housing (1940s–1950s)<br>• Housing Corporation created (1964) | • Fully amortizing bank loans with regular payments | • New Towns Act (1946)<br>• Town and Country Planning Act (1947) |
| 1970s to 1980s | • New investors into the market: mutual funds, pensions (1980s)<br>• Right to Buy Scheme (1980s)<br>• Decent Homes Program (1980s)<br>• Housing associations more involved (since 1980s) |  | • Removal of bank interest rate ceilings (1979)<br>• Housing Act (1980s)<br>• Deregulation of mortgage market (1982)<br>• Basle I capital adequacy (1980s) |
| 1990s to 2000s | • Barings Bank collapse (1994)<br>• Homes and Communities Agency created (2008)<br>• Tenant Services Authority created (2008) | • Euro currency created (1999)<br>• Expansion of credit derivatives (1990s–2000s)<br>• Credit score and AVM models (2000s)<br>• Affordability lending models (2000s)<br>• Fixed, tracker, flexi' and offset mortgages (2000s) | • Financial Services and Markets Act (2000)<br>• Basle II capital adequacy (2000s)<br>• Special Liquidity Scheme (2008)<br>• Housing and Regeneration Act (2008) |

*Figure 5.4* Evolution of the UK housing finance system

Recall from Chapter 2 that our A2F (Access-to-Finance) indicator of housing stress would generally closely reflect the ratio of house prices to income. In the 2000s, average UK house prices have grown at an average rate of about 14 percent per annum. The exception is the crisis year of 2008, when prices corrected and recorded a fall of eight percent, providing temporary respite. On the back of the long-term trend to higher prices, the average mortgage has ballooned relative to borrower income: ten years ago, nearly 85 percent of all loans to first-time buyers were at advance-to-income multiples of less than three, but now the proportion is only 40 percent (Cunningham, 2005). The house price to average

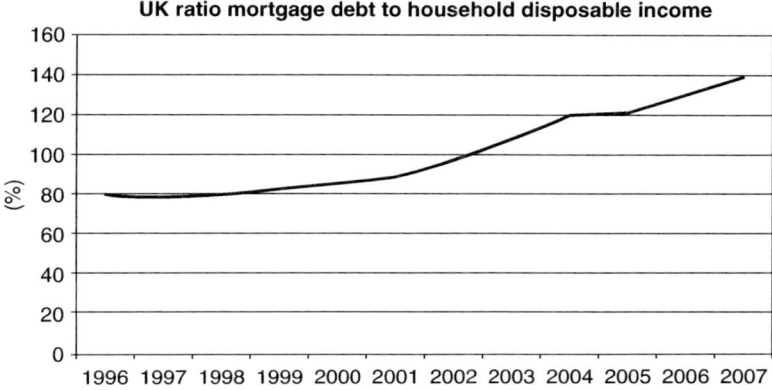

*Figure 5.5* UK housing finance burden, 1996–2007

*Source:* Chart data from Organisation for Economic Cooperation and Development (OECD), *Economic Outlook*, No. 84, October 2008, Annex table 58.

earnings ratio (median multiple equivalent), which was around four for most of the nineties, trended up to around six in the 2000s. With the onset of the crisis, the ratio fell back somewhat, to its lowest level in five years, according to a report from HBOS at the close of 2008. At the end of the crisis-ridden year, the ratio of house prices to average earnings ended at 4.56, down from a peak of 5.84 recorded in the previous year.

Despite this welcome relief, the long-term trend in the mortgage finance burden, depicted in Figure 5.5, is upwards. The burden ratio for Britain is significantly higher than in the case of the US, by about 40 percent. Low-cost home ownership is increasingly slipping out of reach for average British families.

International data confirm the comparative affordability problem in the UK (refer Figure 1.1). In the 2009 *Demographia Survey*, in contrast to housing markets in the US, Britain has no cities classed as "affordable". Of British cities surveyed, one-third are "seriously" unaffordable and the remaining two-thirds are "severely" unaffordable, the worst category. Overall, the median multiple has escalated sharply in the UK: the national multiple in the UK is put at 5.2, which is well above the historic maximum norm of 3.0. Not surprisingly, London is the most unaffordable, with a median multiple of 6.9, along with Belfast. The southwest region (6.8) and London exurbs (6.7) are close behind, and most other UK metro markets are rated severely unaffordable, defined as having a median multiple above 5. The least affordable cities are listed in Figure 5.6.

| Metro market | Median multiple |
|---|---|
| Belfast | 6.9 |
| London | 6.9 |
| Southwest region | 6.8 |
| London exurbs | 6.7 |
| Aberdeen | 5.9 |
| Edinburgh | 5.5 |
| Wales | 5.4 |
| West Midlands | 5.2 |
| East Midlands | 5.1 |
| Perth | 5.1 |

*Figure 5.6* UK metros with lowest affordability

*Source:* 5th Annual Demographia International Housing Affordability Survey (Cox and Pavletich, 2009).
*Note:* Median multiple is the ratio of median house price to median household income.

In applying the A2F dual indicator of housing stress, besides measures such as the LTV ratio and ratio of median family income to mortgage qualifying income, we can look at the experience of first-time home buyers.

Young people in Britain are faced with rising financial stress from housing. Based on data from the Survey of Mortgage Lenders, the proportion of home purchasers who are first-time buyers, which traditionally hovered around 50 percent in the 1980s and 1990s, has since declined to around 30 percent (Cunningham, 2005). This decline occurred in the 2000s, especially in the few years leading up to the credit crisis. Analysis by the Joseph Rowntree Foundation found that 20 percent of households under 40 years of age in Britain have income that is too high to qualify for social housing benefit, but too low to afford a mortgage on the cheapest ten percent of median homes for sale in their locality. One in three young households falls into this category in London, the southeast, and the southwest and other unaffordable areas (Wilcox, 2005). Moreover, there is evidence that financial stress is beginning to crowd the younger generation of Britons out of home ownership. In the under-25 age group, just 50 percent say ownership is their goal, well below the 79 percent recorded back in 1989. Ownership rates for the under-25s have been falling in Britain.

A recent paper compares the transition of young adults from renters to first-time homeowners, in Britain and the US; it seeks to identify behavioral similarities and differences in transitions in the two countries. The study finds that ownership rates among British young adults are higher than in the US. Yet longitudinal data suggest that demographic and housing market variables have similar effects in both countries. By the same token, young adults' transitions to homeowners in Britain are more responsive to income and wealth variables (Andrew et al., 2005).

In summary, both, the recent rise in house prices in Great Britain and then the credit meltdown, have disrupted the availability and affordability of home ownership. The credit crisis has shifted risk and changed the affordability equation for both private open market purchase and the HAs as key providers. These developments have highlighted the issue of providing for that "sandwich" group identified in the Rowntree Report, who are unable to purchase even the cheapest market housing but at the same time are able to afford open market rents and hence do not qualify for the Housing Benefit. As affordability worsens, this at-risk cohort is liable to grow. A post-crisis analysis of the housing stress situation by the Cambridge Centre for Housing and Planning Research (CCHPR) concluded that "a greater number of households struggle to access home ownership as affordability tightens" (Whitehead et al., 2008).

## The current debate in the UK

At the start of the millennium, the UK government embarked on an ambitious agenda for reform of the access, pricing, and subsidy of social housing. This set in train a vigorous policy debate in recent years.

One aspect has encouraged low-cost home ownership. In 2000, faced with emerging housing pressures, the UK government released a white paper, *Quality and Choice; A Decent Home for All: The Way Forward for Housing*. It messaged a new focus on home ownership and included the Starter Home Initiative. In 2003, this was followed up when the Low Cost Home Ownership Task Force recommended a range of improvements to the LCHO program, and in 2005 the Labour government set out reforms which included rationalizing the product range and expanding opportunities for social housing tenants to acquire equity stake in their homes.

Another side to the debate has been about stimulating the supply of new dwellings. In 2004 and 2006, Kate Barker released the final report and recommendations of the *Review of housing supply* (Barker, 2006). The Barker review recommended extensive reforms of the land use planning system, as well as new development taxes, including a "planning gain supplement" (PGS), which was effectively to be a new tax levied on developers to help fund the costs of infrastructure provision. In the wake of the *Review*, the Westminster government committed itself to increasing housing supply, and aspired to raise the level of home ownership to 75 percent. Shared equity and social housing were also to receive a boost.

A third aspect of the ongoing debate in Britain involved the housing finance system. The Miles Report on the UK mortgage market was commissioned by HM Treasury and was released in 2004 (Miles, 2004). Since that time, the Treasury has become more involved with housing and the mortgage market, and attention has been given to deepening the UK housing finance system. See also FSA (2003).

The year 2005 saw the release of *Homes for All*, the government's five-year plan for tackling housing shortages; *Extending Home Ownership*, which focussed on adding one million more homeowners by 2010; and *Housing Policy: An overview statement*. In 2006, the Chancellor announced the establishment of the Shared Equity Task Force and this led to seeking input from the private sector on ways to extend access to home ownership. In 2007, the government's aspirations were revised to1.5 million new homeowners while attaining the 75 percent level of home ownership. The government has also committed itself to reach a target of 200,000 net additions to the housing stock, per year, by 2016 (HM Treasury, 2006).

The arrival of the 2008 credit crisis intervened and slowed progress, especially in relation to the financial advances envisaged in the Miles review. In addition, working with builders and the planning profession to develop a policy framework has taken more time than anticipated. Yet 2008 still saw some forward movement, with the Housing and Regeneration Act, and the creation of HCA and TSA.

In a very real sense, the housing sector is changing, restructuring from "social" to affordable housing (Monk and Whitehead, 2000). UK housing is also moving toward a more commercial style of decision-making. A shift has occurred in housing allocation, exemplified by the adoption of choice-based letting (CBL) and by the introduction of "shopping incentives" within the Housing Benefit. The new model requires the customer to indicate preferences based on market information. Initial evaluation suggests positive reactions by customers to the revised lettings process compared with traditional bureaucratic rationing systems (Brown and Yates, 2005).

The current "British experiment" of shifting toward market-oriented reforms and consumer empowerment, creates a new and interesting dynamic. Arguably, recent developments in housing have been congruent with the modernization of the welfare state concept and a convergence with private sector ideas (Malpass, 2004). Some critics argue that there are significant tensions within the reform agenda, relating to the nature of housing market decision-making and the manner in which housing choice is modelled (Marsh, 2004). The policy of CBLs is analyzed with particular relation to rational choice by Brown and King (2005), who suggest that choice has to be "effective", based on the capability to act, which connects choice with access to resources. On this basis, they question the ability of the new policy to empower users of social housing. Pawson and Sinclair (2003) question the implicit model of human action and motivation based on rational choice theory that underlies many of the recent initiatives. They examine evidence from an experiment in three London boroughs to provide under-occupation incentive payments. To encourage "under-occupying" council tenants receiving Housing Benefit to relocate to smaller properties, the program provided a financial incentive scaled to the net reduction in rent consequent upon the move. The analysis concludes that the relatively small financial inducements offered by this scheme had no impact on tenants' housing consumption decisions. Other authors have expressed concerns about the impact on vulnerable groups, and about the efficacy of the new system to rebalance high and low demand in local housing markets (Brown and Yates, 2005).

Over time, all this creates significant challenges for the UK housing finance system. Affordable housing in Britain, more than in the US or Australia, has been regarded as part of the postwar welfare state, yet it is different from other core services because of the presence of a large market sector. The current debate in the UK turns on this axis, the dynamic tension involved in moving from a social housing philosophy to an affordable housing system that is commercially based.

Underpinning the transition is the need for finance. In some areas of mortgage banking the UK is at the forefront of affordable housing finance, such as shared equity. Yet although the mortgage market in Britain is evolving, the suite of retail products is incomplete relative to the US, and the secondary capital market needs to develop further. Related to this, British households are finding A2F housing affordability increasingly beyond their reach, at a time when the funding needs of HAs are becoming more and more complex.

# 6
# Affordable Housing Finance in Australia

## Introduction

This chapter surveys housing markets, housing stress, and housing finance in the Australian context, and reflects on the current debate in that country about housing.

While Australia was not immune from the Global Financial Crisis (GFC) and associated banking fallout its financial system withstood the international banking crisis relatively well, compared with the US and the UK. In the 2008 credit crisis, no Australian bank had to be bailed out, large or abnormal mortgage write-downs were mostly avoided, and no bank saw its credit rating downgraded. Bank lending slowed, reflecting higher cost of funds and uncertainty, but did not "shut down" as it did in the US and the UK.

To explain the remarkable resilience of the Australian banking sector, we can point to the culture of prudent lending that prevails among its banks. In particular, the philosophy of favoring loan origination over securitization means that the quality of Australian bank assets is comparatively high, with nonperforming assets equivalent to less than one percent of on-balance sheet assets, even post-crisis, versus around five percent in the US post-crisis. The IMF made this assessment of Australian banking during the crisis: "The securitization of mortgages in Australia was not widespread before the crisis, with only about 18 percent of housing loans securitized. These mitigating factors implied that Australian banks suffered only limited direct losses, compared to their counterparts in North America and Europe, and their credit ratings remained high throughout the period" (International Monetary Fund, 2008)

Further, the industry is marked by sound corporate governance, and official oversight of banks is effective, involving the "twin peaks" system of one agency, the Reserve Bank of Australia (RBA), for monetary policy and another, the Australian Prudential Regulation Authority (APRA), for prudential regulation. This includes a government-guarantee of deposit safety, and (unlike the US) the separation of commercial banking from social assistance policy. Just the same, Australian banks have always maintained a comfortable level of provisioning. The banks are soundly capitalized, with a well diversified and stable funding base, and a track record of healthy profitability. Return on equity (ROE) for the Australian banks hovered around 15–20 percent from the mid-1990s until the global crisis, compared with 10–15 for US and UK banks.

The Australian banking system is a strong and safe banking system. Yet for all the advantages of this approach, therein lies a problem for affordable housing finance in Australia. Because the housing finance system is so conventional, virtually restricted to prime mortgages, Australia has seen little or no development of housing finance that is significantly innovative, and more "affordable" than a regular prime mortgage.

Rightly or wrongly, this is undoubtedly a contributing factor to the rising level of housing stress in this, our third national case study. Australia has one of the least affordable housing markets in the world.

## Australian housing markets and policy

Historically, Australia has followed a particular pattern of urban development: 90 percent of the population lives along the seaboard, especially the east coast. Vast tracts of the continent are arid and inhospitable. The nation is relatively young, with just 200 years of modern history since European settlement, and the population is not large relative to the size of the landmass. In comparison with the US, Australian land and housing development is therefore spatially concentrated. Compared with the UK and Europe, with their historical large religious and aristocratic land ownership, development patterns in Australia have been largely market-driven. McLoughlin (1992) notes that private capital has circulated freely in the built environment since the early nineteenth century in Australia. Euro-style direct government interventions and town planning controls have not been a major feature of the housing sector in Australia, although there has long been a role for public-owned housing, and also the past ten years have witnessed a sharp rise in zoning intervention by lawmakers.

Australian housing culture is very much based on the dream of home ownership (Apps, 1975), and the nation has a mature home ownership sector. The ownership rate is about 70 percent (Caplin et al., 2003, Scanlon and Whitehead, 2004). Housing policy has generally sought to facilitate access to home ownership through a combination of regulatory and subsidy arrangements (notably, home savings grants, and tax expenditures) and provision of a public housing sector. Up to the 1970s, housing affordability, generally speaking, was not a major concern. With the onset of financial deregulation in the 1980s, Australia began to exhibit a much more pronounced housing price "boom–bust" cycle, and housing affordability emerged as a major focus. In particular, financing issues such as interest rate levels and deposit gaps have, in each successive business cycle, become a national obsession. At a policy level, this led to a focus on targeting public housing to households deemed to be most in need, and a lively debate about housing policy reform.

The private rental sector is a significant part of the Australian housing system. The 2006 census shows that around 23 percent rent their home from a private landlord. The private rental market in Australia has been described as a "cottage industry" (Yates, 1996; Beer, 1999; Berry, 2000b). The sector is not driven by large-scale investors: six out of ten private rented dwellings are owned by individuals, with most of the remainder of the stock owned by partnerships and small companies. The majority of individual landlords (three in four) own only one rental property. There is a significant incidence of what Yates (1996) has termed "accidental landlordism," such as people renting out the house they previously lived in as owner-occupier, or a dwelling they inherited. Given this, it is perhaps not surprising that reported financial rates of return vary very widely across the sector.

The Federal government has not, until recently, had anything resembling a "department of housing". Nor has Australia developed US-style government-sponsored enterprises (GSE) housing finance agencies along the lines of Fannie and Freddie. Indeed, until very recently, housing policy was unofficially domiciled with the Department of Family and Community Services (FACS). The Commonwealth-State Housing Agreement (CSHA) was the key mechanism, between 1945 and 2008, through which federal and state governments negotiated to provide assistance through public housing. The provision of public housing by State Housing Authorities (SHAs) was central to this periodically renewed agreement, which typically involved a mix of programs ranging from capital grants to SHAs for the provision of public housing and crisis accommodation, to grants or loans to private renters to assist them defray initial establishment costs, and to subsidized home lending products aimed at those in need. Over time, there has been a fall in the number of available public housing dwellings across the country, from 365,000 in 1995 to 341,000 in 2006 (Australian Institute of Health and Welfare, 2007), and there is a wait list of up to seven years.

Each Australian state government operates a department of housing and/or urban policy. These authorities have traditionally acted predominantly as landlords of public housing estates within their jurisdiction, yet they depend for their funding on the Federal government, which has often made for political tension in Australian housing policy and tends to work against intellectual innovation in program design. This dynamic may change, now that the Rudd Labor Government has shaken things up (see below). State governments have been criticized for making housing less affordable by levying stamp duty on home sales. Although in recent times some states have made stamp duty concessions for first home buyers, there remain calls for state authorities to abolish stamp duty for first home buyers buying a median-priced home. Stamp duties on housing average almost A$15,000 for a median-priced house, and are an impediment to home ownership, especially for first home buyers. Land tax on residential properties, levied by states, is also a significant disincentive to investors coming into the market, which analysts say contributes to a shortage of rental housing.

A second major prong of social housing policy – besides public housing – for many years has been Rent Assistance, which in Australia provides a nontaxable cash payment to qualified private sector renters. Assistance is paid at the rate of 75 cents for each dollar of rent paid above the rent threshold, up to specified maximum rates. The rate of rent assistance depends on the number of dependents, and whether the recipient is partnered or single. Critics of rent assistance point out that the program lacks horizontal equity, as individuals with similar incomes do not receive the same amount of cash support. In particular, the real proportional value of the rent benefit varies widely across Australia: the maximum dollar amount of rent assistance paid is the same in every city, in Sydney and in Perth, for instance, yet there is a vast gap in the cost of renting between the two locations.

Home ownership assistance in Australia has typically had two aspects: direct assistance to home ownership through deposit grants to first home buyers, and indirect assistance provided through the tax system. Mortgage interest is not tax deductible for Australian consumer households. However, owner-occupied dwellings, up to a threshold value, are exempt from state land taxes, and owner-occupiers are exempt from capital gains tax on the family home (but not on second and subsequent homes). An individual taxpayer can set up a self-administered pension ("superannuation") fund, and include in the fund any second and subsequent properties owned, such as vacation homes, and then enjoy the favorable tax treatment accorded to pension fund investments in Australia.

The impact of taxation on Australian landlords has generally been favorable. "Negative gearing" is an arrangement whereby Australian investors can claim a tax deduction on interest generated by loans used to purchase a rental property, where the interest paid on loans to finance dwelling purchase and renovations is tax-deductible against the landlord's non-property income for personal taxation purposes. Capital gains tax is levied at rates that are effectively lower than those for other income sources. Land taxes levied by state governments, exempt rental dwellings up to a threshold value (Yates, 1996). For the purposes of goods and services tax (GST), which is levied at ten percent, rents are exempt.

About five percent of the population lives in "social housing" in Australia, slightly above the corresponding figure for the US (3%) but well below the figure of 20 percent in the UK (Scanlon and Whitehead, 2004). Housing policy under the conservative Howard Liberal government, in office for ten years from the mid-1990s to the mid-2000s, was minimalist and market-oriented, emphasizing measures such as the one-off First Home Owner's Grant (of A$7000 to assist buyers purchase their first dwelling), no capital gains tax on the family home, and "negative gearing" (a tax concession) for investors. The Howard administration sought to maintain home ownership as the dominant tenure form, and directed its fiscal subsidies accordingly. Established social housing programs, rent subsidies and public housing, were broadly maintained, but not expanded.

Following its election to office in 2007, the Rudd Labor Government altered the name of FACS to FaHCSIA: Department of Families, Housing, Community Services and Indigenous Affairs. This signaled a higher priority for housing policy on the part of the new administration. Indeed, 2008 – the year of the mortgage crisis – saw a string of new measures introduced by the government aimed at overhauling national housing policy:

- Introduction of First Home Saver Accounts, bank saving accounts where the Government will contribute an extra 17 percent on top of funds deposited into the account up to the value A$5000, a potential contribution of A$850 per year. The accounts are available to anyone aged between 18 and 65 who has not previously owned a home, and contributions can be made by the account holder or by a third party. These accounts are designed to encourage saving for a deposit.

- the First Home Owner Grant, a legacy of the previous government, was retained. However, with the First Home Owner Grant pegged at A$7000 for the past eight years, despite house prices doubling in that period, it no longer provided the support it once did for first home buyers. So the Government modified the grant scheme by announcing the First Home Owners Boost, a response to the housing affordability challenge aimed at strengthening residential investment activity in Australia. First home buyers are eligible for grants of up to A$21,000. Under the program, first home buyers who purchase established homes will have their grant doubled from A$7000 to A$14,000; and those who purchase a newly constructed home will receive an extra A$14,000 that would take their grant to A$21,000.
- A National Rental Affordability Scheme (NRAS) to attract private investment into affordable rental housing and to subsidize the construction of 100,000 affordable rental dwellings over ten years. Investors will be offered A$8,000 in tax credits or offsets from federal and state governments for each unit they build and rent out at 20 percent below "market" rental.
- A National Housing Affordability Fund (NHAF), designed to reduce the cost of bringing new homes to market and assist in increasing supply, reducing development costs, and providing support to both renters and first home buyers over the medium and long term. It will reduce infrastructure charges and streamline planning approvals processes over the next five years, helping developers and construction firms with faster, cheaper, and easier approval procedures.
- A Housing Recovery Plan (HRP), for expanding the supply of new housing for both the public and community housing sectors, through a targeted investment that will stimulate construction work and create jobs in the building and related industries. The plan involves a government-approved tender process for the spot purchase of private sector new dwellings, designed to provide a rapid stimulus to economic activity in constructing private sector dwellings.

Overarching the above measures is the new National Affordable Housing Agreement (NAHA), designed to reduce financial stress for those in rental accommodation. A Residential Investment Fund to support infrastructure provision in rapid growth areas is included, as well as new houses for homeless Australians. The Agreement sets a clear national affordable housing target, namely halving the number of low-income households living in unaffordable housing.

These moves by the Australian government in 2008 and 2009, which had been outlined prior to the 2007 national election in a paper coauthored by the soon-to-be prime minister himself (Rudd et al., 2007), represent a milestone in affordable housing policy in that country, and a distinct shift toward greater government intervention in housing markets. While they will undoubtedly make an impact, it is too early to judge how successful they will be. The measures also leave a question mark over the limitations in housing finance in Australia. Despite some financial aspects, the package overall still has a traditional cash-assistance feel and leaves banking and capital markets for housing still largely unchanged.

## Housing finance in Australia

Australian banks' conservative loan policies mean they do not often depart from prime mortgage lending. APRA defines prime or traditional mortgage loans as those satisfying the following criteria:

- debt service to gross-income ratio not exceeding 30 percent;
- loan-to-value (LTV) ratio not exceeding 80 percent;
- loan approval directly by lending institution, rather than through mortgage brokers; and
- full documentation, rather than low-documentation.

As shown in Figure 6.1, the typical LTV ratio – the mortgage divided by the value of the house – of Australian mortgages is 63 percent, which is lower than in both the UK (69%) and the US (73%). This is consistent with Australia's more conservative lending policies. Lenders in Australia will lend up to only 80 percentage of the value of the property, compared with 97 percent in the US and 110 percent in the UK. Fixed rate loans beyond 20 years in maturity are generally not available. Only around 15 percent of Australians have a fixed-rate mortgage (Johnson et al., 2007), below the 25 percent figure in the UK and the 82 percent in the US.

The banking system in Australia has experienced very strong balance-sheet growth for many years now, mostly driven by high demand for residential housing loans (Figure 6.2). Consequently, the ratio of mortgage debt to GDP is at 80 percent and above the OECD (Organisation for Economic Cooperation and Development) average, up from 20 percent at the start of the nineties, when it sat below the OECD average. Nevertheless the proportion of Australian owner-occupiers with current mortgages is only 45 percent, below the figures for both the UK (60%) and the US (62%) (Scanlon and Whitehead, 2004).

| Metric | Indicator |
|---|---|
| Typical LTV | 63% |
| Maximum LTV | 80% |
| Usual length of contract | 25 years |
| Fixed-rate (>20 years) available? | No |

*Figure 6.1* Mortgage characteristics in Australia

Source: Adapted from Green and Wachter (2005), and Scanlon and Whitehead (2004).
Note: LTV = Loan-to-Value ratio.

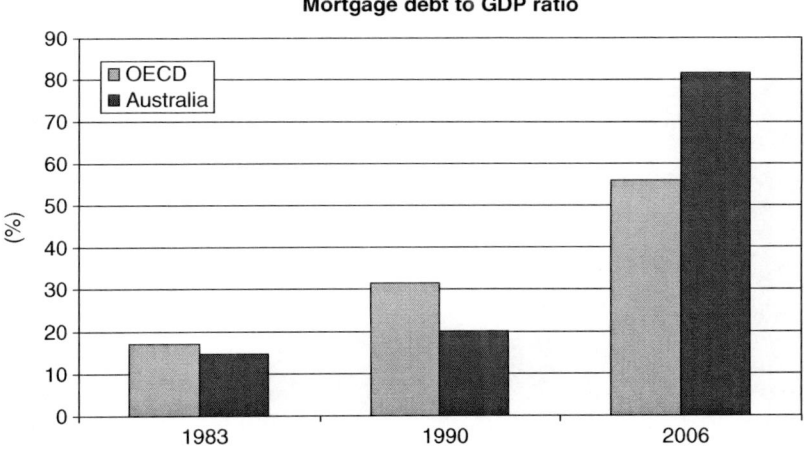

*Figure 6.2* Growth in Australian mortgage debt as percent to GDP

Source: Chart data from International Monetary Fund, *World Economic Outlook*, Data forum, September (2008).

A study by Worthington (2006) of financial stress using data drawn from the Household Expenditure Survey relating to 3268 households found evidence, albeit qualified, that Australia's historically high levels of household debt causes financial stress.

As Figure 6.3 indicates, mortgage lending has outpaced other forms of lending since the early nineties.

Innovations during the past few years in the Australian mortgage market include flexible mortgages with variable repayments, home equity loans, non-conforming loans, redraw facilities, and offset accounts. Some split-purpose loans are also available, which separate the loan into two sub-accounts, giving tax advantages. See Ellis (2006).

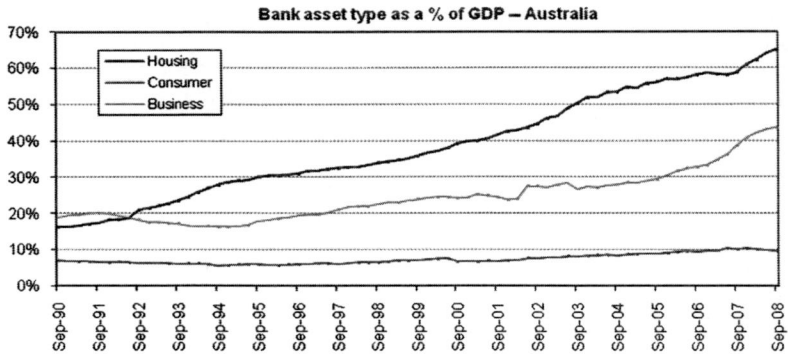

*Figure 6.3* Australian bank lending – by category

*Source:* Australian Prudential Regulation Authority (APRA), Australian Bureau of Statistics (ABS).

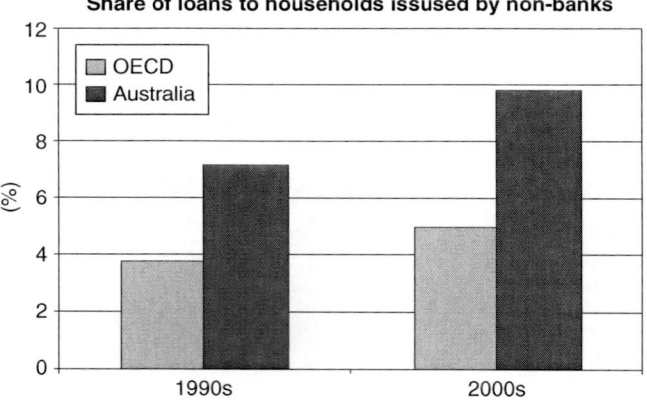

*Figure 6.4* Share of banks and non-banks of Australian mortgage lending

*Source:* Chart data from International Monetary Fund, *World Economic Outlook*, Data forum, September (2008).

The Australian mortgage system has seen an increase in the participation of non-bank players (Figure 6.4), a development reflected in rising prime residential mortgage-backed securities (RMBS) issuance. The Australian market for mortgage-backed securities first emerged in 1984, although there had been trading as early as 1979 (Wright, 1989). More recently, new providers have entered including mortgage originators and brokers, and Australia has seen growth in securitization reflecting the strong demand for housing finance. However, as Black (2008) points out, this is not the full story, as the volume of securitized housing loans has grown faster than housing credit, with the share of housing loans funded through securitization reaching 25 percent. In large part, this reflects the change in the composition of lenders in the market following the entry of non-bank mortgage originators. Prior to the recent turmoil in credit markets, mortgage originators accounted for around 35 percent of RMBS issuance. The bulk of Australian RMBS are prime (95 percent of issuance at the time of the crisis).

Non-conforming RMBS nevertheless became more common over the past five or so years in Australia. These securitized assets are backed by loans to borrowers who have impaired credit histories or other high-risk characteristics: loans with little or no deposit (high LVRs) and low-doc loans. The share of low-doc RMBS increased from being nonexistent in the late 1990s in Australia, to accounting for around ten percent of issuance in recent years. However, the non-conforming market, the closest equivalent to the US subprime market, is still much smaller in relative terms in Australia than in the US, with these loans only provided by a few specialist nondeposit taking lenders, whereas they were provided by a wide range of financial institutions in the US. Non-conforming loans made up only about one percent of outstanding Australian loans heading into the credit storm, well below the corresponding share in the US. Also, the quality of Australian non-conforming loans is higher than US subprime loans; as at the end of 2007, the share of Australian non-conforming loans that were more than 90 days in arrears was less than five percent compared with just below 15 percent for US subprime loans (Black, 2008). This partly reflects the tighter lending standards that were prevalent in the Australian non-conforming market. Owing to the high quality of Australian subprime loans, the spread between full-documentation and low-documentation mortgages narrowed from over one percent in 2000 to virtually zero by 2007 (Johnson et al., 2007).

Financial regulator APRA conducted a profile of Australian mortgages during the credit crunch, collecting data on 112,000 housing loans (APRA, 2008). Prime (full-documentation) loans of the sample had a median loan serviceability ratio (LSR, equal to disposable income/loan payment) of 2.5. Subprime ("low-doc") loans had a lower median LSR of 1.6, and an average LVR of around 70 percent.

Using the APRA model discussed in Chapter 7 (Sy, 2008), stress-testing of a sample of 2006 mortgages found that prime Australian mortgages have low probabilities of default, even when interest rates rise in the

18 months following loan approval in the order of 1.5 percent, provided average property prices are still rising. Subprime loans, not surprisingly, were found to have a lower median LSR of 1.6, leading to higher probabilities of default due to increased difficulties in servicing the mortgages in the same environment, particularly at higher values of LVR. Even in the presence of rising house prices, the default probability of nontraditional loans after two years rose from 3 to 13 percent, as LVR was raised from 70 to 100 percent.

The Australian housing finance system is increasingly deploying Automated Valuation models (AVMs) as a metric tool for credit evaluation (Fortelney and Reed, 2005).

Competition is surprisingly strong in Australian home lending, despite the market being dominated by the "big four" banks. Home loan refinancing data, released by the Australian Bureau of Statistics (ABS), show a high rate of consumers switching to a new lender: over the past three years, around 30 percent of new home loans (owner-occupied) issued by financial institutions were refinances. Competition in home lending in Australia has led to this independent assessment: "we have had a very competitive private mortgage market which has offered a wider range of mortgage products to consumers than that seen in many other countries" (Reserve Bank of Australia, 2008)

Figure 6.5 gives an overview of the development of the Australian system.

Australian housing finance has a history of being quite cyclical in nature (Figure 6.6). This is significant because of the pressure it puts on lending standards during intense periods. APRA found that when increases in Australian house prices run well ahead of wage increases, leading to decreased serviceability of home loans, some lenders seek to maintain market share and business loan volumes to households by lowering lending standards relative to traditional criteria (APRA, 2008).

## Australian housing stress

Our A2F (Access-to-Finance) dual benchmark as defined in Chapter 2 includes the deposit hurdle in applying for a mortgage. In regards to first-home buyers, the RBA found that the "deposit gap" – the difference between median dwelling price and average household borrowing capacity, expressed as a percentage of annual disposable income – went from zero in the mid-1980s to over 100 percent by the mid-2000s. In addition, the RBA measured the percentage of dwellings accessible to persons aged 25–39 years based on assumptions about bank lending

|  | **Institutions** | **Products** | **Legislation** |
|---|---|---|---|
| Up to 1960s | • Creation of licensed banks (1941)<br>• Creation of Reserve Bank (1959) | • Fully amortizing loans with regular re-payments<br>• Maximum LTV up to 80% | • Interest rate ceilings imposed (1942)<br>• Banking Act (1959)<br>• Decimal currency introduced (1966) |
| 1970s to 1980s | • First cash management trust (1980)<br>• Entry of foreign banks (1983, 1985)<br>• Australian Stock Exchange (ASX) deregulated (1985)<br>• New investors enter market: super funds (1980s–1990s) | • Launch of Bankcard (1974)<br>• First options trading (1976)<br>• First Treasury note tenders (1979)<br>• Fixed rate mortgages (1980s) | • Financial Corporations Act (1974)<br>• Campbell Report (1981)<br>• Removal of bank interest rate ceilings (1980s)<br>• Basle I bank capital adequacy framework (1980s)<br>• $A floated (1983) |
| 1990s to 2000s | • First mortgage originator established (1992)<br>• AFIC established (1992)<br>• APRA Created (1998)<br>• ASIC report on mortgage broking (2003) | • Credit scoring models (1990s–2000s)<br>• Expansion of credit derivatives (1990s–2000s)<br>• First mortgage broker lists on ASX (2004)<br>• "Low-doc", home equity and redraw loans (2000s)<br>• RMBS issuance (2000s) | • Superannuation Industry Act (1993)<br>• Wallis Report(1997)<br>• Basle II bank capital adequacy framework (2000s)<br>• National Affordable Housing Agreement (2008) |

*Figure 6.5* Evolution of the Australian Housing Finance System

behavior (30 percent repayment to gross income ratio, ten percent deposit), and concluded that affordability worsened during the decade leading up to the credit crisis. The RBA also found that around 30 percent of Australian households have owner-occupied debt-servicing ratios over 30 percent (*Financial Stability Review*, September 2007). This is consistent with the idea from our A2F dual indicator, that housing stress

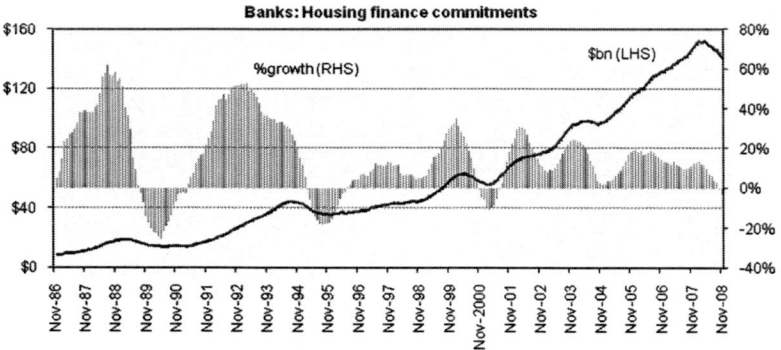

*Figure 6.6* Cyclical nature of Australian housing finance

*Source:* Australian Prudential Regulation Authority (APRA), Australian Bureau of Statistics (ABS).

becomes increasingly important during periods in the business cycle when financiers tighten lending criteria. Prospective home buyers find they have smaller-than-required deposits, and existing owners seeking to refinance at higher LVRs because the market value of their collateral has shrunk.

Research by the RBA finds that housing stress, conventionally defined using the 30-percent-rule, has been rising steadily over the past few decades. The percentage of renters in the lowest income quintile who are in housing stress increased from 40 to 50 percent in the 20 years between the mid-1980s and mid-2000s. More strikingly perhaps, renters in the second lowest quintile in stress soared from 10 to 40 percent in the same period (Richards, 2008).

Again, using the standard 30-rule benchmark, NATSEM data show that 23 percent of Australian households are in stress based on ratio of housing costs to gross income (National Centre for Social and Economic Modelling, 2008). If gross income is used rather than disposable, the figure is 16 percent. A split of those in stress is shown in Figure 6.7, by category of housing tenure.

NATSEM (2008) found that the effective median multiple for Australian housing has essentially doubled since the mid-1980s. The index of house prices today is around five times its level back in 1985, while average earnings of workers have risen by a factor of only 2.5. So, the ratio of median house price to median household income in Australia is twice of what it was back then. In terms of actual level, data produced by international housing survey *Demographia* show Australia's

|  | Private renters | Public renters | Home purchasers | Total Population |
|---|---|---|---|---|
| 30% rule – gross income | 28 | 10 | 26 | 16 |
| 30% rule – disposable income | 35 | 11 | 37 | 23 |

*Figure 6.7* Proportion of Australians in housing stress – by category

Source: Adapted from National Centre for Social and Economic Modelling (2008).

median multiple has risen from around 4.0 in 1985, to almost 8.0 today (Cox and Pavletich, 2009). This matches the trend indicated by NATSEM, and is also confirmed by Yates (2007).

The Real Estate Institute of Australia's (REIA) annual Housing Affordability Report 2008 estimated the proportion of a family's income spent on an average home loan is 36.7 percent, near the highest level recorded by the institute since it began measuring affordability 22 years ago. The institute found that once tax was taken into account, about half a typical family's income was consumed by the mortgage. A 2006 report found that six percent of people surveyed had experienced inability to pay the mortgage or rent on time during the past year (Australian Bureau of Statistics, 2006). Another study shows that mortgage stress in Australia trended up between 2002 and 2007, with the ratio of housing interest payments to disposable income doubling from five to around ten percent over the period. The study estimated that one in ten households were experiencing "severe" mortgage stress by 2007, when the crisis arrived (Johnson et al., 2007).

Private renters are disproportionately represented among the housing-stressed in Australia. Private renters, only one-fifth of the housing population, comprise well over half of all households in housing stress (Robinson and Adams, 2008). Lower-income private renters and purchasers are particularly likely to be affected, with research indicating that the incidence of housing stress for these groups is 65 percent and 49 percent of total households, respectively (Yates and Milligan, 2007). Many families who rent privately not only face rising costs but also face increased difficulty in finding appropriate housing. Vacancy rates for Australian rental properties have been consistently lower than the industry benchmark of 3.0 percent, with vacancy rates ranging from just 1.0 percent in Sydney to 2.6 percent in Canberra in 2007 (Real Estate Institute of Australia, 2008). In recent years, the increase in average rents has outpaced the level of rent assistance available to recipients (Australian Bureau of Statistics, 2006).

In contrast to housing markets in the US, no Australian city was rated "affordable" by the international 2009 *Demographia Survey* (refer Figure 1.1). The median multiple (ratio of median house price to household income) has escalated sharply in Australia and many of the least affordable markets in the world, including Sydney (8.3), Adelaide (7.1), and Melbourne (7.1), are to be found in Australia. These cities are in the same category as San Francisco (8.0), San Jose (7.2), New York (7.0), and London (6.9). Taking the whole survey into account, 100 percent of Australian cities are "seriously" or "severely" unaffordable, compared with just 22 percent in the US (refer Figure 1.1 for details). Figure 6.8 lists Australia's least affordable metro markets. Overall, the median multiple in Australia is 6.0, double the historic maximum norm of 3.0 and well above the levels of just a decade ago (Cox and Pavletich, 2009).

Despite the pace of house price increases easing since the crisis, prices in the Australian housing sector continue to put pressure on affordability, and act as a contributor to housing stress. For several years in the lead up to the credit crisis, the house price index was rising at an annualized rate of 10–15 percent (Figure 6.9). This followed an earlier, prolonged boom during the late 1990s and early 2000s, when annual price growth was 15–20 percent.

| Metro market | Median multiple |
|---|---|
| Sunshine Coast | 9.6 |
| Gold Coast | 8.7 |
| Sydney | 8.3 |
| Bundaberg | 7.2 |
| Adelaide | 7.1 |
| Melbourne | 7.1 |
| Mandurah | 7.0 |
| Wollongong | 6.8 |
| Newcastle | 6.6 |
| Perth | 6.4 |

*Figure 6.8* Australian metros with lowest affordability

*Source:* 5th Annual Demographia International Housing Affordability Survey (Cox and Pavletich, 2009).
*Note:* Median multiple is the ratio of median house price to median household income.

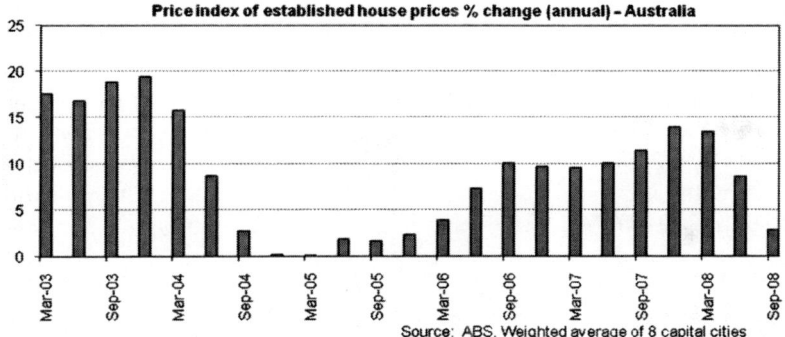

*Figure 6.9* Price index of established houses (annual percent change)—Australia

*Source:* Australian Bureau of Statistics (ABS).

## The current debate in Australia

The affordable housing debate in Australia is active and ongoing. In 2001, a major set of reports was released by the Affordable Housing National Research Consortium, a peak body of industry and government leaders that proposed ways of stimulating private investment in affordable housing (AHNRC, 2001; Allen Consulting Group, 2001; Berry and Hall, 2001; Berry et al., 2001). A National Summit on Affordable Housing was held in Canberra in June 2004, and a National Affordable Housing Conference in June 2005, in Sydney. These movements reflected a chorus of concern among stakeholders and a general consensus on the importance of seeking solutions to housing affordability.

The arrival of the global credit crisis brought the issue to a head, and saw the newly elected Labor Government in 2008 announce a suite of measures that, in large part, mirrored the groundwork laid by the various peak bodies and events. Over the course of the next decade, the effects will be judged, but as things stand in 2009, industry reports calculate that the number of homes built nationally in Australia each year is tens of thousands less than the number required by the growing population. The Federal Government's NRAS program announced in 2008 will, over ten years, go toward making up the housing gap by adding about one-tenth of the needed housing supply per year.

Yet significant new dimensions of the Australian debate are already developing. In June 2008, the Federal Senate Committee on Housing Affordability produced a report on many of the issues driving housing affordability problems in Australia. It observed that both demand and supply factors influence affordability, both for purchasers and renters, and that the question of affordable housing, and housing finance, is multidimensional. Yates (2008) concurs.

For instance, it is likely that Australia at some stage in the future will conduct a review of the tax system as it affects housing. The REIA argues that any review must take into account the full range of taxation provisions affecting the housing market, including state property taxes, as well as the likely impacts on the rental property sector if changes to capital gains tax and negative gearing provisions are proposed. The Senate Committee recommended that all state governments should consider stamp duty exemptions for first home buyers and retirees who are downsizing their primary residence. An exemption for retirees, it is argued by some, will assist in freeing up the supply of family homes close to employment opportunities, and will provide an incentive for retirees to consider housing options more suitable for their household size. Although stamp duty concessions or exemptions for first home buyers are already in place in some states, other states "give the First Home Owners Grant with one hand and take it away in stamp duty with the other", argues the REIA. For example, in the ACT, the first home buyer still has to find another A$10,475 to pay stamp duty on the median-priced home, while an additional $7995 is required in the state of Victoria (REIA media release, June 7, 2008).

Another debate is based on whether the First Home Owners Grant should be reduced for buyers of existing dwellings. Critics argue this would remove choice from first home buyers, particularly those who want to buy a home in established areas close to employment and other infrastructure, and that it is not practical or equitable to suggest that first homeowners should be concentrated in new housing developments, often distant from schools and employment opportunities.

The debate in Australia also involves striking the right ongoing balance between direct and indirect measures. This relates, for example, to existing negative gearing arrangements for landlords, and whether tax deductibility on mortgage interest should be introduced for homeowners. An analysis of Australia's home ownership policies is found in Yates (2003). Indirect (tax based) assistance is shown to dominate direct (cash payment) assistance and is poorly targeted, with the greatest amount of assistance being provided to those households who need it least. On a per household basis, outright owners receive more than five times the amount received by those with a mortgage. High-income outright owners receive an estimated benefit close to A$9000 per annum, while lower-to-middle income purchasers get less than A$500. In another study of Australian tax effects, however, it was found that low-bracket taxpayers are able to obtain rental housing at a cost lower than if they purchased the same quantity of housing for owner occupation. A study using a dataset of 1907 properties owned by Australian landlords shows that tax arbitrage opportunities in rental housing markets mean potential occupants with marginal tax rates below the breakeven tax rate find renting to be a relative cost advantage over home purchase (Wood, 2001). This finding is consistent with Australian tenure patterns.

Given public sector fiscal constraints, there is increasing discussion of transferring tranches of public housing assets to not-for-profit providers. Such transfers will enable the unencumbered value in those assets to be released, and help to build the asset base of those providers and hence, their borrowing potential (Milligan, 2005). This move would also help to establish a more competitive multi-provider system, and mirror the direction of policy in the UK, where we have witnessed an associated spurt of innovation in financing arrangements.

Notwithstanding all the above, the scale of the Australian affordable housing sector remains undersized, in the sense that the country has one of the most unaffordable housing markets in the world. The seven largest providers in the entire nation have developed little more than 1200 housing units in total over the last decade (Milligan et al., 2004). Contrast this dismal number with the situation in the UK, where one community housing association alone, the Leeds Federated Housing Association in England, since the early 1990s has developed 2000 new-build dwellings. Or compare the estimated number of constructions needed to ease affordability: property forecaster BIS Shrapnel estimates that Australia needs 180,000 new dwellings a year to meet demand and yet only 150,000 are being built (Bullock, 2008). Even with the new programs and measures announced in 2008, it is unlikely that enough affordable housing units will be added through the public sector, and equally unlikely that the private sector will move beyond small-scale, one-off project developments.

This brings us back to the question of affordable housing finance. The traditional bank-based housing finance system in Australia is robust and efficient, yet it is proving to be something of a bottleneck that is contributing to high housing costs. Australia needs more capital market involvement, but has not yet developed the full suite of retail products and wholesale capital market capabilities that can be envisaged in a comprehensive system. Meanwhile, Australian mutual funds are constantly seeking new asset classes to invest in, fresh locations for their burgeoning asset book that remained unsatisfied. These investment funds, now huge because of superannuation contributions from

Australia's workers, can potentially provide the supply of investment funds in multigrade mortgages, just like they already do with corporate bonds of various grades, provided the products are well defined. Finance for multigrade housing, both owner-occupied and rental, could become much more flexible and leveraged in Australia. In this way, a serious volume of new private finance could be enlisted for future investment in various grades of affordable housing, which would make a quantum leap in volume of supply and ease pressure on government budgets.

It is to this issue that we turn in the next chapter. The three-country survey in Chapters 4, 5, and 6 has demonstrated that advanced countries share a common, unmet, and constantly growing demand for more affordable housing. The world's financial system, by default, sought to supply this demand in the years between 9/11 and the global credit storm, but unsuccessfully: capital market imbalances resulted because of a lack of sustainability, precision, and articulation, as the banking system collided with the ever-growing need for affordable housing finance. In the next three chapters, we turn to the search for solutions.

# 7
# Capital Market Solutions

## Introduction

From our survey of conditions in the US, the UK, and Australia, we observe that affordable housing finance is a global concern, with common patterns across countries. We also note that, to varying degrees, each of these countries suffered a mortgage-related economic shock from the 2008 credit chaos in subprime lending.

These two observations are intimately connected. What stands apart in this latest crisis is the key part played by the pricing of credit risk. The global crisis has exposed the shortcomings of the credit risk models used, which resulted in poor transparency and pricing of instruments. The rapid growth in asset-backed bonds prior to the fall in worldwide liquidity in 2008 was driven by the securitization of residential mortgages, which grew rapidly between the mid-1990s and 2008, the year of the global crisis. Residential mortgage-backed securities (RMBS) account for a large share of the asset-backed paper on issue, with collateralized debt obligations (CDOs) and commercial mortgage-backed securities (CMBS) making up the remaining portion.

Globally, following 2008, there was a widespread reappraisal of the risks associated with investing in these structured credit products. The securitization market had been dislocated, and investors became cautious about returning the market (Black, 2008). This saw issuance of asset-backed securities (ABS) fall sharply and risk premia widen. Financial institutions that relied on securitization for funding had to scale back their lending, and as a result, the process of dis-intermediation that was evident throughout the past decade, was partly reversed. This amounts to capital market failure.

The agenda, post-crisis, is one of revitalizing and reconfiguring the securitization market. How was it that all those so-called Ninja loans and "liar" or low-doc loans could be dressed up by Wall Street and sold to investors as prime paper? When will the market for residential mortgage backed paper (RMBS) develop a graduated approach to risk-based pricing, as already applies in the market for corporate paper, and when will the subprime market be integrated with the mainstream market? Would a more liquid secondary market in RMBS enable more forms of risk sharing and spawn the development of derivative contracts on residential housing? The situation calls for developing a fresh, intentional approach to investor finance for multigrade housing, through enhanced use of the modern capital market. This new set of arrangements must be information-rich and sustainable.

A study by the European Mortgage Federation estimates the potential gains from improving efficiency and completeness in mortgage markets. "Efficiency gains", such as reductions in servicing, distribution, origination, and funding costs could deliver benefits equating to 0.15–0.30 percent of EU residential mortgage balances. "Completeness gains", flowing from greater product availability via the closure of observed product gaps, could result in a market expansion of up to ten percent, and increased consumer benefit for up to 25 percent of mortgage borrowers, equal to a further 0.15–0.30 percent. Many of these benefits can be achieved through changes at the national level, whereas others will require greater integration across markets in order to be realized (Mercer Oliver Wyman, 2003).

Research suggests that smoothly functioning secondary mortgage markets help the primary mortgage market, and also smooth macroeconomic fluctuations. In recessions, in the absence of mortgage securitization, depository institutions bear all the weight of declines in mortgage flows. In the presence of a securitized secondary housing loan market, banks are able to partially offset this with accumulations of RMBS. As the less procyclical secondary mortgage markets grow and mature, they increasingly stabilize mortgage flows. During periods of financial crises or economic duress, evidence indicates that RMBS markets may have been particularly effective in stabilizing mortgage markets and moderating business cycles (Peek and Wilcox, 2003). The challenge, therefore, is to the private professional capital market, to develop greater prohousing capability. To address the market shortcomings outlined in Chapter 3, and to make a quantum impact on the future supply of affordable housing finance, a capital market solution is required, which involves a fresh appreciation as to how the need for affordable housing intersects with the interests of large investors.

This will involve a measured and nuanced role for regulators. A survey in the UK shows that regulation is a major driver of change in the mortgage underwriting market: almost all lenders that have introduced an "affordability model" (see Chapter 8 for discussion) nominated regulatory guidance as the most important driver. The British market authority Financial Services Authority (FSA) introduced regulation for mortgage providers with rules that explicitly state that mortgage financiers must assess applicants' ability to repay (van Dijk and Garga, 2006).

In this chapter, the ambit of the term "capital markets" includes credit rating agencies. It is apparent the agencies failed to pick the crisis, before it was too late. A more arms-length role is needed for them, like a genuine impartial auditor. This will require structural reforms in the ratings industry. Although rating agency attitudes do not constitute official regulation, they are very influential in determining lender and investor behavior. An example is the attitude of lenders toward using Automated Valuation models (AVMs). Downie and Robson (2007) note that as AVM experience has become established, agencies have abandoned testing and "haircuts" in favor of placing responsibility on lenders to demonstrate that they regularly justify, test, and audit their policies for AVM use. Yet rating agencies' relationship with AVMs is a work in progress (Fitch, 2007). There continues to be significant innovation with AVMs, including the integration of valuation, credit and capacity data, and decision rules in electronic loan decision-making platforms. As AVMs increasingly become integrated into credit decision-making processes to create a unified risk management solution, rating agencies (and regulators) need to be vigilant to ensure quality control.

This chapter outlines how private capital markets can review, re-group, and re-invent themselves, in order to overcome the past shortcomings of technique and infrastructure, and change from being part of the problem to part of the solution to housing provision in the future. This will require wholesale institutional investors to be better engaged, by routinely including the affordable housing sector in their trustee portfolios. Despite fingers being burned during the 2008 crisis, investment in low-income housing paper – correctly specified and supported by appropriate market infrastructure – offers potential portfolio benefits for institutional investors, provided the challenge of creating a defined asset class can be overcome.

## Investment hurdles

Mortgage lenders finance their activities from two main funding sources: retail and wholesale. Retail funding is raised from individuals, mostly through bank deposits. Wholesale funding is raised from companies and capital markets – in the secondary market – where funds are raised by issuing securities backed by existing mortgages. The proceeds are used to finance the next batch of mortgage lending or to replace other funding sources.

RMBS are a method by which lenders raise funds. A particular tranche of existing mortgage loans in the bank's portfolio is identified and acts as collateral for the new investment security that will be created, a mortgage-backed security issued via the process of securitization. The chosen tranche of assets is transferred from the balance sheet of the mortgage lender (the originator) to a company that is legally distinct, known as a special purpose vehicle (SPV). The SPV acquires legal title to these assets and issues the RMBS. Payments to investors are derived exclusively from the performance of that specific pool of loans. Lenders need hold regulatory capital only against assets on the balance sheet; securitizing and taking them off balance sheet allows them to avoid this cost. Where structuring of the issue is required, lenders will usually incur charges from investment banking advisers, usually including a fee for underwriting and for credit enhancements.

The legal separation means the loans are protected should the originator go bankrupt, and also allows the security to be rated independently of the originator, which may have a poor credit rating. Further, the lender no longer has to set aside regulatory capital for the asset tranche that has been securitized. Figure 7.1 provides an overview of the

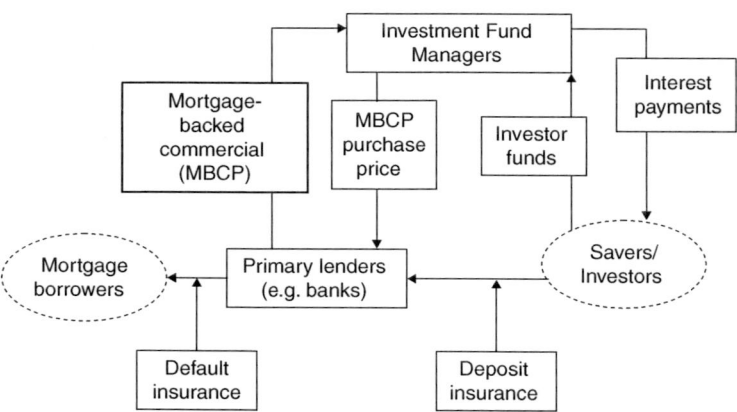

*Figure 7.1* Overview of links between housing financiers and investment fund managers

links between lenders and capital markets, in the provision of housing finance.

RMBS are securities backed by mortgage loans and commonly take the form of mortgage pass-through securities. A selected parcel of original mortgages, acting as collateral, is bundled up to create a new bond-like instrument, and sold to investors. The originating bank, upon receiving monthly repayments from borrowers, passes the income flows through to the new owners, minus any handling fees. A benefit of the RMBS to banks is that they get the mortgages off the balance sheet, freeing up space to write new business.

Collateralized mortgage obligations (CMOs) are a particular type of RMBS that began in 1983 and have grown strongly. Unlike regular RMBS, CMOs generate semiannual interest payments to holders, rather than monthly as with RMBS. CMOs are divided into tranches base on maturity, and can also be split into interest-only (IO) and principal-only (PO) versions. Also, several classes can be purchased: holders of second-class CMOs purchase these instruments based on the knowledge that they will not receive any principal repayments until holders of first-class CMOs are fully repaid. Concerns about CMOs involve what happens when interest rates increase, or decrease. A rise in rates can trigger defaults on underlying loans. A fall in rates can lead to early prepayments of underlying mortgages, forcing investors to reinvest elsewhere, which exposes them to rollover risk.

Professional investment managers and mutual funds operate in a highly competitive environment and need to remain focused on meeting client objectives and on being meaningful contributors to overall portfolio outcomes. Moreover, the trustees of mutual and other investment funds operate under a set of fiduciary obligations to both the regulatory authorities and their members, that may currently be seen as incompatible with lower-grade mortgage investments. Trustees of pension and similar investor funds have a mandate requiring them to seek maximum returns with acceptable risk, and to invest with an eye to increasing their members' wealth. The discipline of the marketplace through competition also means that unless a particular investment promises a safe and attractive reward, it is likely to be eschewed in favor of more desirable alternatives.

A number of investment hurdles and product specification issues are faced by nontraditional securities, specifically diverse-grade housing. Low-income housing paper, as traditionally perceived, faces a perception that the risk profile is high, based on concerns about tenant rental arrears and the potential for property damage. At the same time, expectations about anticipated yields may be below-market on account of the modest internal rates of return that often attach to such housing, because it is targeted at the lower end of the income scale. A risk-neutral investor such as an institution would expect a real rate of return of two to three percent above the "risk-free" rate to justify investment in residential real estate.

The main difficulty facing issuers of unlisted, subprime-rated securities is keeping the apparent promises made to investors of the security of regular income and capital certainty. This is especially problematic when property (and especially property development) is the underlying asset; as the security is both illiquid and cyclical, valuation problems can arise and cash flows depend on sales to be made on project completion. Problems may also arise if the issuer has allowed holders an early withdrawal mechanism. The main difficulties facing would-be investors in unlisted, subprime-rated securities would seem to be the technical challenge of estimating the investment attraction of property, inadequate information on and understanding of risk, and underestimation of the benefits of diversification (Erskine, 2008).

## Portfolio diversification

Yet despite these hurdles, there are good theoretic and business reasons why private asset funds should look at nontraditional housing asset classes, under the right conditions, as being in the long-term interest of investors.

Private investors typically hold fixed-interest debt securities in their portfolios for three reasons: income, diversification, and protection against uncertain economic times. The second of these, diversification, is highly relevant here. The addition of a new and distinct asset class adds diversification to the portfolio, assuming the new asset exhibits defined investment metrics. The principle of portfolio diversification implies that (subject to certain assumptions) the greater the spread of the portfolio across different asset classes, the better. Diversification, even including asset classes that by themselves have unusual or risky characteristics, can reduce portfolio risk overall for a given rate of return (or increase returns for a given level of risk). Housing-linked securities are consequently useful in a Markowitz mean-variance framework for diversifying away risk. House prices often tend to be uncorrelated with other investment classes, and can therefore provide institutional participants with significant diversification gains. Mutual funds are often attracted to holding equity in residential property because house price volatility is dramatically less than stock market volatility.

Research shows that the subprime market serves a diversity of needs. These include credit repair, evidenced by the high proportion of re-mortgages into the sector (Stephens and Quilgars, 2008). Such a spectrum of credit grades creates potential for portfolio diversification.

## From "beta" to "alpha" investing

Increasingly, a revolution in professional investment methodology is seeing nontraditional assets (such as affordable housing) being regarded in a whole new light. While most mutual funds still rely on a framework of a relatively static Strategic Asset Allocation (SAA) developed in the 1990s, there is an emerging trend away from this traditional approach, to one aimed at achieving client objectives more finely. The emerging technique uses strategies designed to separate "alpha" (active) and "beta" (mandate) returns, concepts that come from finance theory and reflect the language of capital asset pricing models. Investors are now able to target specific fixed interest risk premiums and structure a portfolio to effectively meet a variety of investment objectives. Buckley (2008) argues that this trend will see the eventual dilution of the traditional style of funds management, in which fixed income assets were used mainly as a risk-reducing allocation tied to an active return target that was generally low.

Under the emerging approach, beta policy is developed to provide a market return stream (not necessarily a benchmark return). Typical allocations include setting sector exposures (e.g., corporate, high yield, subprime, emerging markets) and credit limits. Alpha policy is aimed at constructing an absolute return portfolio that provides diversification (multiple alpha sources), a consistent return stream, and an outcome that is not tied to any changes to the beta portfolio (Buckley, 2008).

The capital asset pricing model (CAPM) of investing traditionally focussed on the market benchmark and beta, which measures the correlation of a given asset with the benchmark:

$$r_p(t) = \alpha_p + \beta_p r_M(t) + \xi_p(t)$$

where $r_p(t)$ is the return on asset p in period $t$, $\alpha_p$ is a constant, $\beta_p$ is the asset's historical beta, $r_M(t)$ is the market rate of return, and $\xi_p(t)$ is a random error term. The strategist's focus was on beta, and the forecast return on asset p was only as good as the forecast of beta. The contribution of alpha to $r_p$ was virtually irrelevant.

Alpha investing, by contrast, sees $\alpha_p$ as highly relevant. It involves a structured approach to active asset management, a three-stage process involving researching market data, followed by forecasting above-market returns, then constructing and implementing the implied portfolio. It involves outperforming the market benchmark by identifying extraordinary stocks or stock features, based on researching the underlying asset characteristics. This generates an "information ratio", the ratio of the expected annual residual return to the annual volatility of the residual return (Grinold and Kahn, 2000). The focus is on the residual component of the return on an asset, the part that is uncorrelated with the market index. The value added by the strategist-manager is proportional to the square of the information ratio, so a large ratio is better. The better the skill of the researcher, and the more frequently that skill gets to be used (say, daily), the higher the information ratio is likely to be. It is a research-driven investment strategy, that depends on asset classes which display a different pattern of returns to the benchmark return. Affordable housing, in the form of multigrade RMBS, offers a highly suitable asset class for this approach.

In this new alpha-seeking environment, the fixed interest market is constantly looking for new vehicles, searching out a wider and ever increasing range of investment options. The more vast the size and diversity of the fixed-interest market, the better for this new philosophy. Growth in the breadth of fixed-interest opportunities is constantly looked for, as it facilitates the delivery of scalable and capital-efficient pure alpha strategies that can sit over any beta return (Buckley, 2008). For this reason, the world of fixed interest continues to evolve from traditional government and corporate bonds to more innovative sub-asset classes and derivative instruments: the rapid growth in credit default swaps (CDS) to total outstanding of over US$50 trillion (Bank for International Settlements, 2008) is a good example.

Figure 7.2 provides a stylized depiction of a range of possibilities. Even distressed debt can play a constructive role in the portfolio, in the new philosophy. This is precisely where assets such as affordable housing come into play. Such assets, of varying credit qualities, sit somewhere along the generic risk-return spectrum in Figure 7.2, and as such can help the fund manager generate alpha. Instrument innovations allow the new breed of active managers to generate high alpha returns for investors, and thereby drive fixed interest returns harder.

The establishment of an investment framework of independent alpha and beta policy decisions to achieve long-term client investment objectives addresses the weaknesses of the traditional SAA approach, and opens up a new role for multigrade mortgage securities. Besides a preoccupation with benchmarks and the fact that strategic asset allocations

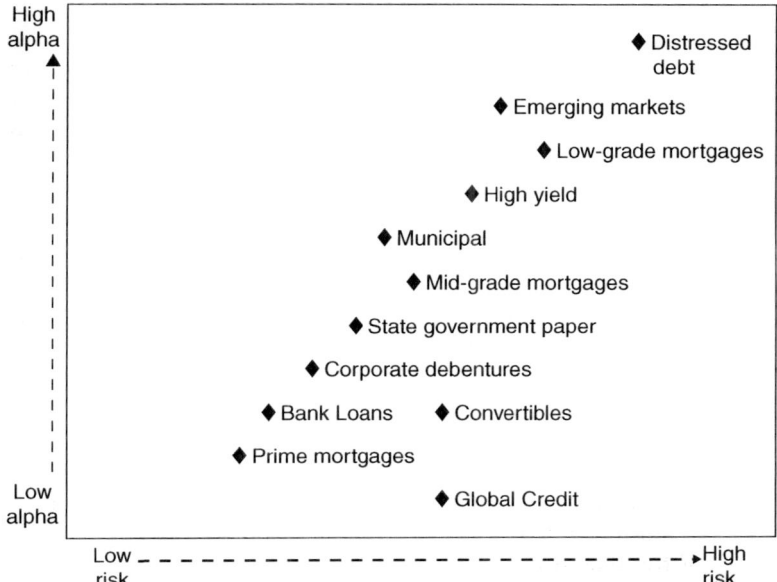

*Figure 7.2* Credit markets' alpha opportunity set

tended to be static for long periods, the old system carried a reluctance to hold significant allocations to assets that fall outside the benchmark. By operating independent alpha and beta policies, as in the emerging approach, a fund manager seeking to better reflect the investment objectives of the clients will be more likely to include such assets in the portfolio (Grinold and Kahn, 2000). At total fund level, fixed interest alpha is meaningful because of the flexibility to adjust underlying betas without disrupting alpha sources, low correlation to beta, greater capital efficiency, and enhanced scalability of alpha.

## Developing a defined asset class

In order for private investors to invest in various grades of housing-backed securities, issued under a variety of modes, the asset class must be well defined. In the Markowitz mean-variance sense, a well-articulated set of housing-backed securities that creates a new asset category can enhance the "optimal" portfolio (Figure 7.3), with participants being motivated to dedicate a share of their capital to such an asset class.

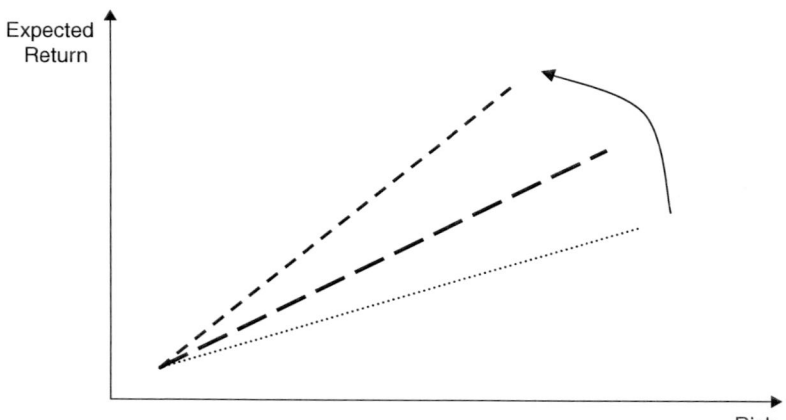

*Figure 7.3* Effect of greater capital market flexibility on the mixed asset-class efficient frontier

An existing barrier to alpha investment in affordable housing, however, is the lack of well-defined and easily accessible vehicles for investing in different grades of housing debt. There are few long time series of historical relationships that investors can use to estimate the probability of default associated with new instruments. Trading in this sector is not straightforward and is often not even available, in comparison to (say) buying a Treasury bond or trading corporate paper. Compared to alternative investments, transactions costs are high which act to further reduce the effective rate of return. Just about the only way that institutional investors could include affordable housing in their portfolios is via direct investment, involving the investor or fund manager in hands-on property management skills and time consuming day-to-day supervision.

The situation is not made any easier by the complexity of the market. In the US context, the common approach used by Fannie and Freddie to hedge against interest rate changes and to reduce the volatility of duration has been to slice mortgage-backed securities (MBSs) into one of four broad derivative types: sequential tranches, planned amortization class (PAC) bonds, "strips", and "floaters" (Green and Wachter, 2005). In the first case, a sequential tranche, the cash flows from the MBSs are divided into rating classes. In the PAC structure, which accounts for over 50 percent of American RMBS derivatives on issue, investors are guaranteed the timing of their cash flows. "Stripped" securities divide the payments from a security into separate instruments: PO strips that pay investors only principal or IO. Finally, floaters are linked to some specified spread over the benchmark London interbank offered rate (LIBOR).

As these are quite complex, and there exist few securitized forms for true "affordable housing" investment and no dealing exchange on which trades can readily be made, a significant barrier in the present circumstances is the lack of cheap, accurate information on the performance of investments in graded affordable housing, making it extremely difficult for a fund manager to assess their viability. An infrastructure-style vehicle for investment in segmented housing that establishes a defined, viable asset class would need to exhibit certain characteristics:

- an estimable market rate of return for an acceptable level of risk,
- existence of market information for comparison with other investments,
- maximum risk exposure,
- expected net revenue flows, and
- legally enforceable contracts that clearly spell out obligations and rights.

This is a minimum list of requirements if a new "affordable housing asset class" is to attract large-scale investment by trustee-constrained mutual fund managers.

The implied informational requirements are essential. The fair value of a financial instrument will be based on the following factors: time value of money, credit and other exposure, volatility reflecting the magnitude of future price changes, foreign exchange, interest rate, equity or commodity prices, prepayment costs, and servicing costs. Identifying exposures of an instrument will depend partly on relevance to investor objectives, but generally involves these five types of exposure: interest rate, credit exposure, illiquidity, currency risk, and volatility risk.

Can these technical requirements be met? We are in a much better position today with respect to meeting the information requirements than, say 10 or 20 years ago, because of the widespread prevalence today of credit scoring and similar quantitative lending techniques. This increasingly provides a dataset of metrics needed to assist asset class development, to evaluate grades of creditworthiness, and to correctly price the associated mortgage underwriting decisions. An example of this type of analysis is found in Chomsisengphet and Elul (2006), who develop and test a model of mortgage underwriting with particular reference to the role of generic credit bureau scores. In their model, scores are used in a standardized fashion, which reflects the prevalence of automated underwriting in industry practice.

The growth of AVMs promises to enrich the database of credit markets over time. Although AVM use is fully established in only three countries to date, its adoption is accelerating in a large number of others. Britain and Australia are fast developing established and widespread AVM use (Figure 7.4). The spread of AVMs reflects a desire by the industry to cut the cost and time taken for valuation, impeded only by caution over possible inaccuracy (Downie and Robson, 2007).

It is unfortunate that AVMs were not already better established prior to the credit crisis of 2008. They might have alerted investors earlier. It also means that AVMs in most countries have not yet been fully tested in a falling housing market, and a proper stress test will have to wait until the next downturn. The market is also still evolving: the list of ways that AVMs are used is expanding beyond their basic function as rapid low-cost collateral valuations. The effect, over time, will be to vastly improve the metrics available to investors when assessing alternative investments. There are growing calls in the US for standardization of AVMs, notably to better enable end users to make comparisons. Eventually, changes in the quality of a mortgage bundle will be able to be tracked in real time.

The Merton (1974) model, a theory of risk premium determination based on a bond market at equilibrium, provides an intellectual starting point for credit risk modeling. The model is a theory about security prices if the borrower can default and it identifies the expectation of loss from insolvency. The equilibrium assumptions of the Merton model are restrictive in the traditional case of non-traded bank loans, but as mortgages have increasingly become funded through traded bond markets, this problem recedes. The Merton model estimates the probability that

|  | 1st mortgage | 2nd mortgage | Portfolios |
|---|---|---|---|
| Australia | Yes | Yes | No |
| UK | Some | Some | Some |
| US | Some | Yes | Yes |

*Figure 7.4* Usage of AVMs – by country

*Source*: Adapted from Downie and Robson, 2007.

the stochastic insolvency variable, the borrower solvency ratio (BSR), will fall below unity, where

$$BSR = \frac{\text{Assets}}{\text{Liabilities}}$$

If BSR falls below one, it indicates that the borrower has negative equity. The value of BSR fluctuates according to some stochastic process while the amount of outstanding bonds (liabilities) is assumed fixed. If we assume the stochastic process to be a standard random walk of a Gaussian process, the Merton model generates a solution along the lines of the Black and Scholes option pricing formula. Over time, the model has had various extensions.

However, it can be argued that there is incomplete default causality in the Merton model, that insolvency is not sufficiently general as a driver of default (Sy, 2008). The existence of other possible causes means that insolvency may neither be a necessary nor a sufficient condition for default of secured loans such as mortgages. Bankruptcy, illiquidity, or shortfalls in cash flow may be the explanation, where a borrower is "asset-rich but cash-poor", solvent but in arrears. Alternatively, homeowners may be technically insolvent but may still be able to stave off default because they continue to make the necessary debt repayments. In other words, ability to service loan commitments is a decisive factor in the actual occurrence of default. Accordingly, Sy (2008) develops a model that assumes that the primary cause of credit default is insufficient cash flow to service mortgage obligations. The model estimates the probability that a stochastic delinquency variable measuring loan service ratio (cash flow to service loan, divided by monthly loan payment) falls below unity. Kealhofer (2003) provides another example of such a modeling.

Other, related theoretical and modeling challenges could also be overcome. For instance, different qualities of collateral can be incorporated into financial models. Plaut (1985), for instance, develops a model of the loan market, noting interrelationships between size of loan, collateral arrangements, and interest rate, in which collateral quality is explored. Similarly, Quigley and Van Order (1991) analyze credit risk for residential mortgages, making estimates of the hazard of mortgage default based upon a large sample of conventional loans. Mean returns are estimated, together with variances and covariances for various loan-to-value (LTV) ratios and geographic groups. The results indicate that credit risk varies "powerfully" by both LTV and geographical diversification. Danis and Pennington-Cross (2008) use a nested logit specification to grade young loans made to low credit score borrowers with low or no documentation in housing markets with moderately volatile and flat or declining nominal house prices.

In a further example of fine-grained credit analysis for different grades of housing debt, Goldberg and Harding (2003) analyze the investment characteristics of mortgage loans made to low- and moderate-income US households. They combine loan level and borrower data provided by a major state housing finance authority with housing transaction data. For various interest rates and house price scenarios, they generate the expected cash flows and calculate traditional investment characteristics such as duration and yield spreads. Then they compare the investment characteristics of lower-income loans with those of conventional mortgages. Surprisingly, the termination rate from mobility for the low- and moderate-income loans can be higher or lower than that of conventional mortgage loans, depending on the nature of the scenario. Overall, the low- and moderate-income loan portfolio has a longer duration but less negative convexity than the conventional mortgage portfolio. Other works on the evaluation of non-prime loans can be found in Quercia (1997), which provides a methodology for assessing the performance of affordable loans.

The use of private mortgage insurance, to protect the lender against losses arising from foreclosure, is another important avenue for enhancing capital market development. Access to mortgage insurance can enable the market to offer higher risk products, because the insurance underwriter can take on the risk rather than the lender, and can do this more efficiently due to the greater diversification of risk. In particular, high LTV loans (above 80%) are prime cases to be covered through this means. Research suggests that markets where mortgage insurance is more common such as the UK have shown greater willingness to offer higher LTV products and loans to higher risk borrower groups (Mercer Oliver Wyman, 2003). Lenders in both the US and the UK utilize mortgage indemnity insurance as risk mitigation, especially as a strategy to manage high-credit risk loans.

In summary, there is no technical barrier to developing a defined affordable housing asset class, in terms of the generic investment information requirements being satisfied, subject to the discussion in the next section.

## How regulators can assist

The rate of progress in private capital markets depends on the policy environment and the participation of policymakers.

In his seminal paper, Akerlof (1970) identified asymmetric information as a key ingredient for market failure, where buyers are less informed than sellers. This factor has clearly been present in the credit market crisis for MBSs. In another landmark paper in economic theory, Minsky (1992) anticipated that the flawed incentives of the mortgage securitization process would create loans of low credit quality, again because the securitization process leads to asymmetric information, because not all information about the loans the mortgage brokers had at loan approval was transmitted to the buyers of the RMBS (Sy, 2008).

Information asymmetry was a crucial ingredient in the credit crisis. Financial innovation in recent years saw an increase in the number and complexity of capital market products. For instance, a level one instrument such as an ABS would transmogrify into a level two instrument, a structured credit product such as a CDO, which would be based on portfolios of ABS, and this in turn would be the basis of a level three instrument, like a CDO-squared (CDOs of ABS that hold CDOs as collateral). A definite lack of transparency developed, a problem exacerbated by the banking system not clearly accounting for these transactions on balance sheet, which often were issued indirectly through SPVs (Black, 2008). A "shadow banking system" evolved, making it harder for investors to accurately assess their counterparties' business and their own exposures.

Information asymmetries were associated with incentive and agency problems: borrowers knew more about their true financial condition than their bank. The "principal–agent problem" is a situation in which agents (mortgage originators) may have different incentives than the principals (mortgage investors), resulting in losses for the principals. In the traditional banking model, banks performed due diligence to gain as much information about the borrower as they could muster and this helped reduce information asymmetry. In the new world of securitization, third party investors did not fully understand the different products they were buying. The difficulties in measuring risk, coupled with limited transparency, meant that many investors were content to outsource loss assessment to credit rating agencies.

Those agencies, it turned out, did not adequately redress the information asymmetry problem. Information transparency going into the credit crisis was not high. A recent UK survey found that only 30 percent of lenders had over five years' data history for probability of default (PD) models required under Basel II, and only 65 percent had at least five years' data for loss given default (LGD) models (Jaggar, 2007).

While markets therefore need to significantly enhance the depth and quality of customer and risk data, to enable reliable appropriate pricing and underwriting decisions, regulators need to address the principal–agent problem. This says that the opportunity exists for some issuers of RMBS to improve their economic payoffs by taking advantage of the inferior information set available to investors outside the banking firm that originated the paper. Issuers have an information advantage and this information asymmetry – and the resulting inefficiencies – should inform governance of the RMBS market.

When investing in mortgage-backed loans, investors are concerned about two issues: the yield they receive and the risk level. The yield demanded, however, itself affects the actions of RMBS originators (lenders) and engenders "moral hazard". Here adverse selection may occur: in order to determine who the good originators are, the investor can use the rate of return as a screening device, but unfortunately originators who are willing to pay yields may be bad originators because they perceive their probability of repayment to be low (Kern, 2004). Therefore, as yields on RMBS in the secondary mortgage market rise, the average riskiness of originators also rises, hence expected returns to the investor are lower. The behavior of the loan originator is often a function of the interest rate on the RMBS. At higher interest rates, originators are induced to undertake projects with higher payoffs but – adversely for the end-investor – with lower probabilities of success.

To deal with these issues, regulators can help by improving the flow of information. The originators' performance history produces valuable information that evolves over time. Secondary RMBS markets are therefore repositories of information, which in itself becomes a valuable asset that allows investors – and regulators – to ascertain good originators from the bad as also to ascertain price risk more efficiently. Regulatory intervention in these potential agency problems can help correct incentive problems that can make RMBS markets subject to inherent instability. This may require enhanced internal control systems within banks and other originators to address the inherent asymmetries of information and the potential market failure that may result. Government intervention might help achieve a Pareto improvement in welfare and might also help to mitigate the systemic threat to market stability that the principal–agent problem poses (Kern, 2004). The financial regulator represents the public's interest in seeing that players are regulated efficiently so as to reduce systemic risk. In a recent report, the International Organization of Securities Commissions (IOSCO) adopted internal corporate governance standards for investment firms to conduct themselves in a manner that would protect their clients and ensure the integrity and stability of financial markets.

As regulators need to design tomorrow's financial architecture with an informational theory of markets in mind, how can they address the credit market failure discussed in this chapter, which we have argued is essentially a failure of information and infrastructure? The authorities can take a number of steps to promote the development of secondary markets for such nontraditional securities such as an affordable housing asset class. It is recommended that new disclosure requirements that strengthen transparency be considered for improving information mechanisms for investors including retail investors. Erskine (2008) argues that new measures designed to promote enhanced disclosure should encourage and help investors to be interested in and be better informed in assessing the risks that they take on their investments.

An example can be drawn from the UK situation. Longer-term fixed-rate mortgages are generally not available in the UK, but can be financed through the issuance of fixed-rate debt by British lenders. This would be one way in which interest rate risk for lenders could be sterilized: the lender's balance sheet mismatch would be rectified, by matching fixed-rate revenues from mortgage interest payments made by the borrower, with fixed-rate outlays from cash flows to holders of fixed-rate debt issued by the lender. Covered bonds are one form of fixed-rate debt where the securities that are issued are collateralized by a specific pool of mortgages (Miles, 2004). Unlike MBSs, covered bonds remain on the lender's balance sheet. In many European countries, covered bonds are already an important source of finance for fixed-rate mortgages. Covered bonds are similar to RMBS, but differ because the mortgage assets are not removed from the balance sheet. The first covered bonds were issued in the UK in 2003.

The problem is that in the UK, as in most European countries, there is no specific covered bond legislation that sets out how security is enhanced for investors in covered bonds in the case of bankruptcy. A covered bond legislation entails that in the case of default by the issuer, the assets backing covered bonds are normally fire-walled thereby enhancing the credit of covered bonds. A UK Treasury Report identified the lack of this legislation as an obstacle to the development of a liquid and efficient covered bond market in the UK (Miles, 2004). The lack of specific covered bond legislation retards the emergence of a longer-term fixed-rate mortgage market, because costs are increased due to uncertainties, and it creates an obstacle to the recognition of covered bonds under the Co-ordination Directive on Undertakings for Collective Investments in Transferable Securities (UCITS). Such lack of recognition affects the extent to which European funds could invest in them. Accordingly, the

Miles Report for HM Treasury recommended that the FSA should provide a definitive view on whether or not current UK insolvency law is sufficient to allow for the recognition of covered bonds under UCITS.

Yet herein lies a delicate trade-off for regulators. Some argue that the last thing secondary market instruments such as covered bonds need is more administrative cost. Regulators affect funding markets through the legal and administrative costs that are associated with different funding methods. The legal documentation required for a covered bond issue in Britain, for instance, is lower since there is no transfer of assets from the balance sheet, yet capital markets are sensitive to such costs. Raising retail funding is administratively more expensive because the costs of maintaining a branch network are attributable to savings, but once raised is relatively cheap to hold. Short-term wholesale funding such as commercial paper is relatively quick and cheap to raise, and tends to be high value and low volume. Longer-term secondary market paper, like RMBS, are significantly more expensive because of the legal documentation required to launch and issue them. In the UK, for instance, each RMBS requires its own detailed prospectus, and the costs of legal documentation in securitization issues can be routinely in hundreds of thousands. One estimate in the UK context puts the cost of wholesale funding (RMBS) at (+)13 basis points, versus a cost of (−)89 basis points for retail funding (Earley, 2005a).

The above discussion illustrates some of the issues regulators must grapple with when enhancing credit markets and helping multigrade mortgage securities gain acceptance by fund managers. The development of more sustainable secondary markets for multigrade mortgage securities should be seen as a positive regulatory objective. Greater standardization of capital market mortgage products, with a view to articulated market trading, should be fostered. This might require a preference for exchange-traded rather than over-the-counter instruments. Authorities should seek to encourage competition among lenders, consistent with financial soundness, and trustworthy accounting and auditing, with different mortgage terms being offered by different lenders. Well-developed title, liability, mortgage, and hazard insurance are desirable, to properly underpin the market, along with a full suite of capital-raising instruments such as MBSs of varying grades and appropriate matching credit derivatives. All this should be nested in a supportive legal environment, including capital requirements.

An example of such a proactive regulator is the Australian Prudential Regulation Authority (APRA, 2008). Credit risk models need to be predicated on an understanding of the causality of the credit default process according to the regulator. This facilitates the building of deductive models capable of making predictions in a changing environment. Application frameworks are therefore being developed within APRA for assessing residential mortgage default risk using a causality model for typical households that takes into account house prices, wages, inflation, consumer credit usage, and interest rates. In the APRA example, related to the work of Sy (2008), a delinquency variable is chosen, the loan serviceability ratio (LSR), defined by the following equation:

$$\text{LSR} = \frac{\text{After-tax income} - \text{Living costs} - \text{Other expenses}}{\text{Mortgage payment}}$$

An insolvency variable is chosen too, assumed to be the reciprocal of the LTV ratio (LVR). The loan approval process captures the relevant data from a sample of borrowers to provide estimates of LSR and LVR at origination for each loan. Regulators, by virtue of their role, are usually in a position to collect these confidential data from banks. Given assumptions about how microeconomic and macroeconomic conditions may change in the simulation period, model parameters are estimated that allow to predict as to how LSR and LVR will evolve over time. From these time-dependent probability distributions, the regulator can calculate into the future the probability of default, loss given default, and expected loss for any given loan.

A further illustration of APRA's approach to mortgage regulation is "Project Panama", an exercise involving stress tests to assess Australian banks' capacity to endure economic downturns (Laker, 2003). Project Panama involved a major data collection and analysis exercise to test the resilience of Australia's banks to a very significant hypothetical increase in mortgage defaults and property price declines. The scenario assumptions used were as follows:

- over a one-year period, house prices decline by 30 percent
- mortgage defaults increase to an average of 3.5 percent.

The second assumption is quite stringent, considering the 20-year average home mortgage default at the time for Australian banks was just 0.12 percent a year. To put this in added perspective, note that the default rate on US mortgages by October 2008, in the heat of the global credit crisis, was 3.3 percent and rising toward five percent.

Regulations have an impact on the funding mix adopted by mortgage lenders. For commercial banks, regulatory capital adequacy requirements are a factor. Differences in the risk weightings on various assets may affect the relative attractiveness of different funding instruments. The Basel II international accord reduced the capital weighting of mortgage assets and this reduces the advantage of removing assets from the balance sheet to avoid the regulatory capital charge. This may be reducing the relative attraction of RMBS as a way to raise funds, particularly as a competitor to structured covered bonds. Non-banking institutions are also affected. In the UK, for instance, the amount of secondary market funding that building societies can access, and the cost of funds, are impacted by Building Societies (BS) nature limits (Earley, 2005a).

There appears to be a need for information, training, and discussion about AVM use. Regulators can help enhance the metrics available to issuers and investors by encouraging literacy in such matters as the choice of valuation service level, use of AVMs by valuers, policies for integration into loan decision processes, testing, and audit. Some authorities are already moving in this direction (APRA, 2005).

Governments can also consider strengthening the market for mortgage insurance. Methods include streamlined legislation, stakeholder communication, and appropriate industry regulation. The coverage of default risk on mortgages is ultimately borne by the borrower, regardless of whether that coverage is implicit or explicit. In the presence of explicit mortgage indemnity insurance, it is prepaid by the borrower in the form of an annual charge. Where lenders do not use explicit contract insurance, there remains an implicit cost, one the customer effectively pays for indirectly, via higher mortgage rates. It can be argued that an explicit system is to be preferred, because it unbundles the insurance function from the lending function, and therefore makes pricing more visible and increases allocative efficiency. Importantly, it improves confidence and decision-making among investors in mortgage-backed assets, which facilitates the orderly development of the capital market.

The dividend for regulators, of nurturing more sustainable mortgage capital markets, will be greater economic efficiencies. Housing finance systems should, ideally, be designed to maximize cost savings in funding, managing portfolios, and generating investment vehicles. Regulatory uniformity across jurisdictions, as has happened with Basel, would enhance global capital market arbitrage and integration. Operational efficiency in the sector and streamlined regulatory arrangements, coupled with maximum prudent flexibility and transparency in the capital market, is to be viewed by lawmakers as a source of potential cost-savings concerning the financing of housing development and supply.

The Miles Report in the UK lists four criteria for the "ideal" mortgage system (Miles, 2004).

- There would be a range of mortgage products, with various risk/return characteristics and various profiles of repayment.
- Borrowers would understand the overall characteristics of various mortgage products and make decisions in an informed, forward-looking way.
- Products would be funded efficiently and risk parceled out (or removed) in a way that makes the cost minimal while generating acceptable returns for providers of financing and those that accept risk.
- Costs of intermediation would be minimized – there would be no unnecessary switching of mortgages, which generates costs, if there are better ways to achieve the same ends.

The report at the same time concludes that while the UK system has some of these characteristics, it does not have them all. We might add that in the light of the credit debacle, the US to date has lacked at least one of the above characteristics, namely that products would be priced efficiently and risk parceled out effectively. And Australia lacks on several points too, notably the first one.

A further dimension to the role of policymakers is that fiscally minded regulatory authorities have the capacity to tax away the gains from trade, so that new developments are stymied before they even get underway. This can be through the imposition of new levies, or the rigid interpretation of existing ones. The antidote to this way of thinking is to recognize that the true dividend from regulation is not realized in the form of direct levies on capital transactions, which create allocation distortions, but rather in the form of stronger macroeconomic performance resulting from healthy financial commerce, which in turn generates higher general tax revenue (or minimizes tax expenditures to clean up the mess left behind by crises). Taxpayers will ultimately bear the burden of the capital market failure in 2008 by paying for a share of the massive financial bailout needed to repair the damage caused by the collapse of global financial markets. This amounts to over US$300 billion for banking firm interventions alone, not to mention the general economic stimulus package. Governments will also pay a price in terms of lower tax revenues and higher social amelioration expenditures. The budgetary cost of a "do nothing" approach, in other words, is not zero. Conversely, the fiscal reward to positive regulatory initiatives that improve the housing finance system will also come in the form of a better outcome for taxpayers and for government revenues.

It is significant that government actions have had considerable influence in shaping the move by banks to link mortgages with the capital market, through a series of steps, starting with the formation of Fannie Mae and Freddie Mac in the late 1960s. This led to the introduction of CMOs by Freddie Mac in the 1980s. The 1986 Tax Reform Act which included the Real Estate Mortgage Investment Conduit (REMIC) rules which can issue multiple-class pass-through securities without an entity-level tax, greatly enhanced the attractiveness of mortgage securitization. The purpose of the 1995 Community Reinvestment Act (CRA) was to assist low-income earners and minorities toward the goal of home ownership, and called for private commercial banks to devote a certain proportion of their excess reserves to such loans. The Bush Administration's 2004 American Dreampackage of housing measures that sought to assist low-income groups through zero equity lending fueled the flow of subprime mortgages that stoked the subsequent lending frenzy and house price bubble. But together these measures contributed to the subprime crisis. According to the Organisation for Economic Cooperation and Development (OECD), the 2004 American Dream in particular was a key factor, and a key reason why the toxic activities that led to the meltdown were so much stronger in the US than elsewhere (Blundell-Wignall et al., 2008). See also Figure 4.4.

The above-mentioned initiatives, well intentioned at the time, arguably had the unforeseen combined effect of forming part of a set of drivers that altered incentives and behavior of US banking firms. They stimulated the overproduction of subprime mortgages in the US banking system, ultimately with disastrous consequences. Coupled with other forces, such as the Federal Reserve's low interest rate regime, these policies caused American banks to accelerate their off-balance sheet mortgage securitization in order to enhance revenue streams and share price appreciation. The result was a marked acceleration in subprime leverage over time, beyond the normal limits of prudent balance sheet management.

Another factor is that the implicit government guarantees for Fannie Mae and Freddie Mac created a "moral hazard" problem, encouraging too many risky loans to be made on the assumption that the government would not allow a default to occur. This had the effect of making the market for MBSs appear as a safe haven in times of financial distress (Green and Wachter, 2005). Before the crisis emerged, Jaffe (2003) expressed concerns about Fannie Mae and Freddie Mac not being regulated in a sufficiently rigorous manner.

In terms of the final scorecard, when we look at what failed in the US in the 2008 episode, it was mostly investment banks, which were largely unregulated and operated with high leverage ratios, around 30:1. By contrast, commercial banks were less prone to fail. They are better regulated, and carry leverage ratios like 10:1. Moreover, the GSEs failed. They were supposed to be prudently supervised, but that turned out to be thin. Overall, this summary argues for reformed regulation in the future.

Ultimately, reductions in the cost of finance can be passed on to consumers in lower mortgage costs and rents. By better matching cash flows to investor liabilities, finance costs can be shaved. An increasingly sophisticated capital market for subprime housing credit, with innovative financial products, will contribute to regulatory efficiency.

## Conclusions and next steps

A flourishing market for RMBS is essential on a number of grounds. Benefits include a significant expansion in the supply of housing finance, greater flexibility and continuity, improved affordability, diversification in funding sources, increased competition with the effect of lowering cost, and a decline in the need for public subsidies. Until recently, the US housing finance system with its securitization approach was the model for the world. It showed the way in terms of expanding home ownership, diversifying mortgage markets, and maximizing housing finance flexibility. With the onset of the 2008 crisis, that has now been called into question.

This chapter has argued that the original thrust of the US model – diversifying housing finance through the private capital market – still promises many benefits. Equally, in the wake of the 2008 crisis, we need a more accurate and sustainable capital market infrastructure for pricing and trading nontraditional asset classes, including multigrade housing.

Despite the complexity and lack of transparency associated with securitized mortgage instruments, many investors nevertheless were not deterred from investing. We may never learn why investors were willing to invest in such darkness. But the capital market can do an improved job in the future by evaluating and pricing risk. It can devolve better and more sustainable Remiss: self-contained, MBSs with accurate risk pricing and transparent information, across multiple classes of risk.

This chapter has outlined an agenda for private, wholesale capital markets to regroup, reinvent and retool in the domain of housing finance. This will necessitate developing improved systems that are better equipped to take account of the role of risks and returns associated with investments in affordable housing. The chapter has argued for the potential role of a better-articulated affordable housing asset class in diversifying portfolio risk and assisting investment managers to generate "alpha" returns. The ultimate objective, from the consumers' point of view, is to ease the housing-related A2F (Access-to-Finance) stress measure of affordability, by enhancing the mortgage markets of the future.

This thesis is compatible with research which shows that the significantly higher levels of default found in the subprime segment owe much to information deficiency. Subprime lending is conducted disproportionately through centralized lenders relying on securitization for funding and using brokers to originate loans. This builds a series of information asymmetries into the system. As seen in the global credit crisis, borrowers that rely on securitized funding are vulnerable to such markets drying up (Stephens and Quilgars, 2008).

The risks could be better handled by integrating the subprime market with the mainstream market, and by applying a graduated approach to risk-based pricing. This is needed to redress a corner inefficiency that currently exists in the economy, in regard to portfolio optimization, because investor appetite for multigrade mortgage assets mostly goes unsatisfied due to a lack of reliable technical benchmark data and modeling to determine pricing.

Regulators have a role in contributing to the stabilizing of the sector, and in so doing, the economy. There is a relatively recent, growing recognition about the importance of the interaction between housing markets and the macroeconomy. This nexus has been shown to operate through several channels, including housing taxation, housing cycles, and housing market–urban structural form (Leung, 2004).

Residential property accounts for around half of all wealth assets in the developed countries of the world, and is of the same order of magnitude as government debt and traded equity securities combined (Caplin et al., 2003). The rapid expansion of secondary mortgage markets has been remarkable. Yet the need for a reappraisal and re-tooling is obvious in the wake of the subprime crisis. The crisis was essentially a failure of information, not a rebuttal to the very idea of evolving more and better household debt markets.

In the next chapter, we turn attention from the wholesale level to the retail side of the housing finance market.

# 8
# Retail Finance Solutions

## Introduction

This chapter explores emerging approaches to making housing finance more innovative at the retail level, so that it can become more accessible and affordable.

In many developed countries, there is growing evidence at the retail banking level of an increasingly large group of households who, while in full-time employment, do not meet the standard lending criteria of lending institutions and are at risk of being precluded from home ownership through a prime bank loan. Or if they do manage to obtain a loan, they are vulnerable to the burden of a traditional mortgage. A report by the British Treasury concludes that there are a significant number of "intermediate" households that cannot afford to enter home ownership (HM Treasury, 2006). Diaz-Serrano (2005), investigating the socioeconomic determinants of mortgage delinquency in eight EU mortgage markets, observes that a growing proportion of borrowers may not be able to accumulate the precautionary savings needed for a "rainy day", to maintain mortgage payments after a shock to income. In the US, a Federal Housing Administration (FHA) analysis of the spatial distribution of subprime lending, aggregated by metropolitan statistical area, shows subprime lenders are more active in cities with worse economic risk characteristics, and historically high risk locations (Fannie Mae, 2003). In the Australian context, research found that access to mortgage finance was steeply skewed toward refinancing existing, rather than new, dwellings and in favor of those who are well placed in the "new knowledge economy" (Berry, 1999). More recently, as housing has become less affordable, researchers have found more families who are "trapped" in the rental market (Yates and Milligan, 2007). This is creating a growing housing "underclass", a segment of the population in advanced countries that are terminally renting, and at risk of never aspiring to own. Renting is becoming a permanent housing tenure for a significant and growing number of people.

While recent years have seen some innovation in bank products, much of this has been at the margin. There remains a need to think outside the box. One commentator has said: "For centuries now, businesses in need of funds have been able to avail themselves of both debt and equity. Yet for households who aspire to expand, mortgage finance has been their one and only option. And so, despite the ever-growing sophistication of corporate capital markets, consumers around the world are forced to use only the crudest of financial instruments" (Caplin et al., 2003). Addressing this asymmetry between corporate and household capital markets – an exercise akin to a kind of product design arbitrage between sectors – is a useful agenda that has the potential to expand the flow of affordable housing finance.

One avenue for addressing the situation is to develop a wider range of affordable housing finance options at household and small investor level. Lending institutions are currently shifting toward affordable lending models, and are introducing a range of products to try to ease entry into home ownership such as low start, discounted, and 100% + mortgages. Credit-impaired mortgages ease access for higher risk buyers. Guarantor arrangements and group mortgages have also come onto the market, along with intergenerational loans. Shared equity arrangements and housing equity investment pools are on the agenda, and community-based approaches are gaining interest, as lenders seek to cater to the full spectrum of would-be buyers. The new wave of products, by improving households' immediate purchasing power, offer a flexible route into home ownership. In what follows, efficient and flexible mortgage design, as well as creative ways of garnering affordable housing finance "on the ground", out in the community, are discussed.

## Affordability-based lending

The development of affordable mortgage business models and products by lenders is on the increase. Historically, the borrower adjusted to the rules and requirements of the lending institution, but increasingly lenders are taking a more flexible approach and tailoring loan terms to the situation of the borrower. The standard annuity mortgage is increasingly being supplanted by mortgages with features to make them more affordable, such as longer terms or interest-only payments. Often, the aim is to reduce the borrower's monthly debt service in the initial period of the loan, to help households into owner-occupation, and to vary their expenditure patterns across the life cycle.

In this context, lenders are increasingly switching from simple income multiples by adopting "affordability models" of loan evaluation. Affordability criteria look more closely at the borrower's debt servicing capacity, and tailor the mortgage product appropriately to fit the customer's economic profile. These involve ability-to-repay assessments, and form part of formal credit assessment process, often as a substitute for conventional evaluations based on income multiples. This is part of the wider trend toward greater sophistication in underwriting and credit assessment in many advanced countries.

In the UK, the Mortgage Conduct of Business (MCOB) rules introduced in 2004 require lenders, as part of the loan application process, to issue a key facts illustration (KFI) to mortgage applicants.

The KFI must illustrate to the borrower the cost of the specific mortgage contract under consideration and how the monthly repayment would change if the loan interest rate were to rise by one percent. In turn, this acts as an affordability guide to the lender. Generally, it is an FSA requirement that lenders lend responsibly. The British market authority introduced regulation that explicitly requires mortgage providers to assess applicants' ability to repay. Banks must be able to show that in the credit assessment process, due account is taken of the customer's capacity to service the loan, including the impact of changes in the customer's circumstances and the effect of higher interest rates. As a result, over 50 percent of British lenders now use an affordability model compared with less than ten percent at the start of the millennium (van Dijk and Garga, 2006). Over the next few years, the proportion of UK lenders using affordability models is expected to rise further, to around 70 percent.

Affordable home mortgage loans, and the investor equivalent in the form of affordable housing development loans, are also part of the scene in the US. Legislation requires US banks to report periodically on Fair Lending and the banking industry has made concentrated efforts to reach emerging submarkets (American Bankers Association, 2009). This is seeing an emerging trend toward private lenders introducing affordable products, not dissimilar to those offered already by government-sponsored enterprises (GSEs), such as Freddie Mac's Alt 97 in the early 2000s which permits the three percent down payment to come from non-borrower sources.

The rise of affordability credit models has seen growth in interest-only loans, which help ease the initial debt service burden for those who have to stretch to gain access to the mortgage market. "Interest-only" loans require no repayment of principal in the early years, and allow the borrower to front-end load the interest repayments. This is often for an initial period of three to five years, but some lenders do not require any principal repayment for as long as 20 years. The benefits for affordability are twofold: the borrower's initial repayments of principal are reduced, and in the US where mortgage interest is tax-deductible for home buyers, the deduction can be maximized. For investors, these loans release cash flow that can be utilized for other purposes. In countries where there are tax deductions for commercial owner-landlords on the interest paid to service loans used to buy the property, such as Australia, the effect is to encourage investor housing by allowing greater deductibility in the early years. A variation on this theme is loans that allow payment of one year's interest in advance, allowing the investor to bring forward tax gains. A downside of interest-only loans can be that such products pose the risk of non-amortization (or lack of equity building).

In terms of affordable loan products, in the US these are often low down payment mortgages. However, when the collateral values are too high, the monthly mortgage payment becomes burdensome for typical households, all else held constant. To remedy this payment affordability problem, lenders in the US have increasingly issued various interest-only loan products.

Graduated-payment mortgages (GPMs) are loans to low-income earners where the repayments start low in the early years, then increase as the years go on, as the principal grows. This allow borrowers to make small payments initially, then raise the level of payments over a five to ten year period as their capacity to pay improves. After a defined period, the monthly repayments level off. Thus, GPMs are tailored to suit households' varying in affordability capacity over the life cycle, by essentially delaying a proportion of the mortgage repayment.

Similar to GPMs are growing-equity mortgages (GEMs). Here too the initial repayments are low and rise with time; however, unlike GPMs the monthly instalments do not plateau but continue to rise throughout the life of the loan. This suits borrowers who wish to start affordably but then with the passage of time, shift gear into repaying the loan increasingly faster.

"Balloon" loans have a long maturity (15 or 30 years in the US), but a shorter repayment pattern. The borrower makes regular repayments for the first few years, perhaps up to five years, then at the end of that period, must repay the full amount of the mortgage principal. This final payout is the balloon payment. The advantage is that no principal repayments are made until maturity, which helps keep monthly payments lower and more affordable. The disadvantage is that the borrower may not be in a position to make the balloon payment at the end of five years, so must refinance with a new mortgage, which carries the risk that the interest rate on the new loan might be higher.

Deposit bonds are a product that delays the need for the home buyer to pay a deposit on the house. Instead, the issuer of the deposit bond (usually an underwriter, broking firm, or insurer) guarantees that the deposit will be paid at a later date. In return, the home purchaser pays a guarantee fee. For individual home buyers, this can buy precious time to save and bridge the deposit gap. For investors, it can provide highly geared entry into the property market at an early date with little outlay, especially when buying "off-the-plan" without the need to part with the deposit during the construction phase.

In Australia, a lateral affordability model involves a national insurance company partnering with a union-based industry pension (superannuation) fund to establish the Superannuation Members Home Loans Scheme. The purpose is to create a vehicle for the pension funds to advance mortgage loans to their members at affordable interest rates. The resulting vehicle issues RMBS by packaging the individual loans together, which are then bought by the pension fund as a portfolio investment. Clark (2000) describes this trend as "pension fund capitalism".

What has been the impact to date of affordable lending efforts on home ownership rates? The result, by and large, has been an increase in mortgage loans to minority borrowers, and progress in developing loan programs that meet the needs of low-income communities. A study in the US assessed the impact of using flexible underwriting guidelines, primarily changes in the down payment and repayment requirements, on the affordability and home ownership of targeted populations. Based on national American Housing Survey (AHS) data, the findings indicate that affordable lending efforts are likely to increase home ownership opportunities for underserved populations, but not equally across all population groups. Recent movers and central city dwellers receive less benefit; young people and African Americans benefit most (Quercia et al., 2003). In the same study, changes in lending guidelines were found to have greater impact than simple reductions in the mortgage interest rate, for all sub-groups. The overall impact of affordability credit models on mortgage access and loan sustainability appears to be highly significant.

Some, however, point out that such mortgages can also be more risky. A study of evidence of 13 developed countries of house prices, debt, and affordability over a ten-year period, in relation to the prevalence of interest-only mortgages, found that interest-only borrowers can end up paying more in the long run, and the housing finance system may be more fragile (Scanlon et al., 2008). The danger is that an interest-only borrower does not accumulate equity as an annuity borrower does.

## Shared equity

Conventional mortgages have an all-or-nothing format, where the borrower alone purchases the house, and pays the purchase price in full. The scale of this is daunting to many home purchasers, especially younger buyers, because of the high median house price-to-income multiples they face, as documented in Chapters 4–6. The all-or-nothing mortgage model therefore can be a barrier to affordability and access to finance.

It is also less than efficient from an economic theory point of view, because it limits housing finance outcomes in the economy to a restrictive corner solution. Moreover, from a financial portfolio perspective, the indivisibility of the asset and the associated liability causes a conflation of the consumption and portfolio decisions of households that are inevitably embedded in any home purchase (Caplin et al., 2003). By preventing homeowner-occupiers from separating their housing consumption and housing investment decisions, the all-or-nothing mortgage creates a housing finance constraint on portfolio optimization, with all the implied welfare loss that this involves.

Shared-equity conversion products seek to address this traditional "indivisibility" of housing finance, by allowing individuals to hold less than 100 percent of the equity in their home, while still having an ownership stake and taking out a mortgage. The home buyer still gets to accumulate equity in the property over time. The shared-equity investor, often a bank or similar lender, takes an equity position in the residential property. In return, the investor receives a pro rata share of any future capital gains. Because these products reduce the required mortgage for the home buyer and bring new borrowers into the market that were previously excluded, they can consequently improve low-cost home-ownership (LCHO) opportunities, and increase the supply of finance for affordable housing. The rate of home ownership will rise. These products support a move toward greater tenure flexibility with a view to helping people move up and down the home ownership ladder as their circumstances change.

A shared-appreciation mortgage (SAM) allows the home purchaser to obtain a mortgage at below-market interest rate. In return, the lender providing the loan on attractive terms will share in the future appreciation of the capital value of the property. It is a two-way partnership between bank and mortgagee. The exact split of future price appreciation between lender and borrower, as well as the interest rate discount involved on the mortgage, can vary and is a matter for negotiation between the parties, yet a typical mix might be a 50 percent interest-bearing equity loan and 50 percent mortgage. A SAM gives the mortgagee the right to a specified portion of the increase in value of the house over the life of the loan. The mortgagee's proportion of the capital gain on the residence usually occurs upon maturity date of the mortgage, or upon sale of the residence and discharge of the mortgage. The homeowner's right to a portion of any increase in value may need to be set against any interest and principal still payable under the mortgage. A SAM can apply equally to incumbent dwellers too, by refinancing.

The shared-appreciation model is typically based on no interest on the equity loan until the person sells the property. In a sense, a SAM can be viewed as a variation on an interest-only loan, or "honeymoon" loan. A SAM enables users to pay lower interest today in exchange for sharing some of the inflation-induced increase in the value of the residence in the future. This reduces the financial stress borrowers experience and makes foreclosures less likely in bad times.

Upon disposal of the property, equity is distributed on a like-for-like basis: for example, a participant who originally borrowed 50 percent of the property's value would repay the same proportion, 50 percent of the sale value, when the property is sold. A borrower who can fund a deposit toward the mortgage is likely to obtain a cheaper interest rate. Mortgage deposits are usually based on the price of the equity share that the resident initially purchases. For example, if a property's full market value is $200,000 and the purchaser buys a 25 percent share, the mortgage would be $50,000. A five percent deposit toward the mortgage would be $5000. In addition, would-be shared-equity purchasers would need extra funds to pay the transactions costs of buying a property such as legal fees, mortgage arrangement fees, and the like. Nevertheless the deposit required is less than that for a full mortgage, a factor that is especially helpful for buyers seeking to get "into the market" for the first time. By trading some future capital gains for lower upfront financing costs, home ownership can become more accessible to households on lower incomes.

Equity sharing products are available in the US, emergent in the UK, and rare in Australia.

In the US, early SAMs were developed amidst the inflationary experience during the 1970s (Murphy, 1991).

Because mortgage debt interest is tax deductible to the homeowner, an important question surrounding SAMs in the US has always been their status as debt or equity. If classified by the Internal Revenue

Service (IRS) as equity, then access to the mortgage interest deduction enjoyed by the majority of home buyers could be denied.

After deliberation, the IRS decided that the interest payments on SAMs were indeed deductible. Consequently, the SAM sector of US mortgages is viable. An example is a "flexishare" mortgage, a product targeted at those who can afford a mortgage of at least 65 percent of the value of the property. That is then topped up with an equity injection, a residential ownership loan (ROL) of up to 30 percent. Typically, the household needs to find a five percent deposit, and there is a charge (of say three percent per annum) on the ROL for the lifetime of the loan. When customers repay the ROL, they repay the loan at its current open market value, so the lender will share in any increase in the value of the residence.

A US case study is Northbay Family Homes, a not-for-profit organization in San Francisco. Northbay offers a product called the "Community-Assisted Shared Appreciation" (CASA) contract. Investors obtain an equity stake in the house in the form of a second mortgage, which is then backed up by the local authorities with a third mortgage. The second and third mortgages each equal ten percent of house price, and both the investor and the government agency receive their principal back when the homeowner sells the property. If the occupiers have not sold after 14 years, they are required to refinance and buy out the investors if they can afford to do so. When the house is disposed of, the family receives 40 percent of the capital appreciation, while the equity partners collect 60 percent (Caplin et al.2003).

In Britain, SAMS are less common than shared-equity mortgages (SEMs). SEMs involve three parties to the mortgage contract: the homeowner, an investor, and a mortgage lender. There are positive signs of development in the UK equity-sharing market. An early report found that shared equity remained small and fragmented (Williams and Bennett, 2004), but a more recent study shows shared equity sales have tripled in the UK over the past five years or so (Whitehead et al., 2008). In England and Wales, part-mortgage/part-rent vehicles include Shared Ownership and HomeBuy. There is currently little or no shared-equity vehicle in Scotland; Northern Ireland has the NI Co-ownership Housing Association (NICOHA). HomeBuy is a good example of the range of products on offer. Some examples are as follows:

- Direct equity loans toward the purchase of a new-build property on designated developments.
- Shared equity loans of between 15 and 50 percent toward the purchase of a home on the open market, with a discounted interest rate of 1.75 percent on the shared equity loan.

- A "rent-to-buy" plan that offers brand new homes to rent at a subsidized rate, with the opportunity to purchase a share in the property after two or three years.
- Shared equity loans of between 20 and 40 percent toward the purchase of a property on the open market; the shared equity loan is interest free for the first five years.

In addition, HomeBuy also offers various other options to qualified households on a shared-equity basis that involve government assistance.

Another UK example is Assettrust Housing, a private company investing in affordable homes including intermediate or key worker rental and shared ownership properties. Assettrust enters into commitments to acquire new completed units from developers and landowners and then offers them for rent at affordable housing rates. The homes are managed by local housing authorities (HAs) on their behalf; the company operates without any government grant.

The role and development of SEMs in the UK appears to be gathering pace. The HM Treasury *Report of the Shared Equity Task Force* (2006) found healthy signs of competition in the market, with HAs increasingly having to compete with the shared ownership schemes now being offered by private developers, although the target clienteles are different. For instance, in 2005, Barratt Homes launched "Dream Start", a shared equity scheme for first time buyers in which customers acquire a 100 percent stake in their home but are only paid for 75 percent, with the remaining 25 percent held by Barratt, interest free for up to ten years. To encourage home ownership, the UK has introduced an equity/debt mix as low as a 25 percent interest bearing equity loan and 75 percent mortgage, which can act as a stepping stone to full home ownership. Significantly, the report sees SEMs as a means of tackling housing affordability, by addressing the long-term challenges posed by the UK's low and unresponsive housing supply in the face of rising demand, particularly for younger households and similar "intermediate market" groups.

In 2006, an Australian industry report recommended exploring a Securities Housing Trust Scheme (SHOTS) to stimulate privately financed affordable housing (Property Council of Australia, 2006). A SHOTS would provide rental returns to the unit holders (investors), and split the capital returns between unit holders and the occupant.

However, at this stage it is little more than a proposal, and the availability of SAMs and SEMs in Australia remains limited.

The potential market for shared equity, however, would appear to be promising in Australia. A model was tested on consumers using focus groups, to gauge the attitudes of nonowning households. Given the unrestricted freedom to choose their debt/equity mix on a scale of zero to 100 percent, respondents prefer to invest about 40 percent of their overall wealth in home equity, and one in two would be interested in supplying housing-related equity claims, even when subject to pessimistic assumptions. Nine out of ten liquidity-constrained dwellers (those on social welfare) thought the introduction of a shared-equity scheme would boost the likelihood of them acquiring a home of their own (Caplin et al., 2003).

In schemes of "co-ownership", where a purchaser benefits from lower mortgage payments in exchange for sharing any appreciation in the value of their home with another party, the partner can take several forms. The equity partner can be silent or active, an equity loan provider, or a shared owner. It need not be a bank (as in the US), or a housing authority (as often applies in the UK). The partner could be an institutional investor. Caplin et al. (2003) recommend housing to be financed with the combination of a mortgage and a passive institutional equity partner. This model links the retail-level equity sharing with the wholesale capital markets. In this variation on the SEM approach, the third party investment partner would contribute equity capital to the dwelling in exchange for a share of the ultimate sale proceeds, with no other monetary payments made between the parties. This associate would be a "silent" partner, as the householder retains most of the decision-making rights (timing of sale, additions, maintenance) free and unencumbered, just as in traditional corporate loan markets.

In return, the occupant would have several obligations such as keeping the residence in reasonable condition, and paying all operating expenses. An advantage of this approach is that since the investor is the limited partner, the investor has no personal liability from ownership of the property, and the associated financial claim can be readily sold or securitized. Caplin and Joye (2002) provides further discussion.

The Caplin study finds that such a model would accelerate the household's transition from the rental to the home ownership market while significantly increasing its disposable income and expected wealth at retirement. The model lowers mortgage costs, and financial analysis suggests that using a mix of debt and equity, the upfront costs of home ownership, and the subsequent repayments, decline by around 30 percent. There is also a dramatic reduction in the household's risk of default, and a 70 percent rise in their liquid assets once they leave the workforce. This exercise assumes that an institutional partner contributes 30 percent of the house price up front in exchange for the return of its principal plus 60 percent of the price appreciation and 30 percent of the depreciation (Caplin et al., 2003)

Generally SEMs, including the Caplin version, create a greater role for the capital market, by linking the retail-level equity-sharing concept discussed in this chapter with the wholesale capital markets discussed in Chapter 7. SAMs can be regarded as a special case of SEMs, where the lender and the equity partner are the same. Under SAMs, the investor's equity capital (owned by the bank) can be put out to market and traded indirectly, if the bank chooses to securitize its house and land-equity assets. In the case of SEMS, especially the Caplin case, the investor's equity capital is issued directly to a third party and the link with the wholesale capital market is explicit. In the UK-style SEMs, the third party investor is at the local level (typically a HA) and the market for the equity capital is relatively constrained and illiquid. In Caplin-style SEMs, by contrast, the units of equity capital would be tradable among investors in a dedicated and liquid capital market.

The development of split equity models of home buying, in conjunction with the capital market reforms discussed in Chapter 7, aimed at creating a vibrant secondary market in multigrade housing debt and equity; it has the potential to bring about considerable structural change in finance for affordable housing.

Critics of SAMs, SEMs, and the like, point to the risk profile of shared-equity products, for both lender and borrower. Lenders already take implicit house price risk in standard mortgages but this is heightened significantly through taking an explicit partial equity stake in real estate. This makes the risk on the equity portion far less standardized than that on a regular loan, making it harder for mortgage insurers to underwrite SAMs. Lenders also already take credit risk on standard mortgages, but if SAMs mean the bank ends up extending home ownership to underserved groups that are currently excluded, then that will raise the bank's credit risk. Commentators also point out that there is no cash flow for the bank on the equity portion of the contract.

From the borrower's perspective, Sanders and Slawson (2005) argue that the borrower faces a moral hazard. They view the lender's share of appreciation in SAMs as a dynamic prepayment penalty imposed on the borrower. However, due to the ability to affect the penalty by reducing maintenance, the borrower can affect the lender's outcome.

These competing risks will be incorporated into the mortgage-pricing model.

## Equity release

A by-product of accelerating house prices in recent years has been greater attention being given by established homeowners to tapping into the existing financial equity tied up in their home, and using it as collateral to obtain a line of credit. This has fostered a growing trend in "dequity" or home-equity-conversion products at the retail level, including second mortgages and reverse mortgages.

This process, where "housing-rich and income-poor" households extract equity to release funds for other purposes, has been observed in the US, the UK, and Australia. Data show that net housing equity withdrawal, expressed as a percentage of household disposable income, in the current decade, has run at around 0.5 percent per year in the US, two percent per annum in the UK, and one percent in Australia (Reserve Bank of Australia, 2003). The differences in these figures may reflect the fact that house prices increased faster in the UK and Australia than in the US, and rising home value is a major driver of equity withdrawal.

In one sense, equity extraction has been going on for centuries, with the transfer of deceased estates to descendents in the form of bequests. The new twist is that baby boomers and the elderly are increasingly extracting the equity before they die, rather than their children doing it upon inheritance, thus bringing the process forward. While the age-old method for housing assistance to the younger generation, through inheritance, continues, in modern times, life expectancy has increased, and with parents living longer, it means offspring are frequently entering the home market when parents are still – in actuarial terms – expected to live for a long time to come. The new breed of equity withdrawal products, also known as "lifetime mortgages", can be viewed as a means of bridging this timing mismatch, by allowing still-living parents to transfer or advance home equity to adult children at a point in the life cycle when young people arguably need it most, as first home buyers. The trend in these products, therefore, is a reflection of demographic changes in the form of the ageing of the population in industrialized countries.

A home equity line of credit (HELOC) or home-equity loan is a mortgage loan that enables the borrower to obtain cash drawn against the equity of his or her home, up to a pre-determined amount. Home equity loans allow borrowers to tap the accumulated value in their property with either a loan for a specific amount, or a line of credit. The proceeds can be used to invest in another property, an investment property, perhaps even a defined affordable housing property. In some cases, no repayments are required provided the size of the outstanding debt remains below a pre-determined threshold. It also leads to a rise in the long-time householder's outstanding mortgage debt, often after years of steady decline in the principal. A further complication is that while banks can foreclose on a first-line mortgage, they typically have little recourse when trying to collect on a delinquent home-equity loan, especially if another bank holds the first mortgage. The second bank cannot usually claim the house as collateral. The consumer can use the funds to renovate the property or consolidate debt. Home equity loans are available in the US, the UK, and Australia.

A reverse mortgage or reverse-annuity mortgage (RAM) is an arrangement in which homeowners borrow against the equity in their home and receive regular monthly tax-free payments from the lender. FinancialFreedom is an example of a reverse mortgage specialist in the US. Instruments such as these provide a stream of cash flows from the bank to the homeowner, funded by running down the owner's equity in the home. The bank has a contractual arrangement whereby upon expiry of the agreement (usually at the death of the homeowner), the property will be sold and part of the proceeds used to refund the stream of reverse payments, with interest. The equity an owner has in the home is calculated as the difference between the market value of the residence and the outstanding mortgage debt (if any) still owing on the property. Reverse mortgages, more often than not, provide a way for elderly households to fund their old age, rather than to facilitate intergenerational transfer. However, if the effect is to alleviate the offspring from the fiscal pressure of costly housing, and from medical and other bills associated with the care of aging parents, then effectively the RAM serves to free up the childrens' cash flow, making it easier for them to afford their own housing. In this situation, the RAM indirectly constitutes a housing-based financial instrument that contributes to improving the supply of affordable housing finance.

A related intergenerational trend more directly connected with affordable housing is the growing role of parents in assisting young people into the home market. A British study found that over the past decade, first-time buyers appear to be relying more and more on parents and others to help with their deposits. The research, using regulated mortgage survey (RMS) data, estimates that 38 percent of first-time buyers under 30 years of age received such financial assistance in 2006 (Tatch, 2007). Assisted buyers were found to have low LTVs because they can put down substantial deposits, and borrow more in relation to their income. In contrast, unassisted buyers have higher LTVs but lower income multiples. Another study also showed that entry into the British housing market is being substantially underpinned by a number of factors including help from existing owners, typically parents, whose own capacity to assist has been enhanced by sustained house price growth and the capacity to borrow against the value of their home (Pannell, 2007).

An international comparison of home equity withdrawal trends is supplied by Williams (2008). In both Australia (ASIC, 2005) and the US, the market is developed and there is clear evidence of strong demand from younger households. The UK market, by contrast, has developed more slowly. Of the three countries, the US is the only one where the government has played a role in developing the market. This has been by supporting the creation of Home Equity Conversion Mortgages (HECMs) that allow homeowners 62 years or older to access a line of credit through their homes with the government guaranteeing the lenders against loss. HECMs make up about 90 percent of the US market.

## Pooled investor vehicles

The establishment of vehicles for private sector investment in affordable housing, including small investors, is a relatively unexplored frontier.

A REMIC is a Real Estate Mortgage Investment Conduit. The vehicle could be a mutual fund, a unit trust, or a stock exchange listed company. A unit trust does not alter its portfolio over time. Real Estate Investment Trusts (REITS) are being introduced in a number of countries, with varying degrees of success. Residential REITs have been established successfully in the US, slowly in the UK, but unsuccessfully in Australia (Jones, 2007). By contrast, a mutual fund is actively managed and the portfolio is adjusted regularly to take advantage of market expectations. A listed company would invest in affordable housing with its funds drawn from two sources: private sector equity investors and borrowed debt funds.

Such vehicles can be utilized in the community housing context (McNelis et al., 2002). A US example of a REIT is the Community Development Trust (CDT). It was established in 1998 and is the only private real estate trust in the US with a public purpose. After ten years of operations, CDT has invested around US$700 million in housing projects, involving 27,000 units of affordable housing stock. At the same time, CDT earns attractive returns for its shareholders, operating like a mutual fund that harnesses the capital of institutional investors to acquire or build affordable housing. All CDT investments must satisfy Community Reinvestment Act (CRA) requirements. The trust operates nationally in order to build up a spatially diversified property portfolio.

A REIT or a similar vehicle, rather than building/managing residences in its own right, can invest in multiple-class mortgage-backed securities that meet defined affordable housing criteria. Mortgage-backed securities for small investors represent a market niche that can become more fully developed. Traditionally, RMBS have been the domain of large investors. In the US, for instance, the minimum denomination of Ginnie Mae pass-throughs is US$25,000 which places them beyond the scope of direct investment for most small investors. However, indirect investment by small investors can be facilitated by the creation of special-purpose vehicles. Unit trusts have been created in the US and these allow access to the market by small players, starting with amounts as low as US$1000. The individual effectively buys a tiny slice, a "unit", like buying stock in a company, of the portfolio of investments held by the unit trust concerned (Clark, 2000).

Investors in general are motivated by more than one consideration. Appropriately specified, the vehicle can market itself as an avenue for ethical investment, alternative investment products (AIPs), or economically targeted investments (ETIs). Ethical investors invest for a mix of commercial and noncommercial reasons, including social and moral causes. They voluntarily accept a less-than-commercial rate of return on their investments in order to also achieve the ethical returns they value. In the US, this type of investment is known as socially responsible investing (SRI).

AIPs are economically targeted investments for socially responsible purposes, like affordable housing. An example in the US is the Wilmington Housing Partnership (WHP), established in 1989. WHP provides affordable homes by teaming up with local community groups and participating with investors to stabilize the neighborhoods in the City of Wilmington, Delaware. It collaborates with select private, nonprofit, and governmental entities to increase the city's housing stock by promoting renovation of existing homes or construction of new homes in strategically selected areas. In 2003, the WHP established the Residential Improvement and Stabilization Effort (RISE), an initiative involving three targeted city neighborhoods and five local housing organizations. One of the objectives of RISE is the stimulation of private investment from ethical investors, charitable foundations, and government in low-cost housing, and the generation of US$18 million in the mortgage financing community.

ETIs deliver minimum economic rates of return, coupled with collateral economic and social benefits. For example, a religious organization might donate land to a community housing association. The housing co-op or Community Development Corporations (CDCs) would then raise funding to develop housing on the land, by sourcing contributions from socially concerned investors.

A Partial Debt Finance (PDF) model can be employed by the community housing group, where private finance at market rates is employed for construction work. Upon completion, tenants can enjoy below-market rents compared to a fully commercial situation, because the development was partly financed by the gift of land.

The Zero-Coupon Bonds (ZCBs) model provides a variation on the theme. The affordability housing project seeks to provide dwellings financed by zero-coupon (zero interest) debentures. Investors purchase the dwellings with interest-free ZCBs, then receive capital gains not on the finance but on the properties acquired using these funds.

In the US, an interesting program is the Community Development Financial Institutions Fund (CDFI). It is a three-way partnership between banks, community groups, and government. The CDFI assists people to gain access to affordable finance, by expanding the capacity of financial institutions to provide credit, capital, and financial services to underserved populations and communities in the US. This is principally through investment in and assistance to community development financial institutions (CDFIs). The program makes use of assistance through the New Markets Tax Credit (NMTC) Program by providing an allocation of tax credits to community development entities which enables them to attract investment from the private sector and reinvest these amounts in low-income communities. Since its inception, the CDFI Fund has awarded US$864 million to community development organizations and financial institutions, and made allocations of NMTCs (see Chapter 9) to attract private-sector investments totaling US$16 billion (American Bankers Association, 2009). The CDFI Fund was established by the Riegle Community Development and Regulatory Improvement Act of 1994. The National Community Reinvestment Coalition (NCRC) is an association of more than 600 community-based organizations that promote access to basic banking services, including credit and savings, to create and sustain affordable housing, job development, and vibrant communities for America's families.

Another emerging model is community microfinance in rich countries. Microfinance, that involves lending out small amounts of money to the poor to start income-generating business ventures, is already well established in developing countries. Mohammad Yunus, along with his Bangladesh-originated Grameen Bank established in 1983, won the 2006 Nobel Peace Prize for the work. In 2008, the US onshore equivalent was initiated. Called Grameen America, and located in New York city, this new lender makes small loans to entrepreneurs for such ventures as taxi registrations and sewing machines. Grameen claims that 98 percent of its loans get repaid, despite no collateral or credit checks used. The philosophy is based on trust, in keeping with the meaning of the original word for "credit" from the Latin *credere* (to believe or trust). Reputation and "credit" in the local community act as enforcement mechanisms. The desire to keep open the line of microcredit is strong, so borrowers think carefully before defaulting, and self interest explains the remarkably low rate of arrears (Parker, 2008). The right to shelter is a basic human right, according to Grameen's founder: credit creates the possibility of employment, employment leads to income, and income finances housing and makes housing affordable. It is a community-based strategy that employs a social business model: affordable housing finance on a human scale. See Flood (1983).

A different way to finance housing at community level is known as "sweat equity". An example from the UK is the Accord program in Birmingham, a low-income self-build housing scheme. This group of residents, spanning various ages and stages in life, has built each other's houses. Although they had no prior construction experience, they each did a two-year part-time training course, women included, and each resident specialized in a particular skill (for example, electrical or bricklaying). A by-product is that each team member picks up a possible new career option, as a building worker. In four years, they built 11 "kit" homes, each identical to the other, in a single street. In return for their work, the residents get a 25 percent share in the value of their home, called sweat equity. The land was provided by a local HA, which retains a 75 percent share. Upon completion, the tenants can increase their equity stake by taking out a mortgage with a bank, or sell their share back to the HA. The HA forms and manages the team, advertising for interested participants willing to devote 20 hours per week. Team members can "bank" their hours in a flexitime system, to get time off the project for special events. Effectively, 25 percent of the housing is affordably financed by resident labor.

## Conclusions and next steps

The household sector has for too long been constrained by limited choices when it comes to financing housing affordably. As outlined in this chapter, there are signs that the market is innovating. Access to a richer array of debt and equity instruments is likely to become an everyday fact in future. This may even involve the development of housing hybrids, securities that combine debt and equity features.

The effect is likely to be a significant increase in the diversity and flexibility of housing finance, a reduction in the occupier's cost of capital, and improved affordability and home ownership opportunities. By enhancing consumer choice and expanding the average borrower's universe of available opportunities, these retail solutions have a significant contribution to make to easing A2F (Access-to-Finance) housing stress. By enabling households to get a foot on the housing ladder in the face of the increasingly steep deposit gaps and income multiples documented in Chapters 4 through 6, an enhanced retail product menu will enable vulnerable households to take a more balanced exposure to interest rate and house price risks.

A role for government at retail level is to improve financial literacy. In the UK, the Miles report (2004) identified this as an important need, and in Australia the Federal government has launched a national financial literacy agenda, which is being led by the Financial Literacy Foundation and supported by the Australian Bankers Association. Research on the effectiveness of programs such as credit counseling shows that it makes a difference. Using US data from a counseling program developed as a result of collaboration between a large midwest bank, churches, and a local community development company, a study found that counseled borrowers defaulted less often than non-counseled borrowers and that counseling affects the optimal exercise of the default option (Hartarska and Gonzalez-Vega, 2006). Governments and community groups should explore programs that help borrowers better appreciate the range of possibilities available for housing finance.

# 9
# Public Sector Solutions

## Introduction

Whether we like it or not, housing is always and everywhere a matter of public–private partnership (PPP), at least to some minimal degree. By definition, housing markets do not occur in a spatial or taxation vacuum, nor are they unaffected by banking regulations and business cycle risk. Rather, housing markets are situated in a wider economic matrix of transport networks, county lines, tax settings, market regulations, Fed policymaking, immigration rates, urban planning history, and the like. It is simply impossible, in other words, to entirely divorce government decisions from housing outcomes. For instance, evidence shows that increasing the property tax reduces city size unambiguously (Song and Zenou, 2006), and that government-sponsored enterprise (GSE) affordable housing goals increase the supply of mortgage credit (Ambrose and Thibodeau, 2004). The implication is that complete policy neutrality with respect to housing markets is unlikely to prevail. Even the most minimalist, free market oriented policy framework we could propose, would still involve a significant degree of de facto government "intervention". The private housing market, in other words, cannot be viewed in isolation from the rest of the society.

The same principle operates in reverse: the public policy process cannot be divorced from private sector decision-making. Policy interventions by overzealous government lawmakers, even if well-intentioned at the time, do not occur in a vacuum, and can have adverse unforeseen effects. For instance, research indicates that public rental housing crowds out private investment (Lee, 2007), and that policymakers face an information problem in trying to help borrowers with negative equity avoid foreclosure (as in the Obama administration's housing rescue policy of 2009), because it is hard to determine which owners really need help in order to stay in their homes (Foote et al., 2008). In short, the unforeseen ripple effects of policies onto the private sector, coupled with information asymmetry, can undo the original intent of government actions and should make us cautious about public sector interventions.

In light of the above, we cannot afford to assume that the public sector has all the answers, neither can we pretend that the government has no role to play in housing outcomes. Rather, the challenge is to negotiate this dynamic tension, and derive the optimum settings for government, in a housing market where private actors predominate. To that end, this chapter considers the role of government inaffordable housing.

## Incentives and disincentives

Our particular focus is on affordable housing finance. There is a long-running debate in the literature about the role of the public sector in housing in general (Struyk and Tuccillo, 1983). Much of this debate has focused on traditional fiscal strategies of housing policy, involving direct government expenditures on the physical housing stock or on subsidies to tenants. Important issues such as government in the landlord role through the provision of public housing, construction programs versus vouchers, the efficacy of the housing benefit system (Stephens, 2005), and whether different types of rental assistance contribute to work disincentives (Hulse and Randolph, 2005), to name just a few, are covered in that literature. However, since our concern in this text is with housing finance rather than physical aspects of housing policy (such as zoning, construction, or delivery), we will not cover that side of the debate.

In this chapter, we focus on the public sector in relation to affordable housing finance and capital. While government can play a direct role as quasi-banker (as in the United States' GSEs), more likely will the government tend to play an indirect role instead, through the setting up of incentives and disincentives to private behavior. Previous chapters have already emphasized that there is a valuable part regulators can play in fostering the development of private wholesale and retail housing finance markets, through thoughtful regulation and education. Now we explore the ways in which central government budget decisions on taxation and subsidies can best set the scene for private financing and investment decisions in affordable housing.

In a perfectly developed mortgage market, there might be little or no role for the government to play in the arena of housing finance. Yet as we have seen in earlier chapters, especially Chapters 3 and 7, the housing credit market is currently far from perfect. It is subject to significant corner constraints, information deficiencies, and incompleteness both at wholesale and retail levels. In this context, when housing finance markets are constrained, theory indicates that there may be a constructive welfare-enhancing role for the public sector. For instance, Jin and Zeng (2007) articulate a general equilibrium model of a two-sector economy where real estate entrepreneurs borrow from households subject to a credit constraint. Real estate serves as collateral in entrepreneurs' debt contracts and credit markets are not unconstrained. Public policies involving subsidizing are found to open up a wide range of possibilities for Pareto improvement when the supply of real estate is endogenous.

The potential for government to leverage private finance for affordable housing at a gearing ratio greater than one, and thereby reap efficiency gains, adds a further dimension to our discussion. Studies find that new construction of affordable dwellings is considerably more costly than other methods of housing support (Shroder and Reiger, 2002), and that subsidized construction is an extremely expensive method to increase the home ownership rate of low-income households (Green and Malpezi, 2003). If the supply of affordable housing and housing capital can instead be stimulated from the private sector, perhaps by the strategic use of government incentives at far less cost, then affordable housing policy will be fiscally more efficient (Hawtrey, 2001).

There can be a role for joint ventures (JVs) and PPPs. The United States (US) experience shows the importance of PPPs in affordable housing finance, involving collaboration among large intermediaries, community organizations, and state and local housing agencies. According to HUD, this has extended to the design of new products (HUD, 2006). JVs involve governments developing partnerships with private investors and non-profit organizations to deliver housing services. These variously involve leasing, sale-and-leaseback, and corporate vehicle arrangements. For example, the government authority can head-lease dwellings management to selected community housing groups. Alternatively, housing authorities (HAs) can lease from private landlords and on-rent to low-income tenants. If structured correctly, these pass taxation benefits related to depreciation and other allowances onto private investors in return for lower rent payments. These avenues, by enabling a partnership between the private and public sectors, can also allow governments to access the large amount of investment dollars available in mutual funds and the like. In so doing, the public sector gets more value for the taxpayers' dollar: governments can address the matter of affordable housing at a much lower overall cost than would otherwise be the case, were they acting without private sector involvement. PPPs, through government participation, help create the critical mass required to attract large investors, and to bridge the gap between actual and required rates of return to private investors.

The latter is particularly important, as affordable housing, in the eyes of private investors, does not always look immediately appealing. There can be a number of reasons for this perception, including inadequate rental yields, illiquidity, regulatory restrictions, poor market information, location not conducive to capital gains, high management costs, and small project scale (Milligan, 2005). Investors may doubt the income earning and portfolio diversification benefits of low-end residential investing, and prefer the middle or upper residential markets as less risky. Experience since 2000 in the UK, however, suggests this can be turned around. In that country, a number of critical ingredients have coalesced to change investor perceptions in a positive direction, including the "right" mix of policy certainty and rules of engagement to give confidence to potential investors, and an adequate level of subsidies (or tax offsets) that are sufficient to close the gap between the required rate of return for investors and the income stream that is generated by "affordable" prices or rents. Significantly, the ingredients also encompass housing financiers: the ability of lenders to have first call on the housing assets (with second mortgages or other charges over the asset held by government funders), and a sufficient scale of opportunity to generate commitment from the financial sector, to attract large players (such as banks and pension funds) and/or a regime, and underwrite the risk of private investors, thereby reducing the cost of finance (Berry 2003; Youren, 2005a).

In order to nurture fledgling markets for private investment in affordable housing, with large-scale financial sector involvement, government can play a leadership role. Evidence suggests that this makes a critical difference, by imparting a level of clarity and predictability to the investment environment. Equally, however, this public sector role is best viewed as transitional.

As far as possible, a commercial approach to housing is to be preferred in the long run, and private sector outcomes to be seen as the default position. Governments should only intervene when it is essential, and minimize that intervention, and attach a sunset clause.

The optimal role for government is not to supplant the private sector but be a catalyst for it. Governments should be involved only for the duration required to nurture affordable housing capital markets until they attain self-sustainability, and with appropriate calibration of its actions to the efficient minimum required to succeed and no more.

There are essentially two ways that government can act: tax incentives and risk mitigation.

## Tax incentives

An international survey of taxes and subsidies on housing is found in Scanlon and Whitehead (2004). A comparison of arrangements in the US, the UK, and Australia is shown in Figure 9.1.

Comparatively speaking, the US emphasizes tax incentives to make housing finance affordable, while the other two countries tend to emphasize subsidies to make housing itself affordable. The US employs tax-deductibility on the owner-occupier's mortgage interest payments, a subsidy to savings for a home deposit, subsidized mortgage interest rates, and assistance to low-income earners with mortgage repayments. The GSEs play a big part in this system. In addition, the US has its Low-Income Housing Tax Credit (LIHTC) to subsidize developers who provide affordable housing (see discussion below). It is significant, however, that despite these policies, the rate of home ownership is no higher in the US than in the UK or Australia (see Chapters 4 through 6).

|  | US | UK | Australia |
|---|---|---|---|
| Owner mortgage tax relief | Y | N | N |
| Tax on imputed rental income | N | N | N |
| No capital gains tax family home | Y | Y | Y |
| Subsidy to savings to buy home | Y | N | Y |
| No stamp duty on home sales | Y | N | N |
| Grants for home buyers | Y | N | Y |
| Subsidized mortgage interest rates | Y | N | N |
| Improvement grants for owners | Y | Y | N |
| Assist low-income with repayments | Y | N | Y |
| Tax relief landlord rental income | N | N | N |
| Depreciation deductible landlords | Y | N | Y |
| Tax relief for renters | N | N | Y |
| Assist low-income pay rent | Y | Y | Y |
| Low-income developer tax credit | Y | N | N |
| Negative gearing | N | N | Y |

*Figure 9.1* Housing taxes and subsidies – by country

*Source:* Adapted from Scanlon and Whitehead (2004) with updates and extensions by author.

By contrast, the UK majors on tax relief for renters and grants for home improvers. Britain used to provide mortgage tax relief and grants for first home buyers, but these were abolished by the year 2000. Interest deductibility, known as income support for mortgage interest (ISMI) was phased out gradually in the UK after 1980. Williams (2007) demonstrates that the reduction in financial support for home ownership from the mid-1990s has been steep in Britain, as measured by the combined effect of mortgage interest tax relief, and the abolition of ISMI, stamp duty, and inheritance tax. The net tax/benefit treatment has gone from positive to negative since the mid-1990s, from around +£3000 to almost −£5000 per annum, on an average.

Australia majors on help for first home buyers in the form of subsidies to deposit savings and grants for home purchase, and on renter assistance via payments to low-income renters and "negative gearing" for landlords. Australia also assists low-income earners with mortgage repayments. The subsidy to savings for a home deposit was introduced only recently, in 2008. Grants for first home buyers have been available for most of the 2000s.

Mortgage interest deductibility has been criticized on the grounds of encouraging higher homeowner leverage. Others argue that deductibility is needed to treat debt and equity financing of houses symmetrically. Britain provides an interesting test case, for interest deductibility paid by homeowners for income taxation purposes was phased out in Britain over a period of more than a decade. A study of 117,000 British mortgage originations found that removal of interest deductibility reduced initial loan-to-value (LTV) ratios by 30 percent on average. That is, the leverage of borrowers declined (Hendershott et al., 2003). This result says that the amount home buyers borrow is sensitive to the debt tax penalty or break implied by interest deductibility. Homeowners with existing mortgages will also pay down their loans, if deductibility is removed. Another similar study using UK mortgages found that limiting deductibility imposes a debt tax penalty that leads households to shift from debt toward equity financing, reducing debt from 40 to 32 percent of house financing (Hendershott and Pryce, 2006).

Mortgage interest relief via the tax system has also been criticized as inefficient. Analysis has demonstrated that the revenue-neutral replacement of home interest deductibility and property taxes with a tax credit of the appropriate level alone can increase aggregate home ownership rates in the range of three to five percent (Green and Vandell, 1999). Moreover, the increases were found to be even higher in lower-income neighborhoods. Others point out that borrowing subsidies such as the interest deduction have limited effect when housing supply is constrained. In markets with limited supply, credit subsidies push up housing prices, and make housing less, not more, affordable (Glaeser and Gyourko, 2008).

Turning to the rental sector, investors in the private rental sector are at a disadvantage in the UK because there are no depreciation allowances for landlords. At the same time, when house prices are rising, landlords have to pay capital gains tax. By contrast, in Australia, owners of rental property enjoy "negative gearing", the ability to set losses on rental property against income from other sources for tax purposes. Negative gearing is a form of leveraged investment in which an investor borrows money to buy a rental property, but the income generated by that asset does not cover the interest on the loan. The strategy is motivated by the taxation system which allows deduction of ongoing speculative losses against highly taxed income, but taxes capital gains at a much lower rate. A negative gearing strategy can make a profit only if the asset rises so much in price that the capital is more than the sum of the ongoing losses over the life of the speculation.

In the US, capital investment in the rental sector is supported by the LIHTC program, as well as by depreciation allowances for landlords. The LIHTC involves an indirect Federal subsidy used to finance the development of affordable rental housing for low-income households, and is a primary tool for subsidizing housing supply. The program delivers tax credits to selected developers who must contract to maintain low to moderate income occupancy of the dwellings for a period of 30 years. The LIHTC is a tax credit created under the Tax Reform Act of 1986 (TRA86) that gives incentives for the utilization of private equity in the development of affordable housing aimed at low-income Americans. The credits are also commonly called Section 42 credits in reference to the applicable section of the Internal Revenue Code. The tax credits are more attractive than tax deductions as they provide a dollar-for-dollar reduction in a taxpayer's federal income tax, whereas a tax deduction only provides a reduction in taxable income. The LIHTC provides funding for the development costs of low-income housing by allowing a taxpayer (usually the partners of a partnership that owns the housing) to take a federal tax credit equal to a percentage of the cost incurred for development of the low-income units in a rental housing project. To qualify for tax credits, developments must have a minimum percentage of units occupied by tenants with a household income less than the metropolitan median in which they live, and rents charged must not exceed 30 percent of metropolitan-wide household median income.

Evaluations of the effectiveness of LIHTC are generally positive (Cummings and DiPasquale, 1999; McClure, 2000). The program generates more than half a million units per decade that would not otherwise have been built, covering a wide variety of housing types and serving a range of populations. A major advantage of using a tax-based strategy is the versatility that it engenders. The funding is not necessarily tied to any particular estate or provider. Rather, the flexibility of the program's design allows governments, housing groups, and developers to pursue their own goals to a large extent.

Critics contend that the LIHTC, which was introduced to provide incentives for private sector production of low-income housing, rather than adding to the low-income housing stock has simply substituted for unsubsidized units that otherwise would have been built. Malpezzi and Vandell (2002) examined this question, and found no significant relationship between the number of LIHTC units built in a given state and the size of the current housing stock, suggesting a high rate of substitution. However, they caution that their test is not sufficiently powerful to be conclusive.

Another tax-based affordable housing strategy in the US is Tax Increment Financing (TIF), a tool to use future gains in taxes to finance the current improvements that will create those gains. When an infrastructure project such as an affordable housing development is carried out, there is often an increase in the value of surrounding real estate, and an inflow of new investment into the area. This increased site value and investment generates increased future tax revenues, known as the "tax increment". TIF dedicates tax increments within a certain district to finance debt issued to pay for the project, and is especially used in distressed areas where development would not otherwise occur. For example, Chicago has a long history of TIF investment and more than 130 established TIF districts, comprising over 29 percent of the city's total acreage and approximately 19 percent of the total real property tax base. A study of TIF in the Chicago multifamily real estate market found that designating an area a TIF district has an impact on real property appreciation rates. Properties located within a designated TIF district exhibit higher rates of appreciation after the area is designated TIF, when compared with those properties selling outside TIF districts. The findings provide support for the hypothesis that TIF policy impacts property values through increased investment (Smith, 2006).

Also in the US, the New Markets Tax Credit (NMTC) Program permits taxpayers to receive a credit against Federal income taxes for making qualified equity investments in designated Community Development

Entities (CDEs). The credit provided to the investor totals 39 percent of the cost of the investment and is claimed over a seven-year credit allowance period (American Bankers Association, 2009). In each of the first three years, the investor receives a credit equal to five percent of the total amount paid for the stock or capital interest at the time of purchase. For the final four years, the value of the credit is six percent annually. Investors may not redeem their investments in CDEs prior to the conclusion of the seven-year period, and the entire funds must in turn be used by the CDE to provide investments in low-income communities. CDEs can be granted authority to issue up to a total of $23 billion in equity to investors with NMTC claim eligibility. To qualify under the NMTC program, an organization must be certified as a CDE. To gain certification, a CDE must demonstrate a primary mission of providing investment capital for low-income communities and persons. To date, the fund has made 364 awards totaling US$19.5 billion in allocation authority.

Tax breaks can be used to support housing bond programs. The California Communities Housing Bond Program is designed to assist both profit and nonprofit developers in accessing tax-exempt bonds for the financing of low-income multifamily and senior housing projects. The developer agrees to set aside all, or a portion, of the units in a project for individuals and families of very low, low, or moderate income. A developer can finance a project at a lower interest rate than available through conventional financing because the interest paid to bondholders is exempt from federal (and in some case state) income taxes. Since inception, this program has issued over US$6.6 billion in bonds for more than 777 multifamily and senior housing projects throughout California.

In summary, although the results for tax-based strategies are mixed in some respects, a tax incentive approach represents an important tool. Assistance into first home ownership, coupled with beneficial tax treatment of income from investment in defined affordable housing, is a considerable twin strategy.

## Risk mitigation

Economists have long recognized the financial risks implicit in household property investing. Not only cash flow, but also the volatility of that cash flow, therefore, is important to homeowners and investors. The more unpredictable the future cash flows, the greater the risk and the lower the risk-adjusted expected return. Looked at in another way, the higher the uncertainty, the higher is the effective cost of capital. The most critical category is credit risk, and after that on two subcategories of risk: interest rate risk and capital value risk. Through laying off some of these risks, government can encourage the supply of finance for affordable housing. In some cases, this may be more cost-effective than tax subsidies.

An international survey of housing risk mitigation on housing is found in Scanlon and Whitehead (2004). A comparison of arrangements in the US, the UK, and Australia is shown in Figure 9.2.

The application of risk mitigation policy can apply on two fronts: retail and wholesale. Retail mortgages in the US are classified as conventional or federally insured. Conventional mortgages are almost always privately insured, a mandatory requirement by most lenders, and the insurance premium is paid by the borrower. Federally insured mortgages carry protection against default in the form of a guarantee of loan repayment to the lender. Commonly, the guarantor is the Federal Housing Administration (FHA), and insured mortgages are available to qualified borrowers who satisfy FHA requirements, including an income test. An important factor in the US case is that the majority of mortgages are fixed-rate mortgages with no prepayment penalties (see Chapter 4). Fixed-rate mortgages provide certainty over the profile of nominal payments over a given horizon and represent a form of insurance against the risk of rising interest rates.

In the UK, private mortgage insurance, known as mortgage indemnity insurance (MII), is available, but is not universally required. It is most likely to be required by the lender for high LVR loans. The government provides virtually no mortgage insurance; an exception is the case of those who become unemployed in the long term.

In Australia, where, like in the UK, a higher proportion of mortgages are at floating rate instead of fixed, government formerly provided selected mortgage insurance until the mid-1990s but it has since been

|  | US | UK | Australia |
|---|---|---|---|
| Private insurance available | Y | Y | Y |
| Govt provides mortgage insurance | Y | N | N |
| Mortgage insurance tax deductible | N | N | N |
| Assist low-income with repayments | Y | N | Y |
| Assistance low-income pay rent | Y | Y | Y |
| Govt gaurantees affordable-housing bonds | N | Y | Y |

*Figure 9.2* Housing risk mitigation – by country

*Source:* Adapted from Scanlon and Whitehead (2004) with extensions by author.

abolished. Private mortgage insurance is available in Australia, but is not universal.

By encouraging or facilitating more flexible options in housing insurance, the government can probably improve home ownership rates. Englund et al. (2002) analyze the composition of household investment portfolios and find that for short holding periods, the efficient portfolio contains essentially no housing, whereas for longer periods, low-risk portfolios contain 15–50 percent housing. These results suggest that there are potential gains from policies that would permit households to hedge their lumpy investments in housing. Estimates of the potential value of hedges in reducing risk to households show that the value is especially large for poorer homeowners.

The Miles report (2004) in the UK recommended the government allow the proceeds of mortgage insurance to be tax exempt. The report noted that the UK does not have a high proportion of fixed-rate mortgages to provide certainty, as occurs in the US. Alternative ways in which borrowers can protect themselves against interest rate fluctuations are therefore needed, and these might include capped mortgages. If interest rate caps could be sold separately from the mortgage, they would protect against interest rate movements while offering greater flexibility, but there is uncertainty in the UK about the tax and regulatory treatment of stand-alone interest rate insurance. Accordingly, the Miles report advocated that the government "treat interest payment protection as insurance for tax purposes, provided that the sum assured is no greater than that part of a mortgage with a variable interest rate". The income received as compensation would not be subject to tax.

An allied but slightly different approach to the same question would be for the governments of the UK and Australia to allow the cost of mortgage insurance to be tax deductible. This would encourage a higher take-up of MMIs. The motivation for this or a similar policy is that the comparatively low proportion of fixed-rate mortgages in the UK and Australia affects the risk profile of their respective housing finance systems. Using economic theory, it can be shown that in an optimal loan contract, interest rate risk should be shared between lender and borrower. Conventional adjustable-rate mortgage (ARM) contracts violate this rule since they require complete risk absorption by the borrower (Arvan and Brueckner, 1986).

Turning to risk mitigation in the wholesale housing capital market, here too governments can play a role. Risk guarantees by the government can help minimize housing subsidy costs through efficient targeting and through the contribution of such risk management measures to attracting private capital into affordable housing.

A structured debt finance approach to raising private sector capital for affordable dwelling construction, based on public sector risk underwriting, is one option. The role of government in this model would be similar to that played in the financing of other social infrastructure, such as schools or hospitals. A minimum income threshold would be specified, and when the revenue flow is at or above this level, no government contribution is required; whenever it drops below this threshold, government undertakes to fund the gap.

Under this approach, known as the Guaranteed Housing Bonds (GHB) model, governments raise finance for affordable housing through the issue of a housing bond with a guaranteed minimum after-tax return. The funds can then be loaned to housing authorities, developers, or other eligible providers, at competitive rates, on the condition that the monies are used to construct affordable rental dwellings. The dwellings are then owned and managed by the approved providers. The risk guarantee can be provided in two ways: via a tax concession or through a budget outlay.

In the Australian context, the risk mitigation model was recommended by the Affordable Housing National Research Consortium (AHNRC, 2001). On the criteria of efficiency, equity, and effectiveness, it was rated very highly. This model removes most of the risks of investing in affordable housing perceived by institutional investors, by transferring them to the government. The approach involves a PPP that enables government to access institutional investment dollars.

Notably, the housing bond model was shown to be highly efficient at leveraging private sector investment. Modeling indicates that the leverage ratio is around 5:1, under certain reasonable assumptions. That is, for every $1 of taxpayers' money, about $5 of private money would be raised for affordable housing (Hall, 2001). This makes risk underwriting a vastly less expensive means of assisting affordable housing for governments than direct public sector construction of dwellings.

The bond model emerging from Australia is not unlike the Essential Function Bonds (EFBs) prevalent in the US. EFBs are housing bonds issued by local housing authorities to finance the construction of affordable housing owned by state or local housing finance agencies. As part of a broader effort to reform public housing in the US, the Quality Housing and Work Responsibility (QHWR) Act of 1998 authorized new ways to leverage capital and operating funds, and stimulated interest in bond financing mechanisms. A survey of local housing authorities discovered that since the QHWR Act, the use of EFBs has surged (Apgar and Whiting, 2003).

California has a long history of housing bonds for affordable dwellings. The Department of Housing and Community Development, together with California Housing Finance Agency, administers the program which seeks to provide multifamily and special needs low-cost homes. The program began in 1988 with Proposition 77 which had an allocation of US$150 million, and has grown to where it is today with Proposition 1C at US$2.8 billion.

The bond plan is used to fund affordable home ownership programs. Around 50 percent of the funding helps families become or remain homeowners, including funding for the Building Equity in Neighborhoods Program, CalHome, and California Homebuyers Downpayment Assistance Program.

The GHB/EFB model has the capacity to generate a large volume of private investment for affordable housing, and is simple and flexible to implement. In 2006, an Australian industry report recommended the housing bond risk underwriting approach to stimulate privately financed affordable housing (Property Council of Australia, 2006). The approach is also supported in the literature, for example by Milligan et al. (2004).

## Conclusions and next steps

Figure 9.3 provides an overview of the two public sector approaches: tax subsidies and risk mitigation.

Of the three countries under review, the US provides the strongest example of government policies specifically toward making housing finance more affordable. In addition to the measures listed in Figure 9.1, the US also has regulation that requires financial institutions to invest in affordable housing, plus a requirement on all lending institutions that enjoy federal government guarantees to match their lending profile to the credit needs of the whole community, including low income and excluded households. On top of this, there are the major mortgage finance institutions, Fannie Mae and Freddy Mac, whose mandate is to lend to individuals and not-for-profit agencies for affordable housing. In the wake of the subprime meltdown, some commentators now say that the US experience has shown the weakness of a housing finance system which encourages low-doc loans, and lenders lending to those without sufficient financial resources. Whether or not the American approach is successful is for history to judge, once the dust has settled on the credit crisis. But we should not be too quick to condemn it simply on the basis of the 2008 cyclical episode, for that would be throwing the baby out with the bathwater. As argued in Chapter 7, the crisis was

## Overview of Public Sector Solutions

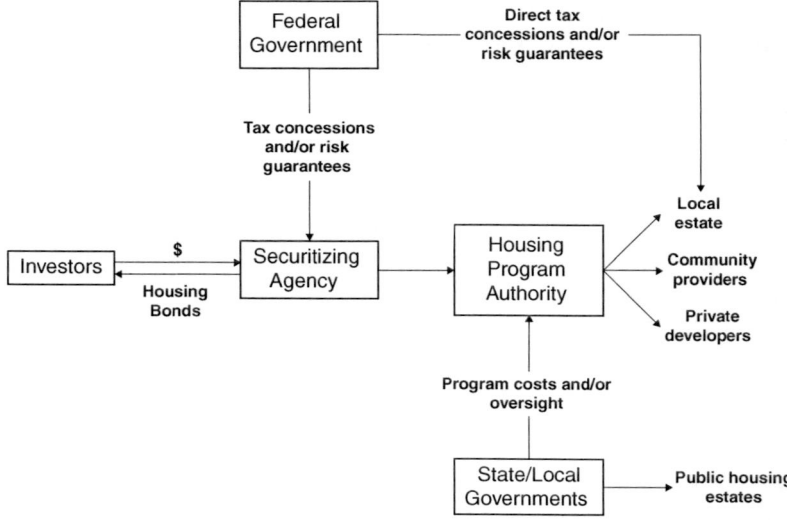

*Figure 9.3* Overview of public sector solutions

caused by market imperfections, not by the idea of multigrade mortgage markets per se.

In the UK, by contrast, government incentive policy in housing finance is minimal. Since the release of the Barker Report (Barker, 2006), the British government has committed to increasing affordable housing supply, and aspired to raise the level of home ownership to 75 percent, yet this is principally by using the physical side of housing, notably the land-use planning system and by selling council houses.

In Australia, the emerging trend is to use tax credits and develop PPPs. Explaining the government's housing plan to a business leaders' forum in 2008, Prime Minister Rudd told his audience that it was "a new partnership with the private sector – a Public Private Partnership in concept", assuring them that the government would "calibrate the future issuing of tax credits to market demand". The government believes it can improve rental affordability while still producing good returns for investors. A subsidy to attract investment in low-cost housing has been introduced.

International policy comparisons are fruitful because they reveal lessons and raise questions. For instance, during the discussion in Chapters 4 through 6, we saw that the US system contains a stronger element of housing finance assistance than Britain or Australia, and affordability is substantially better in the US. At the same time, we noted in the present chapter that despite the myriad measures to assist mortgages in the US, its rate of home ownership is no higher than in the UK and Australia.

This volume has argued that financial markets have a huge role to play in the solution for affordable housing. Uniquely, this book analyzes the interaction between capital markets and housing outcomes. Substantial intellectual progress is being made in the US, the UK, Australia, and elsewhere as an increasing number of analysts and public officials recognize the nexus between the financial system and lower housing affordability.

In that context, rather than just calling for more public sector funding, this chapter has highlighted the potential role of private capital, and then asked whether there is an optimal role for government.

Future government housing policies can combine different financing and nonfinancing elements to exploit diverse opportunities, using the capacity and different interests of private investors, developers, and not-for-profit partners. A new policy mentality can evolve that is less program-based and more project-driven. By encouraging creative partnerships with nongovernment players, governments can make enhanced use of capital markets and improve the gearing ratio, making better use of taxpayers' dollars and in turn making housing, and housing finance, more affordable at the least cost (Berry and Hall, 2006).

# 10
# Future Directions

The housing finance systems of advanced countries remain very much as works in progress. This brief final chapter sketches areas that deserve further attention, by way of a future research agenda.

There are three areas where further work on affordable housing finance is needed: financial markets, government policy settings, and housing imbalances. Below are some suggestions for future work.

- In the wake of the housing correction, global de-leveraging, and the history-making subprime crisis of 2008, will housing credit markets be able to regroup and resume activity in securitized mortgages? If so, how long will it take, and what role do regulators need to play? As revealed by the credit crisis, the infrastructure of capital markets was not up to the task of calibrating and valuing multigrade housing debt, despite having done the same with corporate debt for decades. What are the requisites for the capital markets to retool and be fully functional in a multi-asset-class real estate securities world? Stephens and Quilgars (2008) suggest that currently, "the institutional structure that underpins sub-prime lending appears to amplify the levels of risk unnecessarily". How can these deficiencies be rectified?
- What does it mean for housing credit markets to be "complete"? A template for mortgage markets, based on the notion of industry completeness, is provided by the European Mortgage Federation based on four main criteria: credit risk tolerance, product range, distribution, and availability of information (Mercer Oliver Wyman, 2003). An alternative set of benchmarks for an efficient housing finance system is suggested by the Department of Housing and Urban Development (HUD), based on indicators in three categories: borrower access, capital supply, and low transactions costs (HUD,

2006). How can these – or a different set of criteria – be attested, and where are markets currently incomplete? Where are the existing "corner solutions" for the demand and supply of housing finance, which are producing suboptimal outcomes and welfare loss?

- Where are the gaps in housing data? For example, Listokin et al. (2003) find considerable statistical discrepancies between the American Housing Survey, Consumer Expenditure, National Survey of Families and Households, and Survey of Income and Program Participation. Lam and Kaul (2003) express concern about a lack of reliability on American Housing Survey Data. In the UK and Australia, analysts also regularly appeal for richer data. Can the discrepancies and blank spaces in data be resolved?
- What is the dollar magnitude of the role played by housing as part of the economy's essential infrastructure, akin to the role played by ports, telecommunications, bank payments networks, and so on? Housing is recognized as an investment good, yet there is very little analysis of its contribution to economic growth and employment. What are the measures of housing's value-added? Does a dollar of government spending on housing finance support or generate higher macroeconomic returns than a dollar spent on, say, education or health?
- What are the preconditions for engendering greater flexibility in retail housing finance? It is likely that shared-equity finance will only develop into a major market if there is an underlying commercial rationale, and if it fulfils key community requirements. What are the factors that will drive this development?
- What are the barriers to greater funding of affordable housing by private institutional investors? Can perceived obstacles with low-income housing investment such as illiquidity, below-market returns, management costs, higher risk, and lack of information be overcome without direct government intervention? If not, what is the optimum level of government involvement?
- How is housing finance affecting – and being affected by – the changing generational and demographic patterns of the population, especially the ageing of the populace? Intergenerational equity provides a way for baby boomers who have surfed the wave of housing price gains to give something back to the younger generation that would soon support them in their old age. Yet high house prices are making it harder for young people to enter the housing market. Is the housing finance system operating efficiently to produce an equilibrium in pan-generational outcome?

- Do emerging and developing countries have a housing affordability problem? Are the causes similar to those in advanced economies, or are they different (Kissick and Leibson, 2006)? Can the policies around affordable housing in the North be adopted in the South, or are the emerging economies, including their financial systems, so different as to make this impractical? Do those countries have a sound private rental market, contract savings, and other means to equip households to become homeowners? Why do some emerging economies, such as in the Eastern bloc, have very high loan-to-value ratios (LVRs) (as high as 8–10, versus 3–5 for advanced markets), making for problematic credit risk?
- What contribution to improved affordability and efficiency could be made by lowering transactions costs – such as stamp duties and other taxes levied by federal, state, and local governments – in housing finance markets?

It seems clear that, as the twenty-first century gets underway, we live in an age of evolutionary housing finance. Despite the 2008 credit crisis, secondary mortgage markets will re-emerge; the failure was with the infrastructure of secondary mortgage markets at that particular stage in their history, not with the basic notion of financial engineering per se. In the face of the massive re-intermediation of savings away from banks into pension funds, in effect starving lenders of the in-house flows they once employed to fund mortgages, the involvement of non-bank investors in supplying housing finance remains unavoidable. The way forward is therefore still for investors, large and small, to invest in a menu of housing-linked capital assets – both debt and equity – of multiple grades, originated by banks and other vehicles in a flexible retail environment, but this time around to do a better job of pricing and trading these instruments.

As we saw in Chapter 2, the costs of housing stress, left unresolved, are ultimately borne by communities, business, investors, and governments. These costs include what economists call "negative externalities" and come in a myriad of forms, such as rising credit-card debt, higher community health bills, increased incidence of crime, marriage breakdown, disruption in education, proliferation of ghetto communities, and the like. The private sector bears these costs indirectly in the form of lost output, higher insurance premiums, higher interest rates, and decay in the urban environment. The public sector, for its part, bears the cost directly in the form of lower tax revenue alongside higher budgetary outlays on welfare and rent-assistance payments. In other words, failure to address the shortage of adequate housing infrastructure "up front" often simply leads to high losses to national income in other forms, later.

Each person's need for a zip code is fundamental to the human experience. Shelter occupies a priority position in the hierarchy of human needs – alongside food and clothing – and the demand for it is not easily dissuaded. Moreover, housing expectations tend to increase, not retreat, among the population with time; living standards in advanced countries, measured by per capita income, have tripled since the 1950s, and consumer expectations for ever bigger and better housing have grown accordingly. The need for housing is not going to go away any time soon, nor the need for affordable housing, nor the need for affordable housing finance.

# References

Affordable Housing National Research Consortium (2001), *Affordable Housing in Australia: Pressing Need, Effective Solution*, AHNRC, Sydney, September.

Akerlof, G. (1970), "The market for 'lemons': Quality uncertainty and the market mechanism", *Quarterly Journal of Economics*, 84(3), 488–500.

Allen Consulting Group (2001), *Policy options for Stimulating investment in affordable housing across Australia: Stage Three Report*, Affordable Housing National Research Consortium, Sydney, September.

Ambrose, P. (2001), "Living conditions and health promotion strategies", *Journal of the Royal Society for the Promotion of Health*, 121(1), 9–15.

Ambrose, P. (2003), "Housing standards and NHS costs", paper presented at UnHealthy Housing: Promoting Good Health conference, Warwick University, UK, 19–21 March.

Ambrose, B. and T. Thibodeau (2004), "Have the GSE affordable housing goals increased the supply of mortgage credit?", *Regional Science and Urban Economics*, May, 263–73.

American Bankers Association (2009), website: www.aba.com.

American Dream Coalition (2009), website: http://americandreamcoalition.org/.

Andrew, A., D. Haurin, and A. Munasib (2005), "Explaining the route to owner-occupation: A transatlantic comparison", *Journal of Housing Economics*, 15(3), September, 189–216.

Aoki, K., J. Proudman, and G. Vlieghe (2004), "House prices, consumption, and monetary policy: A financial accelerator approach", *Journal of Financial Intermediation*, October, 414–35.

Apgar, W. and E. Whiting (2003), "Essential function bonds: An emerging tool for affordable housing finance", *KSG Working Paper Series No. RWP03-015*, Harvard University, February.

Apps, P. (1975), "Home ownership: The Australian dream", *Australian Quarterly*, 48, 64–75.

APRA (2005), *Residential valuation practices by ADIs and LMIs*, Australian Prudential Regulation Authority, Sydney.

APRA (2008), "ADI housing lending", *APRA Insight*, Issue 1, Australian Prudential Regulation Authority, Sydney, May.

Arnott, R. (2001), "Housing economics", in N. Smelser and P. Baltes (eds), *International Encyclopedia of the Behavioral and Social Sciences*, Elsevier, Amsterdam, 6939–46.

Arvan, L and J. Brueckner(1986), "Risk sharing in the adjustable-rate loan market: Are existing contracts efficient?", *Economics Letters*, 22(4), 361–36.

Aura, S. and T. Davidoff (2008), "Supply constraints and housing prices", *Economics Letters*, 99(2), May, 275–7.

Australian Bureau of Statistics (2006), *Australian Social Trends, 2006* (Cat. No. 4102.0), Canberra: ABS.

Australian Housing and Urban Research Institute (2002), "Do housing conditions make a difference to our health?", *AHURI Research and Policy Bulletin*, 6, 1–4.

—— (2005), "The health, employment and education benefits of public housing", *AHURI Research and Policy Bulletin*, 54, 1–4.
Australian Institute of Health and Welfare (2007), *Australia's welfare 2007*, Canberra: AIHW.
Australian Securities and Investment Commission (2005), *Equity Release Products*, Report 59, Sydney, Australia: ASIC.
Ayala, L. and C. Navarro (2007), "The dynamics of housing deprivation", *Journal of Housing Economics*, March, 72–97.
Baer, W (1976), "The evolution of housing indicators and housing standards: Some lessons for the future", *Public Policy*, 24(3), 361–93.
Baker-Botts (Law Firm) (2003), *Report to the [Freddie Mac] Board of Directors, Internal Investigation of Certain Accounting Matters*, July 22.
Bank for International Settlements (2008), *OTC Derivatives Market Activity in the Second Half of 2007*, Monetary and Economic Department, May.
Barakova, I., R. Bostic, P. Calem, and S. Wachter (2003), "Does credit quality matter for homeownership?", *Journal of Housing Economics*, December, 318–33.
Barker, K. (2006), *Review of housing supply: Delivering stability, securing our future housing needs: Final report – Recommendations*. Norwich, England: Her Majesty's Stationery Office.
Barrow, M and R. Bachan (1997), *The Real Cost of Poor Homes: Footing the Bill*, London: Royal Institution of Chartered Surveyors.
Beer, A. (1999), "Housing investment and the private rental sector in Australia", *Urban Studies*, 36(2), 255–69
Bernanke, B. (2007b), *Speech at the Federal Reserve Bank of Kansas City's Economic Symposium*, Jackson Hole, Wyoming, August 31.
Bernanke, B. (2007a), "The Subprime mortgage market", *Speech delivered at the Federal Reserve Bank of Chicago's 43rd Annual Conference on Bank Structure and Competition*, Chicago, May 17.
Berry, M. (1999), "Unravelling the Australian housing solution: The post-war years", *Housing, Theory and Society*, 16(3), 106–23.
Berry, M. (2000), "Investment in rental housing in Australia: Small landlords and institutional investors", *Housing Studies*, 15(5).
Berry, M (2003), "Why is it important to boost the supply of affordable housing in Australia, and how can we do it?", *Urban Policy and Research*, 21(4), 413–35.
Berry, M (2006), "Housing affordability and the economy: A review of macroeconomic impacts and policy issues", *AHURI Research Report No. 4*, National research venture 3: Housing affordability for lower income Australians, Canberra: Australian Housing and Urban Research Institute.
Berry, M, C. Whitehead, P. Williams, and J. Yates (2004), "Financing affordable housing: A critical comparative review of the United Kingdom and Australia", *Final Report*, Melbourne: Australian Housing and Urban Research Institute (AHURI).
Berry, M., G. Carter, and J. Hall (2001), *Policy Options for stimulating Investment in Affordable Housing Across Australia: Stage Two Report*, Affordable Housing National Research Consortium, Sydney, September.
Berry, M. and J. Hall (2001), *Policy Options for stimulating Investment in Affordable Housing Across Australia: Stage One Report*, Affordable Housing National Research Consortium, Sydney, September.

Berry, M and J. Hall (2006), "Making housing assistance more efficient: A risk management approach", *Urban Studies*, 43(9), 1581–604.

Black, S. (2008), "Recent developments in securitisation", *Finsia Journal of Applied Finance (JASSA)*, Special Issue: Proceedings of the 13th Annual Melbourne Money and Finance Conference, December, 7–14.

Blundell-Wignall, A., P. Atkinson, and S. Lee (2008), "The current financial crisis: Causes and policy issues", *Financial Market Trends*, Paris: OECD.

Boehm, T. and A. Schlottmann (2006), "A comparison of household mobility for owned manufactured, traditional owned, and rental units using the American Housing Survey", *Journal of Housing Economics*, June, 126–42.

Bonnefoy, X (2007), "Inadequate housing and health: An overview", *International Journal of Environment and Pollution*, 30(3/4), 411–29.

Bostic, R. and S. Gabriel (2006), "Do the GSEs matter to low-income housing markets? An assessment of the effects of the GSE loan purchase goals on California housing outcomes", *Journal of Urban Economics*, 59(3), May, 458–75.

Boehm, T. and A. Schlottmann (1999), "Does home ownership by parents have an economic impact on their children?", *Journal of Housing Economics*, September, 217–32.

Boehm, T. and A. Schlottmann (2002), "Housing and wealth accumulation: Intergenerational impacts", in N. Retsinas and E. Belsky (eds), *Low-income homeownership: Examining the unexamined goal*, Washington, DC: Brookings Institution Press, 407–26.

—— (2004), *Wealth accumulation and homeownership: Evidence for low-income households*, US Department of Housing and Urban Development, Washington.

Böheim, R. and Taylor, M. (2000), "My home was my castle: Evictions and repossessions in Britain", *Journal of Housing Economics*, 9, 287–319.

Bramley, G. (2002), *Evaluation of the Low Cost Home-Ownership Programme*, London: ODPM.

—— (2004), *Scoping the low cost home ownership market in the UK*, London: Council of Mortgage Lenders (CML).

Breunig, R. and D. Cobb-Clark (2004), *Understanding the Factors Associated with Financial Stress in Australian Households*, Canberra: Social Policy Analysis and Research Centre.

Brown, T. and N. Yates (2005), "Allocations and lettings: Taking customer choice forward in England?", *European Journal of Housing Policy*, 5(3), December, 343–57.

Brown, T. and P. King (2005), "The power to choose: Effective choice and housing policy", *European Journal of Housing Policy*, 5(1), April, 59–97.

Bryant, J. (2008), *A guide to the Housing and Regeneration Act 2008*, UK: National Housing Federation.

Buckley, S. (2008), "Fixed income managers: Evolution or revolution?", *Finsia Journal of Applied Finance (JASSA)*, Special Issue: Proceedings of the 13th Annual Melbourne Money and Finance Conference, December.

Bullock, G. (2008), "Inside the housing affordability crisis", *NineMSN news Report* (online), Sydney, March.

Calem, P. and M. LaCour-Little (2004), "Risk-based capital requirements for mortgage loans", *Journal of Banking and Finance*, March, 647–72.

Campbell, J., J. Hilscher, and J. Szilagyi (2005), "In search of distress risk", *Discussion Paper No. 2081*, Harvard Institute of Economic Research, July.

Caplin, A., and C. Joye (2002), *A Primer on a Proposal for Global Housing Finance Reform* (Monograph No. 2), Sydney: The Menzies' Research Centre.

Caplin, A, C. Joye, P. Butt, E. Glaeser, and M. Kuczynski (2003), *Innovative Approaches to Reducing the Costs of Home Ownership*, A Report Commissioned by the Menzies Research Centre for the Prime Minister's Home Ownership Task Force, Sydney, June.

Caplin, A., S. Chan, C. Freeman, and J. Tracy (1997), *Housing Market Partnerships*, Cambridge, MA: MIT Press.

Carbo, S., E. Gardner, and P. Molyneux (2005), *Financial Exclusion*, London: Palgrave Macmillan.

Chaplin, R., S. Martin, J. Yang, and C. Whitehead (1994), *Affordability: Definitions, Measures, and Implications for Lenders*, Cambridge, England: Department of Land Economy, Cambridge University.

Chomsisengphet, S. and R. Elul (2006), "Bankruptcy exemptions, credit history, and the mortgage market", *Journal of Urban Economics*, January, 171–88.

Clapham, D. (2006), "Housing policy and the discourse of globalization", *European Journal of Housing Policy*, 6(1), April, 55–76.

Clark, G. (2000), *Pension Fund Capitalism*, Oxford: Oxford University Press.

Clinch, J. and J. Healy (2000), "Housing standards and excess winter mortality", *Journal of Epidemiol Community Health*, 54, September, 719–20.

CML (2004), *Shared Ownership Joint Guidance for England*, London: Council of Mortgage Lenders (CML).

Colton, K., (2002), "Housing finance in the United States: The transformation of the U.S. housing finance system", *Working Paper W02-5*, Joint Center for Housing Studies, Harvard University, July.

Cox, W. and H. Pavletich (2005), *1st annual Demographia International Housing Affordability survey*, February, Illinois.

Crews Cutts, A., and E. Olsen (2002), "Are Section 8 housing subsidies too high?", *Journal of Housing Economics*, 11(3), September, 214–43.

Crook, A. and P. Kemp (1999), *Financial Institutions and Private Rented Housing*, York: Joseph Rowntree Foundation.

Cummings, J. and D. DiPasquale (1999), "The low-income housing tax credit: An analysis of the first ten years", *Housing Policy Debate*, 10(3), 251–307.

Cunningham, J (2005), "Affordability pressures build", *CML Housing Finance*, November, London: Council of Mortgage Lenders.

Danis, M. and A. Pennington-Cross (2008), "Financing community reinvestment and development: The delinquency of subprime mortgages", *Journal of Economics and Business*, January, 67–90.

Datamonitor (2006), *UK Equity Release Schemes*, London: Datamonitor.

David, P. (2004), *Funding mechanisms for low-income housing: a case study of the USA*, Housing Finance Systems Monograph Series, New York: United Nations Center for Human Settlements, January.

Davis, J.(ed.) (1994), *The Affordable City*, Philadelphia: Temple University Press.

Dewilde, C. and F. De Keulenaer (2003), "Housing and poverty: The 'missing link'", *European Journal of Housing Policy*, 3(2), August, 127–53.

Di, Z., E. Belsky, and X. Liu (2007), "Do homeowners achieve more household wealth in the long run?", *Journal of Housing Economics*, November, 274–90.

Diamond, D. (2000), "Assessing the housing finance system", paper presented at the World Bank Mortgage Finance Workshop, Washington, DC.

Diaz-Serrano, L. (2005), "Income volatility and residential mortgage delinquency across the EU", *Journal of Housing Economics*, September, 153–77.

DiPasquale, D. and E. Glaeser (1999), "Incentives and social capital: Are homeowners better citizens?", *Journal of Urban Economics*, 45, 354–84.

Downie, M. and G. Robson (2007), *Automated valuation models: An international perspective*, London: Council of Mortgage Lenders, October.

Dusansky, R. and Ç. Koç (2007), "The capital gains effect in the demand for housing", *Journal of Housing Economics*, 61(2), March, 287–98.

Earley, F.(2005a), "UK mortgage funding", CML Housing Finance, February, Council of Mortgage Lenders, London.

Earley, F. (2005b), "Mortgage equity withdrawal", *CML HousingFinance*, No. 51, London: Council of Mortgage Lenders, August.

Ellis, L (2006), "Housing and housing finance: The view from Australia and beyond", *Research Discussion Paper, 2006–12*, Sydney: Reserve Bank of Australia, December.

Englund, P., M. Hwang, and J. Quigley (2002), "Hedging housing risk", *Journal of Real Estate, Finance and Economics*, 24(1/2), 167–200.

Erbas, S. and F. Nothaft (2002), "Boosting growth through home ownership", *IMF Survey*, Washington.

Erskine, A.(2008), "The unlisted, unrated debentures market", *Finsia Journal of Applied Finance (JASSA)*, Special Issue: Proceedings of the 13th Annual Melbourne Money and Finance Conference, December.

European Committee for Social Cohesion (2000), *43: Strategy for social cohesion*, Brussels: CDCS.

European Mortgage Federation (2007), *United Kingdom Fact Sheet*, EMF.

Fannie Mae (2003), *Subprime lending in the primary and secondary markets*, White Paper, Fannie Mae Foundation, January.

Fitch (2007), "Criteria for automated valuation models in the UK", May, website: www.fitchratings.com.

Flood, J. (1983), "A scheme for co-operative home ownership", *Polis*, 10(1), 15–19.

Foote, C., K. Gerardi, and P. Willen (2008), "Negative equity and foreclosure: Theory and evidence", *Journal of Urban Economics*, 64(2), September, 234–45.

Fortelney, A. and R. Reed (2005), "The increasing use of automated valuation models in the Australian mortgage market", *Australian Property Journal*, May, 1–7.

FRB New York (2003), "Policies to promote affordable housing", *Federal Reserve Bank of New York Economic Policy Review*, Theme Issue, 9(2), June.

Federal Reserve Board (2008), "February 2008 statistical supplement: Mortgage debt outstanding", *Statistical Supplement of the Federal Reserve Bulletin*, Federal Reserve Board of Governors, New York.

FSA (2003), *Towards a National Strategy for Financial Capability*, London: Financial Services Authority, November.

Gans, J. and S. King (2003), *Policy options for housing for low income households*, A Report for the Prime Minister's Home Ownership Taskforce, University of Melbourne.

Garnett, D. and J. Perry (2005), *Housing Finance*, third edition, Chartered Institute of Housing, UK.

General Accounting Office (US) (1997), *Tax credits: Opportunities to improve oversight of the Low-income Housing Program*, Washington, DC.

Glaeser, E., and B. Sacerdote (2000), "The social consequences of housing", *Journal of Housing Economics*, 9(1–2), March, 1–23.

Glaeser, E. and J. Gyourko (2002), "The impact of zoning on housing affordability", *Working Paper No. 8835*, New York: National Bureau of Economic Research (NBER).

Glaeser, E. and J. Gyourko (2008), *Rethinking Federal Housing Policy*, American Enterprise Institute.

Glaeser, E., J. Gyourko, and A. Saiz (2008), "Housing supply and housing bubbles", *Journal of Urban Economics*, 64(2), September, 198–217.

Goldberg, G. and J. Harding (2003), "Investment characteristics of low- and moderate-income mortgage loans", *Journal of Housing Economics*, September, 151–80.

Goodman, A. (2005), "Central cities and housing supply: Growth and decline in US cities", *Journal of Housing Economics*, 14(4), December, 315–35.

Gobb, K., M. Munro, and M. Satsangi (1999), *Housing Finance in the UK: An Introduction*, : Palgrave Macmillan, Basingstoke

Green, R. and S. Malpezzi (2003), *A Primer on U.S. Housing Markets and Housing Policy*, Washington, DC: Urban Institute Press.

Green, R. and K. Vandell (1999), "Giving households credit: How changes in the U.S. tax code could promote homeownership", *Regional Science and Urban Economics*, 29(4), July, 419–44.

Green, R., and S. Wachter (2005), "The American mortgage in historical and international context", *Journal of Economic Perspectives*, 19(4), 93–114.

Green, R. and M. White (1997), "Measuring the benefits of home owning: Effects on children", *Journal of Urban Economics*, 41, 441–61.

Grinold, R. and R. Kahn (2000), *Active Portfolio Management*, 2e, New York: McGraw Hill.

Hall, J.(2001), *Policy Options for stimulating Investment in Affordable Housing Across Australia: Stage Four Report*, Affordable Housing National Research Consortium, Sydney, September.

Hamnett, C. R. (1996a), "Home ownership, housing wealth and wealth distribution in Britain", in J. Hills (ed.) *New Inequalities: The Changing Distribution of Income & Wealth in the UK*, Cambridge: Cambridge University Press, 348–73.

Hamnett, C. R. (1996b) "Social polarisation, economic restructuring and welfare state regimes", *Urban Studies*, 33, 1407–30.

Harker, L. (2006), "Chance of a lifetime: The impacts of bad housing on children's lives", *Shelter*, UK, September.

Hartarska, V. and C. Gonzalez-Vega (2006), "Evidence on the effect of credit counseling on mortgage loan default by low-income households", *Journal of Housing Economics*, 15(1), March, 63–79.

Haughey, J. (2008), "Housing affordability improves but will not boost home sales", December 11, website: www.reedconstructiondata.com.

Haurin, D., R. Dietz, and B. Weinberg (2003), "Impact of Homeownership on Child Outcomes", *Low-Income Homeownership: Examining the Unexamined Goal*, in N. P. Retsinas and E. S. Belsky (eds), Washington, DC: Brookings Institution Press, 427–46.

Haurin, D., T. Parcel and J. Haurin (2002), Does homeownership affect child outcomes?", *Real Estate Economics*, American Real Estate and Urban Economics Association, 30(4), 635–666.

Hawtrey, K. (2001), "Making affordable housing an asset class", *ASX Perspective*, Australian Stock Exchange, 1st Quarter, 47–50.

Heady, C. (1997), "Labour market transitions and social exclusion", *Journal of European Social Policy*, 7, 119–28.

Healy, J. (2004), *Housing, Fuel Poverty, and Health: A Pan-European Analysis*, London: Ashgate Publishing, Ltd.

Hendershott, P., G. Pryce, and M. White (2003), "Household leverage and the deductability of home mortgage interest: Evidence from UK house puchasers", *Journal of Housing Research*, 14(1), 49–82.

Hendershott, P. and G. Pryce(2006), "The sensitivity of homeowner leverage to the deductibility of home mortgage interest", *Journal of Urban Economics*, 60(1), July, 50–68.

HM Treasury (2006), *Report of the Shared Equity Task Force*, London.

HM Treasury and ODPM (2005a), *The Government's Response to Kate Barker's Review of Housing Supply*, London.

――― (2005b), *Housing Policy: An Overview Statement*, London.

Holmans, A., K. Scanlon, and C. Whitehead (2002), *Fiscal policy instruments to promote affordable housing*, Research Report VII, Cambridge: Cambridge Centre for Housing and Planning Research.

Housing Corporation (2004), *A home of my own: Report of the Government's Low Cost Ownership Task Force*, London: Housing Corporation.

Hronsky, J. and D. Robinson (2008), "Fair or not? Fair value measurement in the subprime crisis", *Finsia Journal of Applied Finance (JASSA)*, Special Issue: Proceedings of the 13th Annual Melbourne Money and Finance Conference, December.

HUD (2006), "Evolution of the US Housing Finance System", Office of Policy Development and Research, US Department of Housing and Urban Development, April.

HUD (2009), "The Federal Housing Administration", US Department of Housing and Urban Development, www.hud.gov.

Hulse, K. and B. Randolph (2005), "Workforce disincentive effects of housing allowances and public housing for low income households in Australia", *European Journal of Housing Policy*, 5(2), August, 147–65.

International Monetary Fund (2008), *Australia: Selected Issues*, International Monetary Fund, Washington, August 18.

Jaffe, D. (2003), "The Interest Rate Risk of Fannie Mae and Freddie Mac", Journal of Financial Services Research, 24:1, 5–29.

Jaggar, B. (2007), *Basel 2 and the UK mortgage market: Challenges and opportunities*, London: Council of Mortgage Lenders, June.

Johnson, B., S. Manning, and D. Disney-Willis (2007), *Australian Mortgage Industry*, Volume 6, Sydney: JP Morgan/Fujitsu Consulting, September.

Jin, Y and Z. Zeng (2007), "Real estate and optimal public policy in a credit-constrained economy", *Journal of Housing Economics*, 16(2), June, 143–66.

Jin, Y. and Z. Zeng (2004), "Housing and the macroeconomy: The nexus between residential investment and house prices in a multi-sector monetary business cycle model", *Journal of Housing Economics*, December, 268–86.

Joint Center for Housing Studies (2008), *The state of the nation's housing 2008*, Boston: Joint Center for Housing Studies, Harvard University.

Jones, O. and L. Grebler (1961), *The secondary mortgage market*, University of California Press.

Jones, C. (2007), "Private investment in rented housing and the role of REITS", *European Journal of Housing Policy*, 7(4), December, 383–400.
Kealhofer, S. (2003), "Quantifying credit risk I: Default prediction", *Financial Analyst Journal*, Jan/Feb, 30–44.
Kern, A. (2004), "Corporate governance and banking regulation", *Working Paper 17*, Cambridge Endowment for Research in Finance, University of Cambridge, June.
King, U., L. Parrish, O. Tanik (2006), *Financial quicksand*, Washington, DC: Center for Responsible Lending.
Kissick, D. and D. Leibson (2006), *Housing for All*, World Urban Forum III.
Kleiman, M. (1996), Housing, welfare and the state: A comparative analysis of Britain, France and Germany, Cheltenham: Edward Arnold.
Kutty, N. (2007), "Housing Affordability in the United States: Income and Price Contributors", *mimeograph*, June.
Lam, K. and B. Kaul (2003), *Analysis of Housing Finance Issues Using the American Housing Survey (AHS)*, US Department of Housing and Urban Development, April.
Laker, J. (2003), "The resilience of housing loan portfolios – APRA's stress test results", *Speech by APRA Chairman*, John Laker, Sydney, October 9.
Lee, C. (2007), "Does provision of public rental housing crowd out private housing investment? A panel VAR approach", *Journal of Housing Economics*, 16(1), March, 1–20.
Leung, C (2004), Macroeconomics and housing: A review of the literature, Journal of Housing Economics, 13(4), December, 249–267.
Listokin, D., E. Wyly, I. Voicu, and B. Schmitt (2003), "Known facts or reasonable assumptions? An examination of alternative sources of housing data", *Journal of Housing Research*, 13(2), 219–51.
Lumpkin, S. (2008), "Resolutions of weak institutions: Lessons learned from previous crises", *Financial Market Trends*, Paris: OECD, September.
Malpass, P. (2004), "Fifty years of British housing policy: Leaving or leading the welfare state?", *European Journal of Housing Policy*, 4(2), August, 209–27.
Malpezzi, S. and K. Vandell (2002), "Does the low-income housing tax credit increase the supply of housing?", *Journal of Housing Economics*, 11(4), December, 360–80.
Malpezzi, S. and D. Maclennan (2001), "The long-run price elasticity of supply of new residential construction in the United States and the United Kingdom", *Journal of Housing Economics*, 10(3), September, 278–306.
Marsh, A. (2000), "Housing deprivation and health: A longitudinal analysis", *Housing Studies*, 15(3), 411–28.
——— (2004), "The inexorable rise of the rational consumer? The Blair government and the reshaping of social housing", *European Journal of HousingPolicy*, 4(2), August, 185–207.
Marsh, D., C. Gordon, P. Pantazis, and S. Heslop (2000), "Home sweet home? The impact of poor housing on health", *British Medical Journal*, 2, 1470–74.
McCarthy, G., S. Van Zandt, and W. Rohe (2001), *The economic benefits and costs of homeownership: A critical assessment of the research*, Working Paper No. 01–02, Research Institute for Housing America, Arlington VA, May.
McCaughey, J. (1992), "Where now? Homeless families in the 1990s", *Policy Background Paper No.8*, Melbourne: Australian Institute of Family Studies.
McClure, K. (2000) "The low-income housing tax credit as an aid to housing finance: How well has it worked?", *Housing Policy Debate*, 11(1), 91–114.

McLoughlin, B. (1992), *Shaping Melbourne's future: Town planning, the state and civil society*, Melbourne: Cambridge University Press.

McNelis, S., D. Hayward, and H. Bissett (2002), *A private rental investment vehicle for the community housing sector*, Final Report, Melbourne: AHURI.

Mercer Oliver Wyman (2003), *Study on the financial integration of European mortgage markets*, for the European Mortgage Federation, Brussels.

Merton, R. (1974), "On the pricing of corporate debt: The risk structure of interest rates", *Journal of Finance*, 29(2), 449–70.

Miceli, T. and C. Sirmans (2007), "The holdout problem, urban sprawl, and eminent domain", *Journal of Housing Economics*, November, 309–19.

Miles, D. (2004), *The UK mortgage market: Taking a longer-term view*, Interim Report to HM Treasury, December.

Milligan, V. (2005), "Directions for affordable housing policy in Australia: Outcomes of a stakeholder forum", *AHURI Research Report No. 2*, National research venture 3: Housing affordability for lower income Australians, Canberra: Australian Housing and Urban Research Institute.

Milligan, V., P. Phibbs, K. Fagan, and N. Gurran (2004), "A practical framework for expanding affordable housing services in Australia: Learning from experience", *AHURI Final Report No. 65*, Sydney: Australian Housing and Urban Research Institute, July.

Minsky, H. (1992), "The capital development of the economy and the structure of financial institutions", *Working Paper No. 72*, The Jerome Levy Economics Institute of Bard College.

Monk, S. and C. Whitehead (eds) (2000), *Restructuring Housing Systems: from Social to Affordable Housing?*, York: Joseph Rowntree Foundation.

Monk, S., T. Crook, D. Lister, S. Rowley, and C. Short (2005), *Land and finance for affordable housing*, Joseph Rowntree Foundation: UK.

Mueller, E. and J. Tighe (2007), "Making the case for affordable housing: Connecting housing with health and education outcomes", *Journal of Planning Literature*, 21, 371–85.

Murphy, A. (1991), "A practical analysis of shared-appreciation mortgages", *Housing Policy Debate*, 2(1), 43–8.

National Centre for Social and Economic Modelling (2008), "Wherever I lay my debt, that's my home: Trends in housing affordability and housing stress, 1995–96 to 2005–06", *AMP-NATSEM Income and Wealth Report*, Issue 19, Sydney, March.

National Low Income Housing Coalition (2004), *America's Neighbors: The Affordable Housing Crisis and the People it Affects*, Washington, DC: NLIHC.

—— (2006), *Out of Reach 2006*, Washington DC: NLIHC.

NHS (1991), *The affordability of Australian housing*, National Housing Strategy, NHS Issue Paper No. 2, Canberra.

Nothaft, F. and B. Surette (2001), "Industrial structure of affordable mortgage lending", *Journal of Housing Research*, 12(2), 239–76.

O'Flaherty B. (1995), "Economic theory of homelessness and housing", *Journal of Housing Economics*, 4(1), March, 13–49.

O'Flaherty, B. and T. Wu (2006), "Fewer subsidized exits and a recession: How New York city's family homeless shelter population became immense", *Journal of Housing Economics*, 15(2), June, 99–125.

Önder, Z. (2002), "Homeownership and FHA mortgage activity in neighborhoods and metropolitan areas", *Journal of Housing Economics*, 11(2), June, 152–81.

Ortalo-Magné, F. and S. Rady (2004), "Housing and the macroeconomy: The nexus housing transactions and macroeconomic fluctuations: a case study of England and Wales", *Journal of Housing Economics*, 13(4), December, 287–303.

Owyang, M., J. Piger, H. Wall, and C. Wheeler (2008), "The economic performance of cities: A Markov-switching aproach", *Journal of Urban Economics*, November, 538–50.

Pain, N. and P. Westaway (1997), "Modelling structural change in the UK housing market: A comparison of alternative house price models", *Economic Modelling*, October, 587–610.

Pannell, B. (2007), "Consumer attitudes to long-term fixed rate mortgages", *CML Housing Finance*, No. 8, London: Council of Mortgage Lenders.

Parker, E. (2008), "Subprime lender", *Wall Street Journal*, March 1.

Property Council of Australia (2006), *Improving housing affordability in NSW: A plan for industry and government*, PCA Report, Canberra, November.

Pawson, H. and S. Sinclair(2003), "Shopping therapy? Incentive payments and tenant behaviour: Lessons from underoccupation schemes in the United Kingdom", *European Journal of Housing Policy*, 13(3), December, 289–311.

Peek, J. and J. Wilcox (2003), "Secondary mortgage markets, GSEs, and the changing cyclicality of mortgage flows", *Research in Finance*, 20, 61–80.

Phibbs, P. (2000), "The social and economic impacts of unmet housing needs", *Housing Policy and Research Occasional Paper 4*, Brisbane: Queensland Government.

Plaut, S. (1985), "The theory of collateral", *Journal of Banking and Finance*, September, 401–19.

Poole, W. (2003), "Housing in the macro economy", *Speech at Office of Federal Housing Enterprise Oversight Symposium*, March.

Putnam, R. (1998), "Social Capital: It's importance to housing community: An empirical investigation", *Housing Policy Debate*, 9(1), 61–88.

Quercia, R. (1997), *A methodology for assessing the performance of affordable loans*, Report to the US Department of Housing and Urban Development, March.

Quercia, R., G. McCarthy, and S. Wachter (2003), "The impacts of affordable lending efforts on homeownership rates", *Journal of Housing Economics*, 12(1), March, 29–59.

Quigley, J. and R.Van Order (1991), "Defaults on mortgage obligations and capital requirements for U.S. savings institutions: a policy perspective", *Journal of Public Economics*, April, 353–69.

Real Estate Institute of Australia (2008), *Real estate market facts*, December, Canberra.

Reserve Bank of Australia (2003), "Housing equity withdrawal", *Reserve Bank of Australia Bulletin*, Sydney, February.

——— (2008), "Financial Aggregates Table 2", *Monthly Statistical Release*, Reserve Bank of Australia, March.

Richards, A. (2008), "Some observations on the cost of housing in Australia", Paper presented to the Economic and Social Outlook Conference, Melbourne Institute of Applied Economic and Social Research, Melbourne, March.

Riddel, M. (2004), "Housing-market disequilibrium: An examination of housing-market price and stock dynamics 1967–1998", *Journal of Housing Economics*, June, 120–35.

Robinson, E. and R. Adams (2008), "Housing stress and the mental health and wellbeing of families", *AFRC Briefing No. 12*, Canberra: Australian Institute of Family Studies, Australian Government.

Rohe William, George McCarthy, and Shannon Van Zandt, The social Benefits and Costs of Homeownership: A Critical Assessment of the Research, Research Institute for Housing America, May, 2000.

Rosenthal, S. and W. Strange (2008), "Mortgages and the housing crash: A symposium",(Editorial), *Journal of Urban Economics*, 64(2), September, 197.

Rudd, K., T. Plibersek, and W. Swan (2007), *New Directions for Affordable Housing*, Policy Discussion Paper, Australian Labor Party, Canberra, June.

Saegert, S. and G. Winkel (1998), "Social capital and the revitalization of New York city's distressed inner-city housing", *Housing Policy Debate*, 9(1), 17–60.

Saks, R. (2008), "Job creation and housing construction: Constraints on metropolitan area employment growth", *Journal of Urban Economics*, July, 178–95.

Sandel M, and J. Zotter (2000), "How substandard housing affects children's health", *Contemporary Pediatrics*, 17(10), 134–39.

Sanders, A. and V. Carlos Slawson, Jr. (2005), "Shared appreciation mortgages: Lessons from the UK", *Journal of Housing Economics*, 14(3), September, 178–93.

Scanlon, K and C. Whitehead (2004), "International trends in housing tenure and mortgage finance", London: Council of Mortgage Lenders.

Scanlon, K., J. Lunde, and C. Whitehead (2008), "Mortgage product innovation in advanced economies: More choice, more risk", *European Journal of Housing Policy*, 8(2), June, 109–131.

Schich, S. (2008), "Financial crisis: Deposit insurance and related financial safety net aspects", *Financial Market Trends*, Paris: OECD, December.

SEH (2007), *Survey of English Housing 2004/05*, CLG.

Shiller, R. and A. Weiss (1998), "Moral hazard in home equity conversion", *Cowles Foundation Discussion Paper no. 1177*.

Schroder, M. and A. Reiger (2002), "Vouchers versus production revisited", *Journal of Housing Research*, 11(1), 107–17.

Smith, B. (2006), "The impact of tax increment finance districts on localized real estate: Evidence from Chicago's multifamily markets", *Journal of Housing Economics*, 15(1), March, 21–37.

Song, Y. and Y. Zenou (2006), "Property tax and urban sprawl: Theory and implications for US cities", *Journal of Urban Economics*, 60(3), November, 519–34.

Stegman, M. (1999), *State and local approaches to affordable housing*, Washington DC: Urban Land Institute.

Stegman, M., R. Quercia, and G. McCarthy (2000), *Housing America's working families*, Washington: Center For Housing Policy.

Stephens, R. (2005), "An assessment of the British housing benefit system", *European Journal of Housing Policy*, 5(2), August, 111–29.

Stephens, M. and D. Quilgars (2008), "Sub-prime mortgage lending in the UK", *European Journal of Housing Policy*, 8(2), June, 197–215.

Stone, M. (2006a), "What is housing affordability?: The case for the residual income approach", *Housing Policy Debate*, 17(1), Fannie Mae Foundation.

——— (2006b), "Housing affordability: One third of a nation", in R. Bratt, M. Stone, and C. Hartman (eds), *A Right to Housing: Foundation for a New Social Agenda*, Philadelphia: Temple University Press, 38–60.

Struyk, R. and J. Tuccillo (1983), "Defining the federal role in housing: Back to basics", *Journal of Urban Economics*, 14(2), September, 206–23.

SustainLane (2009), "City Rankings (Housing Affordability)", website: www.sustainlane.com.

Sweeney, J. (1974), "A commodity hierarchy model of the rental housing market", *Journal of Urban Economics*, 1(3), July, 288–323.

Sy, W. (2008), "Credit risk models: Why they failed in the credit crisis", *Finsia Journal of Applied Finance (JASSA)*, Special Issue: Proceedings of the 13th Annual Melbourne Money and Finance Conference, December.

Tatch, J. (2007), "Affordability: are parents helping?", *CML Housing Finance*, Issue No. 3, London: Council of Mortgage Lenders, May.

Temkin, K. and W. Rohe (1998), "Social capital and neigborhood stability: An empirical investigation", *Housing Policy Debate*, 9(1), 61–68.

Thomson, H., M. Petticrew, and D. Morrison (2001), "Health effects of housing improvement: Systematic review of intervention studies", *British Medical Journal*, 323, July, 187–90.

Thomson H., M. Petticrew M and D. Morrison (2002), *Housing improvement and health gain: a summary and systematic review*, Glasgow: MRC Social and Public Health Sciences Unit

Trimbath, S. and J. Montoya (2002), Housing affordability in three dimensions: Prices, income and interest rates, *Policy Brief*, California: Milken Institute, September.

Turner, B. and Z. Yang (2006), "Security of home ownership: Using equity or benefiting from low debt?", *European Journal of Housing Policy*, 6(3), December, 279–96.

US Department of Agriculture (2004), *County typology*, Washington: Economic Research Services, USDA.

Van Dijk, R. and S. Garga (2006), *UK mortgage underwriting*, London: Council of Mortgage Lenders, April.

Van Kempen, R. and H. Priemus (1999), "Undivided cities in the Netherlands: Present situation and political rhetoric", *Housing Studies*, 14(5), 641–57.

Warnock, V. and F. Warnock (2008), "Markets and housing finance", *Journal of Housing Economics*, September, 239–51.

Wesley Mission (2006), *Financial stress and its impact on the individual, family and the community*, Sydney, website: www.wesleymission.org.

Whitehead, C., G. Burgess, and F. Lyall Grant (2008), *Low cost home ownership: Affordability, risks and issues*, Report for the TSA, Cambridge Centre for Housing and Planning Research, University of Cambridge.

Wilcox, S. (2005), *Affordability and the intermediate housing market: local measures for all local authority areas in Great Britain*, York: Joseph Rowntree Foundation.

Williams, P. (2007), "Home ownership at the crossroads?", *CML Housing Finance*, No. 2, London: Council of Mortgage Lenders, May.

―――― (2008), "Please release me! A review of the equity release market in the UK, its potential and consumer expectations", *CML Research Paper*, London: Council of Mortgage Lenders, March.

Williams, P. and J. Bennett (2004), "Shared futures: Taking home-ownership forward through shared equity", *CML Housing Finance*, London: Council of Mortgage Lenders, winter.

Wood, G. (2001), "Are there tax arbitrage opportunities in private rental housing markets?", *Journal of Housing Economics*, 10(1), March, 1–20.

Worthington, A. (2006a), "Debt as a source of financial stress in Australian households", *International Journal of Consumer Studies*, 30(1), 2–15.

Worthington, A. C. (2006b), "Modelling the usage and understanding of financial products: An empirical analysis of Australian owner-occupied and investor mortgages", *Working Paper Series No. 06/03*, School of Accounting and Finance, University of Wollongong.

Wright, S. (1989), "The future of the market for mortgage-backed securities in Australia", *Economic Papers*, 8(1), March, 12–25.

Yates, J. (1996), "Towards a reassessment of the private rental market", *Housing Studies*, 11(1), 35–50.

Yates, J. (2003), "The more things change? An overview of Australia's recent home ownership policies", *European Journal of Housing Policy*, 3(1), April, 1–33.

Yates, J. (2007), "Housing affordability and financial stress", *Research Paper No. 6*, National research venture 3: Housing affordability for lower income Australians, Australian Housing and Urban Research Institute (AHURI), Sydney Research Centre, October.

Yates, J (2008), "Australia's housing affordability crisis", *Australian Economic Review*, 41(2), 200–14.

Yates, J. and M. Wulff (2000), "W(h)ither low cost private rental housing", *Urban Policy and Research*, 18(1).

Yates, J. and V. Milligan (2007), "Housing affordability: A 21st century problem", *AHURI Final Report No. 105*, National research venture 3: Housing affordability for lower income Australians, Australian Housing and Urban Research Institute, Canberra.

Youren (2005a), Private sector requirements for involvement in affordable housing investments. Keynote address to the National Affordable Housing Conference, Making it Happen Innovation in Policy and Practice, Sydney: Australian Housing and Urban Research Institute (AHURI), June 21–22.

—— (2005b) Developing lending products to service the Australian affordable housing market. Keynote address to the National Affordable Housing Conference, Making it Happen Innovation in Policy and Practice, Sydney: Australian Housing and Urban Research Institute (AHURI), June 21–22.

Ying, J. and S. Park (2000), "Increased homelessness and low rent housing vacancy rates", *Journal of Housing Economics*, March, 76–103.

Zandi, M., C. Chen, C. deRitis, and A Carbacho-Burgos (2009), *Housing in crisis: When will metro markets recover?*, Moodys Investor Services, February.

# Index

access-to-finance (A2F) indicator, 11, 54, 78, 80, 83, 94, 144
adjustable-rate mortgages, 38
affordable housing bonds, 113, 125
affordable housing, defined, 7–12, 23–24
Affordable Housing Goals, 67
affordability-based lending, 128–132
alpha returns, 4, 109–111
Alt-A mortgages, 27, 28, 52
alternative investment products, 141
'American model', 59, 63–65, 125, 157
asymmetric information, 117
Australia, 2–4, 12–13, 31–33, 56, 61–62, 73, 79–80, 85, 88, 90, 93, 98, 114, 121, 140, 149, 150, 154, 158
automated valuation models, 76–77, 94, 105, 114, 122

bailouts, 32–33, 34–35, 65–66
balloon loans, 130
Bank of America, 31, 32
Bank of England, 33, 69
banks, 31–37, 39, 42, 55, 74, 84, 90–92, 94, 117, 121, 124, 129
Barker Review, 81–82
Barclays PLC, 31, 33
Basel guidelines, 42, 55, 78, 95, 122
bequests, 138
Bernanke, Ben, 29, 39, 40, 52
beta returns, 109
borrower solvency ratio, 115
'British experiment', 82–83
Brown Gordon, 75, 82
Bush administration American Dream Package, 124

California Communities Housing Bond Program, 153
capital asset pricing model, 109–110

capital market, 4, 29, 37–41, 45–46, 56, 77, 104–105, 120, 124–126, 127, 147
capital gains tax, 87, 100
choice based letting, 82–83
CDOs-squared, 43, 117
Citibank, 31, 32, 38
collateral, 115
collateralized debt obligations, 37, 40, 43, 117
collateralized mortgage obligations, 52, 107
Commonwealth-State Housing Agreement, 86
Community Development Financial Institutions Fund, 142
Community Development Trust, 140
Community Reinvestment Act, 53, 64, 124, 140
competition, 76, 107
convex payoffs, 41
co-ownership, 136
corner solution, 42, 132
council housing, 70
covered bonds, 119
credit default modeling, 115–116, 120–121
credit default swaps, 110
credit markets, 29, 40–43, 44, 103–105, 127–128, 147
credit rating agencies, 28, 37, 105
credit scoring models, 38, 76–78, 114
Credit Suisse, 31
crime outcomes and housing, 19
debt burden, 10, 54, 75, 79, 90

Department of Housing and Urban Development, 50, 52, 55, 63, 66, 147, 160
deposit bonds, 131
deposit hurdle, 11, 53, 94

Deutsche Bank, 31
distressed debt, 110
Dream Start, 135

economic benefits of housing finance, 43–45, 161
economic costs of housing stress, 13–18
economic influences on housing, 1, 22
economic stimulus package, 32, 66
economically targeted investments, 141
educational outcomes and housing, 15
efficiency gains, 104, 122
elasticity of housing supply, 45, 73
employment, 9, 14–15
equity release, 138–140
essential function bonds, 156
ethical investment, 141
European housing finance, 12, 29, 33–35, 73, 76, 85, 104, 119, 127

Fair Lending, 129
family breakdown and housing, 19
Fannie Mae, 7, 35, 51–52, 55, 56, 57, 60, 64–66, 68, 86, 112, 124, 157
Federal Housing Administration, 28, 50, 55, 64, 65–66, 127
Federal Reserve, 4, 124
financial exclusion, 17
financial influences on housing, 1, 20, 23
financial institutions, 28–29, 31, 42–43, 55, 74, 119, 122, 125
financial instruments, 10, 54, 74–75, 77, 106–107
financial regulation, 77, 84–85, 93, 116–125
Financial Services Authority, 9, 69, 105, 129
first home buyer grants, 87, 100
fixed-rate loans, 54, 74–75, 78, 119
fixed-interest market, 110
floaters, 113
foreclosures, 9, 66–67
Freddie Mac, 35, 51–52, 55, 56, 57, 60, 64–66, 68, 86, 112, 124, 129, 157

gearing ratio, 147, 156, 159
general equilibrium, 42
Ginnie Mae, 51, 141
Global Financial Crisis, 1, 4, 27–41, 43, 47–48, 49–50, 64–66, 69, 77, 84, 103, 114, 124, 162
Goldman Sachs, 30, 31, 32
government sponsored enterprises, 2, 51–52, 59, 64, 67, 86, 145–46, 149
governmental influence on housing, 1, 20, 22–23, 146–149, 158
graduated-payment mortgages, 130
Grameen Bank, 142
growing equity mortgages, 130
Guaranteed housing bonds, 156

health outcomes and housing, 15–16
HM Treasury, 77
HomeBuy, 135
home equity conversion, 138, 140
home equity line of credit, 138
home ownership, 54, 64, 67, 75, 80–81, 86–88, 90, 131–132, 147
homelessness, 6
Home Savers Advance Program, 65
Homes and Communities Agency, 72
'honeymoon' period, 11, 133
Hong Kong Shanghai Banking Corporation, 31, 33
household stability and housing, 17–18
housing affordability, dimensions of, 6–12, 23–24, 82
housing affordability, measures of, 4, 6–12, 13, 60–63, 78–81, 94–97
housing, assets characteristics, 45–46
Housing Associations, 71, 77, 81, 137, 147
Housing Benefit, 82–83
Housing Corporation, 72
housing bubbles, 12, 45–46, 49, 69, 81, 98–99, 124
housing demand, 10, 26, 99
housing exclusion, 9–10, 14, 17
housing finance demand and supply, 11, 26–27
housing finance stress, 6, 9–12, 62–63, 77–81, 94–97

housing finance system, 26–27, 65–66, 68, 74, 123, 160
housing market, 2, 28
housing policy, 20, 22–23, 48, 50–53, 65, 75, 81–83, 85, 87–90, 99–102, 145–159
house prices, 28, 45, 49–50, 64–65, 69, 78, 98–99
housing stress, 1, 3, 6–12, 61, 68, 77–81, 91, 94–97, 162–163
housing stress, effects of, 13–24
housing supply, 10, 26–27, 45, 63, 73, 100, 147
HUD – see Department of Housing and Urban Development

indivisibility problem, 132
information ratio, 110
information, role of, 29, 36–41, 43, 112–113, 117–119
impaired loans, 31–32
International Monetary Fund, 34, 84
interest rates, 53, 57, 66, 93, 122
interest-only mortgage, 128–130, 131–132
intermediate housing, 6, 127
international benchmarks, 3, 56, 61–62, 73, 79–80, 85, 88, 90, 93, 98, 114, 121, 140, 149, 154, 158–159
investors, 104–108, 111, 118, 140–143, 148
investment hurdles, 107–108
investment opportunity set, 111
intergenerational outcomes, 138–139, 161

joint ventures, 147
JP Morgan, 31, 32
jumbo mortgages, 30

Key Facts Illustration, 129

labor market, 9, 14
land tax, 87, 100
Lehman Brothers, 30
leveraging private financing, 147, 156, 159
'liar' loans, 28
LIBOR, 113

Lloyds TSB, 33
low-documentation loans, 90, 93, 95
loan-to-value ratio, 11, 53–54, 66, 75, 90, 94, 115–116, 121, 150
low-income housing tax credit, 52, 149, 151
low-income households, 9–10, 56, 77, 132

macroeconomy and housing, 6, 20, 22, 37, 44, 47, 58, 96, 104
market liberalization, 2, 29, 73, 76
mean-variance framework, 108, 111
median multiple, 4, 13, 62, 79, 96, 98
Merrill Lynch, 30, 31, 33
Merton model, 114
Microcredit, 142
Miles Review, 77, 82, 144, 155
Moodys, 28, 30, 40, 65
moral hazard, 118, 124, 137
Morgan Stanley, 30, 31, 33
mortgage affordability, 59
mortgage-backed securities, 27–29, 38, 40–41, 60, 77, 92, 95, 103–104, 106, 110, 112, 117–120, 124–125, 141
mortgage debt-to-income ratio, 56, 79, 97
mortgage innovation, 58–59, 74, 77–78, 91–92, 127
mortgage insurance, 50–51, 116, 122, 154
mortgages, 10, 40–43, 75–76, 90–91, 128
mortgage-to-GDP ratio, 54–55, 75–76, 90–91
multi-grade housing securities, 37, 39, 40–42, 107–108, 110, 112–113, 124, 141
mutual funds, 107–108

National Association of Realtors, 50
negative gearing, 73, 88, 100, 151
New Markets Tax Credit Program, 142, 152
'ninja' loans, 28

Obama administration housing rescue package, 66–67, 145
OECD, 2, 36, 59, 90, 124

originate-to-distribute model, 40
origination, 118
overcrowding, 9

partial debt finance model, 142
Paulson, Henry, 41
payback period, 9
pooled investor vehicles, 140–143
portfolio diversification, 108–109, 111–112, 132, 140
predatory lending, 27–28
principal-agent problem, 38–39, 117
public housing, 2, 52–53, 87, 101
public private partnership, 145, 147–148

rational choice theory, 83
Real Estate Mortgage Investment Conduit, 124, 140
Real Estate Investment Trusts, 140
Registered Social Landlords, 71
regulators, 105, 116–125
regulatory capital, 106, 119, 121–122
regulatory costs, 120, 123
rent assistance, 87, 98
rental allowance, 72
rental sector, 86–87, 97–98, 127, 151
rental voucher program, 52
Reserve Bank of Australia, 34, 85, 94
residual-income rule, 8
residential ownership loan, 134
retail finance, 127
reverse mortgage, 138
Right-to-Buy scheme, 70–71, 75
risk, 10, 36–38, 41, 43, 46, 64, 103, 108, 113
risk mitigation policies, 153–157
risk-return spectrum, 110, 113, 117
Royal Bank of Scotland, 31, 33
Rudd, Kevin, 87, 88, 90

secondary mortgage market, 104, 106, 118–120
securitization, 28–29, 60, 84, 92, 103–104, 106–107, 124
shadow banking system, 117
shared-appreciation mortgage, 132
shared-equity, 132–137
shared-equity, 134
social capital, 6, 18–19, 87
social housing, 73, 77, 83, 88

socially responsible investing, 141
spatial aspects of housing, 1–2, 20–22, 70, 85
special purpose vehicle, 106
stamp duty, 87, 100
Standard and Poors, 28, 30, 38, 40
strategic asset allocation, 109–111
stress tests, 121
strips, 112–113
subprime mortgages, 1, 27, 28, 29, 37–38, 77, 93, 108, 124
sweat equity, 142

taxation, impact of, 53, 73, 87–88, 100–101,123–124, 133–134, 145, 147, 149–153, 155, 162
tax credits, 53, 54–55, 66, 73, 87–88, 100, 134, 150–151
tax increment financing, 152
Tenant Services Authority, 72, 78
30 rule, 7, 11, 96
30/40 rule, 7, 11, 54
transparency of markets, 36, 117
trickle down effect, 6
Troubled Asset Relief Program, 32

UK housing finance, 2–4, 12–14, 31–33, 45, 56, 61–62, 73, 79–80, 85, 88, 90, 93, 98, 114, 121, 140, 149,150, 154, 158
Union Bank of Switzerland, 31
United Nations, 13
US housing finance, 2–4, 12–14, 31–33, 44, 73, 79–80, 85, 88, 90, 93, 98, 114, 121, 140, 149, 150, 154, 157
US Treasury, 41

vacancy rates, 97
value-to-income ratio, 9

Wall Street, 29
wealth creation and housing, 16–17
welfare state, 83
Wells Fargo, 31, 32
wholesale funding, 29, 105–106, 120
Wilmington Housing Partnership, 141
World Bank, 13

zero coupon bonds, 142